River Rats

The People of the Thousand Islands

Shawn Thompson

Published by

GENERAL STORE PUBLISHING HOUSE INC.

1 Main Street, Burnstown, Ontario, Canada K0J 1G0
Telephone (613)432-7697 Fax (613)432-7184

ISBN 0-919431-07-0
Printed and bound in Canada.

Designed by Marlene McRoberts and Bill Slavin

Copyright ©1989
The General Store Publishing House Inc.
Burnstown, Ontario, Canada

No part of this book may be reproduced, stored in a retrieval system or transmitted in any form or by any means electronic, mechanical, photocopying, recording or otherwise, except for purposes of review, without the prior permission of the publisher.

Canadian Cataloguing in Publication Data

Thompson, Shawn, 1951-
River rats: the people of the thousand islands

ISBN 0-919431-07-0

1. Thousand Islands Region (N.Y. and Ont.) --Biography. I. Title.

FC3095.T48Z48 1989   974.7'58043'092   C89-090138-4

F1059.T48T47 1989

First Printing August 1989

To my
daughter
Caitlin

Table of Contents

Introduction
Charting a Course with the Current...7

Chapter 1
Seven Eyes on the St. Lawrence..11

Chapter 2
Keepers of the River..35

Chapter 3
River Rats..57

Chapter 4
Enterprise and the Castle Builder...99

Chapter 5
Gypsy Summer 125

Chapter 6
Muskie Lords and Muskrat Men..151

Chapter 7
Squatter's Rites...178

Chapter 8
A River for Creators: Getting Metafishical..................................221

Conclusion
Odin's Eye Put to Rest 240

Regional Maps 242

Name Index..250

Acknowledgements..252

Author Information 254

Charting a Course with the Current

Mid-summer heat haze

It is summer in the Thousand Islands.

The solitary, long-lived, shark-toothed muskie buries itself deeper under the waves and waits for the bold fishermen of autumn to drop their lines.

The great blue heron flaps from its self-created natural slum on Ironsides Island to pose coyly, darkly, on a distant rock, like a slender, iron weather vane built in one dimension.

On Hay Island, blind writer Bob Russell cocks an ear that has recorded three decades of river mutterings. He hears the wind filtered through the stiff pine needles, the mechanical purr that distinguishes one boat's motor from another. The white tour boat from Gananoque swings by his dock. Standing in the water, he shampoos his hair and scrapes the stubble from his chin with a wet razor.

Eastward down the channel the windmill atop Rolly McIntosh's barge houseboat whirls with lazy gusto. The windmill traps energy in its big paws. A trap tied to the side of the barge grabs minnows for bait. The river rat fishes through a hole in his living room floor.

Still eastward with the current, past the high Landon's Bay lookout where you can see Allen Cook tending his nets from the granite bluff; past the river farmhouse where an old man remembers catching red-hot rivets when the Thousand Islands bridge was built; past Smugglers' Cove where a boy served drinks in a riverside tavern to Americans escaping Prohibition for one liquid day; then down the ferocious narrow channel under the bridge's arches; there is Rockport.

Rockport --- that small community improbably throned on jagged granite --- attracted boat-building clans of gleeful Andresses and ingenious Hucks.

Even the rock here was fresh, assertive, creative. It did not crumble like a spineless thing. It fell in massive, wolfish shards, opening its bright-red and florid pigment to the sun.

The spot was blessed. That was only fitting, since here was a current of might flowing by rock sturdy beyond measure. On a cliff in front of the white Catholic Church a sculptor longed to put his statue to St. Brendan the seafarer. But that was not to be. It would have to wait until another time.

Still, there is not a moment to lose.

The current does not linger. It flows past Rockport to Tar Island. Here Ralph Hodge, a handsome corn farmer who retired to his memories, presides over a shady slope seeded with his boyhood years. Only he can hear the long-vanished cows crying across the water.

On the far side of Tar is Grenadier Island, an old farm community dwindling to Hodge's one-eyed brother Fred and his wife June Hodge. The only harvests these days near Grenadier are the podlike cakes of ice thrashing in the spring break-up like fish.

There are more dreams and tales and memories in this stretch of the river than islands to count and number.

Listen to the story of the newlyweds who put their bed on the dock and slept exposed to the stars. The next morning they woke dusted lightly with frost.

Family annals swell with pride at the toothless, one-hundred-and-sixty-five-pound sturgeon that a seventy-nine-year-old man heaved into his rowboat.

Among the floating homes, the most regal, *La Duchesse*, is rescued from the river mud. She sank to the bottom after the dreams of George Boldt the castle-builder died. The granddaughter of Boldt reaches back to the life that surged through the great builder.

The river pauses, slows to silence, with the current quickened underneath. Listen closer.

Hear about the immigrants --- Dutch, Irish, French, German --- who flowed into the St. Lawrence valley with vitality and purpose and ingenuity, and made a start here, a fresh evolution and genesis of genealogy. One immigrant built boat engines on his metal lathe. Another fashioned a wooden sailing boat to avoid sleeping inland during the summer.

It is a river of desire, raw as the blast of a freighter's horn, old with pollution. Lives are moulded and lost. Fortunes made. Time passed in pleasure.

Here waste can be dumped out of sight of cities and farms. Here drug smugglers are seduced by fancy boats and marijuana and cocaine, simple, harmless plants that grow out of the earth.

Listen to the tale of disaster. Oil from a broken barge leaks across the water. Ten years later the story is a musical drama and the audience weeps to hear their joy and anguish for the river put into song.

Here, too, life can be rich, desire satisfied, the heart fattened like a wild turkey.

Is the St. Lawrence old enough, dignified enough to stand against the great rivers of the world? This river is no Amazon running through tropical jungle, no Tigris where Daniel saw an angel with burning eyes, no Jordan where Christ was baptized. It does not have the history of the River Babylon or the seclusion of the Nile. It is the St. Lawrence, named after a saint who thought the wealth of the church was its people. It is a river which lets people tell their tales without the burden of measureless time.

But does the river rat really exist? Is it a fiction made from a romantic dream of the river?

"I'm a river rat," asserts Hunter Grimes. "I'm an upper-level predator." He is in a cunning, satirical mood.

Muskie Jake --- the mildest and gentlest of the breed --- demurs. "We're all river rats," and then denies that river rats exist. "It's just a name."

Well, take heart. Somewhere between the bold, gruff outer self and the shy soul in touch with the pulse of the river, lies the river rat, the subject of a labyrinthine tale composed by the hot breath of life.

The St. Lawrence River is what was created here, the fish that spawned, the unions sanctified in small churches, the lives piloted from generation to generation.

The tales of the Thousand Islands are numbered among the spiked chips of pink granite that fall like undying sparks at the bottom of the river cliffs. The tales sing like the broken ice that chimes in the spring break-up along the shoreline. Like the river, the stories have no end.

Listen for a moment. Hear the tales of men and women who sowed what they had and reaped what they could on the banks of a river as old and as mighty as creation.

Rock with a heart, Narrows Lane

Seven Eyes on the St. Lawrence

Coming Home Through the Dark

The Russell Family

In Norse mythology the god Odin traded one eye for a drink from the fountain of wisdom. A giant took his eye as the price of knowledge. However much Odin wanted the bargain, there are mortals who have made even greater trades...

Bob and Elisabeth Russell

A flock of Canada geese wheels around Hay Island. The birds yap and bleat in shrill tones like newcomers on the river. The birds swoop to a spot on the water off the island's bright southwest tip. For Miranda Russell the geese are welcome, reassuring.

For a year the twenty-six-year-old woman suffered through chemotherapy and then radiation treatment. It was a slow, painful process to stop the tide of leukemia in her bloodstream. Then came the excruciating transplant of bone marrow supplied by her brother Richard.

Now Miranda was back on the island near Gananoque where she grew up in the summers. She had romped on the island with her three brothers and took her wedding vows under a cluster of pine trees.

Here, by the St. Lawrence River, the young girl and a friend had imagined they were transformed into witches "when the moon was full and orange." Later, fed by reckless teenage enthusiasm, she hit a shoal or two with the boat. She was always able to rescue the boat herself.

It was to the river and the island and the memories that Miranda returned from her hospital bed. Since her childhood she had become a painter using images as a way to think and feel. Now she needed the memories to endure the mental anguish of the long, wintry days of her illness.

"You always retreat into a place where you're unobstructed and free," she muses. One daydream in particular, nourished from childhood impressions, gave Miranda strength. "I was being taken down a narrow creek --- maybe a smaller version of the river here --- taken along in a very nice skiff. I was being rowed along, just rowed along the creek." Another daydream that helped ease the pain was a Winnie-the-Pooh fantasy. "I was taken up to a tree house where Owl lived, a big house with a smooth, golden oak floor. I was lying in bed. Dad was in his pyjamas and dressing gown and bringing me a cup of tea."

Hay Island was a place for the minds of the children to grow. Ever since Bob and Elisabeth Russell bought their first piece of property on the island in 1956, the children lived double lives. One life was a mundane existence south of the Canada-United States border in the winter. Those times alternated with the excitement of working and playing on the island in the summer.

As a child of five Miranda remembers walking to the end of the dock in the early morning with her father. She watched him catch perch for breakfast. "I fed the little perch to the Siamese cat," she says.

In 1968, the Russells became confirmed Hay Island residents. They bought sixteen acres and the buildings of a former girls' camp. Their property was a scanty layer of soil draped over the rocky end of the island. If the soil was too poor to farm, it was a rich family kingdom bordering the river. With the children gathered around the stone fireplace, Elisabeth Russell, an English teacher, read Tolkien's whimsical fairy tale *The Hobbit* aloud. That same voice, in deep, hearty tones from the English seacoast, read to Miranda in the hospital while she was battling leukemia.

Miranda endured the treatment of the disease bolstered by the love of her husband Bill and her family. And when it was summer again and she was free of the disease, she returned to the island. It was a moment to renew her contact with time and the river and the flow of life. The excitement rushed upon her senses like a fresh, clean wind off the river.

At that moment, when the disease had fallen away and her eyes were bright, the geese descended. It was as though they had been summoned as a sign. The geese "honked and gabbled joyfully" just for her, she says.

It was also a moment that made the choice of Miranda's name at birth almost prophetic. Miranda Russell had a stormy start to life. Labour was induced in her mother at seven months and the doctors thought that the infant had little chance of survival. When the child lived, Elisabeth Russell was struck by the wonder of the occasion. She remembered the name Miranda, which means "to wonder at," from a play of Shakespeare's called *The Tempest.*

Bob Russell remembered Shakespeare's play when he wrote the saga of the family summers on Hay Island. One chapter of Russell's book, *The Island*, is called "Prospero and Miranda" after the father and daughter of *The Tempest*. In Russell's book, father and daughter walk along the rim of Hay Island over the sea-grey granite by the jagged waves. Led by Miranda and enjoying her eyesight --- Russell has been blind since he was a child --- it is a moment that Russell savoured, aware that time was passing, his daughter growing up. He refused to meddle in his daughter's life. Still, there was a meeting of minds across the gulf.

Years later, Miranda says that she can feel what her father is thinking. That is the communication and strength they have in common. It hardly matters that he can not see her paintings, Miranda says. "He really has the same sensibilities I have. I can share my love of painting with him and I can describe things to him. He is conscious of the motivation. It's really the same inspiration."

A freak accident left Bob Russell blind at five years old. A splinter from a croquet mallet pierced one eye and sight was lost in the other through infection. However, Russell did not become a hermit. He did not retreat from what he could not see, which included the power of the river. Russell kept his humour and compassion and thoughtfulness. He earned graduate degrees in English literature by having books read to him and made himself a writer.

Russell also tested himself, starting in the summers when the sightless teenage boy was brought to the edge of the St. Lawrence River in the Thousand Islands.

In *The Island* he recalled the power of the unseen river to a thirteen-year-old. "The St. Lawrence was another world, and all through that first night I lay at its edge, wondering whether I would have the courage to enter upon it... Once out there on the river, for me there would be no land. Only space through which wind and water would ripple and hiss."

Russell was not daunted by the problems of being blind on an island. Among his other adventures, he devised a way to fish for pike alone in a boat. Theoretically, no one can sail a boat if he cannot see. But Russell was not a helpless landlubber. On the end of his dock he put an electric bell which chimed at regular intervals. The sound of the bell was his lifeline on the water.

Russell thus learned to handle the world through images. As with his daughter the painter, a flux of sensations and feelings pours through his mind into thought. He says that the objects on an island are "rough and prickly, not citified." The play of words and images delights him. His voice drifts without impediment, joyfully. The tones sound like a husky chord strummed by a musician in the shadows.

But summer is passing. The point of Hay Island shears the waves. The birds chart new paths through the wind. Across the water in the distance hangs the hazy image of the town of Gananoque. The double-decker tour boats swing past Russell's dock with the frozen, fleeting faces of tourists fixed at the rails.

In the kitchen the blind writer, one hand stroking through the soft, unruffled white bristle on his head, lays his thoughts out orderly, carefully, like fish to be cleaned and filleted. He enjoys choosing his words.

For the moment he ignores the familiar sound of Ahab, the West African grey parrot, cracking peanut shells in his crooked beak. A luxurious pile of scattered husks lies on the floor under the bird. Outside, the chimes on the porch knock in the west wind. An unusually chilly gust in the leaves makes a feverish rustle.

Hay Island

Sometimes a Temporary Notion

Shannon McCune

In Korea it is said that the doorway of a home can be protected from evil spirits by an Ishi Gan Tu stone. Of course, the stone is only a stone, not a spiritual power. Still, there are things in life worth protecting...

Shannon McCune

Spring on an island is a good time for rituals. Winter has been smashed and sent hustling down river with the crusty old blocks of ice. The buds and the wildflowers have broken the locks that held them in thrall under the snow. And Shannon McCune arrives at his tiny river-bound kingdom near Ivy Lea.

In the spring McCune puts out his white Okinawan Ishi Gan Tu stone to ward off evil spirits. He hangs his watch on a nail behind the door to banish the restless spirit of time. "To me the islands have been a refuge," says McCune, who bought the island for six hundred dollars in 1952 during the golden age of real estate. "When I was tired or I was discouraged, I came to the island to get renewed."

McCune could have chosen anywhere on the globe to settle. His parents were Presbyterian missionaries in Korea, where he was raised. He was the civilian administrator of the Japanese Ryukyu Islands and educational director of the United Nations Educational, Scientific and Cultural Organization in Paris. But the exotic country that the world-renown geographer chose was the Thousand Islands.

Here McCune found what he needed when he came in the 1950s, a deep well of solitude and freedom. He had arrived during a lull in the history of the islands, a crack in time. Once, the Thousand Islands had been seen as worthless territory. After the Iroquois and Mississaugua departed in the eighteenth century, few Anglo-Saxons wanted to settle here. They saw little to inspire them other than rocks and swamps. The first real wave of settlers was of refugees from the United States, whose numbers were still relatively small. The United Empire Loyalists were fleeing the fiery division of loyalties in the new republic of the United States.

At the time that McCune came to the islands the turmoil of human history had subsided: the fighting of the War of 1812 was long forgotten; the lusty burst of castle-building at the turn of the century had languished; the booming real estate market of the 1980s lay hidden in the future.

Although McCune was not a refugee like the Loyalists, the island was his safe haven. Here there was protection against senseless change. The island, he says, "gave us a place that we have kept to, that we have retreated to. It's always been there. This was always a constant. There was always the island."

McCune's rock sits remote from the main channels inside a nest of islands. The cottage is wedged among the trees as tightly as a shaft driven by a huge wooden mallet. "That's why we don't like intrusion," he says. "We like to be in the quiet part of the river."

McCune, professor emeritus at the University of Florida, needed to escape time. Even in the university the feverish factorylike clock of American culture pursued him. The lecture periods were cut into fifty-minute blocks and he began to think at that pace.

Summers on the island were a way to make a break, a chance to experiment with life like the Russells up-river.

McCune leads the way through the underbrush of the island to the office he built on the western tip among the white pines. Before McCune bought the island, a second growth had to replace the ravages of a fire. "The only trees that were left were those that could get down to the water," McCune says. His wife Edith --- also the child of Presbyterian missionaries in Korea, where the two met in high school --- replanted the trees over the years.

Along the path, where huckleberry and blueberry bushes clutch at passing feet, the hollow trunk of an old tree doubles as a flower pot. As a geographer making an island his home McCune made few changes aside from a cottage --- "We've got the cabin close to the river so we feel a part of the river" --- and his office. Here, with a portable typewriter, a few books, a cot, a space heater and supply of pipe tobacco, he works on his books and articles about the Far East with the islands and the river outside his window.

While McCune labours at his desk, fishermen linger in the quiet channel at the head of the island. Their lines dangle in water where McCune predicts they will never hook a fish. Upstream is the two-fifths-of-an-acre island that McCune bought for eight hundred dollars to protect his view. He sold the rock to his daughter and son-in-law for a dollar. The McCune island has no official name beyond its number, 60, though McCune has a wooden sign which reads Yundo. *Yun* is the McCune family name in Korean and *Do* means island.

Time is different on the river, McCune says. "Gananoque is a time community. River people are much more influenced by the river." The human calendar is ordered and adjusted in time by events on the St. Lawrence, like storms and freeze-up and low water marks. The river people "time themselves by the river."

"This year the water's way down," McCune remarks out of habit.

The dams and the St. Lawrence Seaway stabilized the fluctuations in the river. Still, the level is a hot topic among islanders, competing with other issues like noisy boaters, septic systems and the beavers' raids on the trees. McCune recalls a story told to him by a longtime resident about the days when the levels of the river were as erratic as storms. In 1933, the water fell so much that the residents had to extend their docks to get past the exposed mud flats. That was the Year of Low Water as measured by time on the river.

The international border which runs through the islands did not divide the ways of life on the river --- apart from the initial differences between United Empire Loyalists and revolutionary warriors, and the flare-up of the War of 1812. Tourism made a greater difference in thinking, McCune says. The river people, however much they like tourists, still resent the loss of independence. Tourism made them servants, subservient to people with no claim on them through tradition or kin. With a laugh, McCune comments that such revolutions are the way of the world. The Okinawa that he once knew has become a tourism empire.

In spite of all his precautions, Shannon McCune has not been able to resist the logic of civilization. His aspirations have fallen into contradictions. He can not ignore the American clock-wound pace that sets him apart even from Canadians. "I, perhaps, move faster and I'm less patient." He gets the *New York Times* a day late, and admits that the newspaper is also a kind of wristwatch, a way of keeping pace with one sense of time. He is annoyed, he says, that invitations to island cocktail parties have a set time, which runs counter to the spirit of the river. "In the old days you'd say, why don't you drop around." Still, he is also impatient with the timing of river people who appear a day or two late for work.

McCune has to be on guard every moment against alien spirits that might infest the island. His wife fights the disease that has attacked the white pines --- leaving the desolate skeleton of a tree beside his office --- and McCune ponders what else should be banished from the island.

"I'm a relatively impatient guy, so that's an evil spirit," he says. Another evil spirit --- with roots in time --- is the advance of age.

But McCune, a spry, thoughtful man, born in 1913, has not been held ransom to time. He and his wife have lived happily since the days in Korea --- McCune jokes that the marriage was *Chakchung,* a loose agreement between parents to consider the marriage of their children. "It worked out very well," he says with a chuckle. And the McCune island resists change like a lily pad sheltered in a reverent corner of the river. There is still some magic on this island. The Ishi Gan Tu stone may be working.

Yundo (Island 60)

Pottery Shards and Past Lives

Patrick Wilder

In the Thousand Islands the mundane world shrinks in significance. There are islands carved by glaciers long ago, fish and birds that live unseen lives. And there is the current of history, narrowing to rush through the chasm of a particular moment in a particular spot...

Patrick Wilder

One blustery day in the 1860s a historian landed at the foot of Carleton Island, where Lake Ontario empties into the St. Lawrence River. He climbed the footpath. The steep rock bluff made his blood pump furiously until he reached the top. Then he paused. On the plateau was the broken link in time that the historian wanted to find. He saw the ruins of a British fort from the previous century. The visit was cut short "by the increasing violence of the wind, which became almost a gale at noon."

In his book on the War of 1812 Benson Lossing recorded his impressions. He recognized that the fort was the key to defence and navigation on Lake Ontario and the St. Lawrence. The maze of channels and islands was strategically important. The channels made blockades and defence easy; but the river was so narrow and the islands so numerous, it was just as easy to launch raiding parties. Smugglers also knew the advantages of the Thousand Islands from the beginning.

Lossing saw the importance of the ruined fort. But like historians for years afterward, he misinterpreted the role played by what he mistakenly called Fort Carleton.

At the beginning of the War of 1812 the fort was a broken shard of its former glory. In his *Pictorial Fieldbook of The War of 1812* Lossing wrote: "A garrison composed of a sergeant, and three invalid soldiers, and two women, occupied the fort when the war broke out." Immediately, a keen revolutionary soldier named Captain Abner Hubbard, sacker of cities, set out in a boat with a man and a boy to capture the fort. It was the smallest armada in naval history. "He succeeded and this was the first seizure of a military post after the declaration of war. He sent a boat the following day to bring away the stores, and soon afterward the barracks were burned. Nine bare chimneys have stood there ever since, grey and solitary tokens of change."

In the spring of 1974, more than a hundred years after Lossing, a historian named Patrick Wilder climbed the cliffs again. He saw what Lossing saw, but with different eyes. The size of the ruins added to his growing suspicion about the significance of the fortifications. "I thought we were going to find little or nothing," Wilder recalls. "After viewing the fort I was astonished to see the ramparts. There was actually a moat on the plain's side."

Wilder, employed at the New York State War of 1812 battlefield site at Sackets Harbor, headed north to Ottawa to read correspondence about the fort in the National Archives of Canada. Wilder opened the correspondence of Frederick Haldimand, governor of the colony of Quebec during the American War of Independence. The letters had gone back and forth between the governor in Quebec and the fort on Carleton Island named in his honour, Fort Haldimand.

Slowly, Wilder put the pieces together. He realized that the history of the fort had been veiled partly because it was a secret British installation and the key to British control of Lake Ontario and the inner continent. "It was a revelation that something of this magnitude could be seen anywhere in the St. Lawrence basin," Wilder recalls.

Climbing to the top of the cliff that earned the fortification the name of "the Gibraltar of the St. Lawrence" Wilder saw also the monolithic chimneys and the remains of the half-star fortifications. He went scuba diving off the island to visit the wreck of an eighteenth-century British troop carrier and supply vessel which was armed with heavy canons. The two-masted ship, called a snow brig because of its extra sails, was eighty feet long and probably built in the 1770s. The meaning of what he was piecing together surprised and stunned Wilder. Before him, historians had shuffled down the wrong path in their re-creation of the history of the Thousand Islands. Far from being an insignificant outpost, the fort helped to secure and then lose Britain's hold on what became the United States.

Misconceptions, wrong assumptions, and a British historical site located on American soil had helped to obscure the past of Fort Haldimand. Lossing thought that it was built by the French and taken over by the English, whereas Wilder learned that the British built it. American historians had overlooked the importance of the fort because the papers were in Canada and the fort, after all, interested Canadians more than Americans. Canadian historians may have suspected the importance of the fort, but as far as Wilder knew no one had done research on the subject.

The Haldimand papers came alive for Wilder. He watched the alarm and anger of the fort's British officers during the American Revolutionary War. Their efforts were coming unravelled. The British wanted to stop settlement of the continent from this point westward to protect the fur trade. The plan was failing miserably. Settlers were ignoring the 1763 Proclamation Line and the rebellion of the American colonies --- partly because of pressure from Fort Haldimand --- was undermining the whole British design.

As his research gathered momentum, Wilder became more absorbed in the work. He dove through the entrancing "yellowish-green" water at Carleton Island and swam over the wreck of the snow brig, finding shards of pottery lying there. It was a moment of discovery that rekindled his boyhood days on the St. Lawrence hunting for Indian arrowheads.

When he was eight years old, Wilder's thirst to uncover the past started. He found a pottery shard and it was as though he had found another way of life. Now he was on the brink of an awakening again. The solitude of the dive over the wreck helped to free his thoughts and emotions. "You hear nothing, just the bubblings of your air tank, your breathing. The loudest thing around you are your thoughts." Wilder marvelled at the craftsmanship and care that went into the old ship. "I could see the ceiling planking over the ribs, the futtocks. I could see very plainly the keel, which was quite massive in size, and I could see the steps into which the bottom of the masts would fit."

After Wilder's work on Fort Haldimand, an archeologist, Joseph Murray, was hired to head the survey of the ship. Items, including old muskets and brass Indian bells and pewter caps, were brought to the surface. Meanwhile Wilder continued pouring over the old documents.

Wilder believes the British realized that Carleton Island was a key to controlling the continent's interior and began fortifying the island in the mid-1770s. Carleton Island, and not Oswego, was the staging area for raids in the Mohawk Valley against the American rebels from 1776 to 1781. The fort also served as a trading post and a supply centre for the Iroquois and Mississaugua allied with the British. Ships, like the wreck at Carleton, allowed the British to meet any threat against their control of Lake Ontario and the St. Lawrence.

In the Haldimand papers Wilder could see Britain's plans falling to pieces. The colonies, Wilder believes, saw the Proclamation Line and the fort at one end of it, as a barrier and an irritation. During the American Revolutionary War the irritation at the British flared and burst into flames. The British at the fort discovered that their Indian allies were slaughtering rebels, Loyalists and neutral people indiscriminately, Wilder says. The settlers were forced to take arms against the British allies, thus swinging loyalists and neutralists to the revolutionary camp.

"I'll never forget the excitement of the research and the material and how it fits into North American history," Wilder says. "I thought, this is amazing. It was such a well-guarded military secret that it fooled later historians."

The day of his first dive to the snow brig in 1974 unleashed strange emotions in Wilder. It was the culmination of the excitement of boyhood discoveries and it also brought a sense of loss. The wreck made Wilder aware of the distance of the past, the cultural differences between the people living in North America and their ancestors.

You cannot re-create the past once it is gone, Wilder says. Time is as pure and inviolable as the old Proclamation Line tried to be. Yet, with a little imagination and fragments from the past for meditation, you can feel what life must have been like. Wilder says that he feels a sense of intimacy with the long-vanished British soldiers. He understands their military discipline, their pride and sense of accomplishment in a wild land.

Wilder thinks the soldiers would be shocked to see Fort Haldimand in ruins, the army and the order it brought banished from the islands. Those were hard times. The river and the new land seemed to need the soldiers. There was no doubt in their minds about their role. "They knew their jobs were important. They knew that they were in the last of a string of outposts in North America. Their mission was to hold the frontier for Great Britain."

Sackets Harbor

Dispatches from Disaster

Mike Sykes

Sight can be both a blessing and a curse. Sight means that you cannot be oblivious to suffering. It might be easier to have eyes and barter away the heart, but then there would be no river to enjoy --- or to lose...

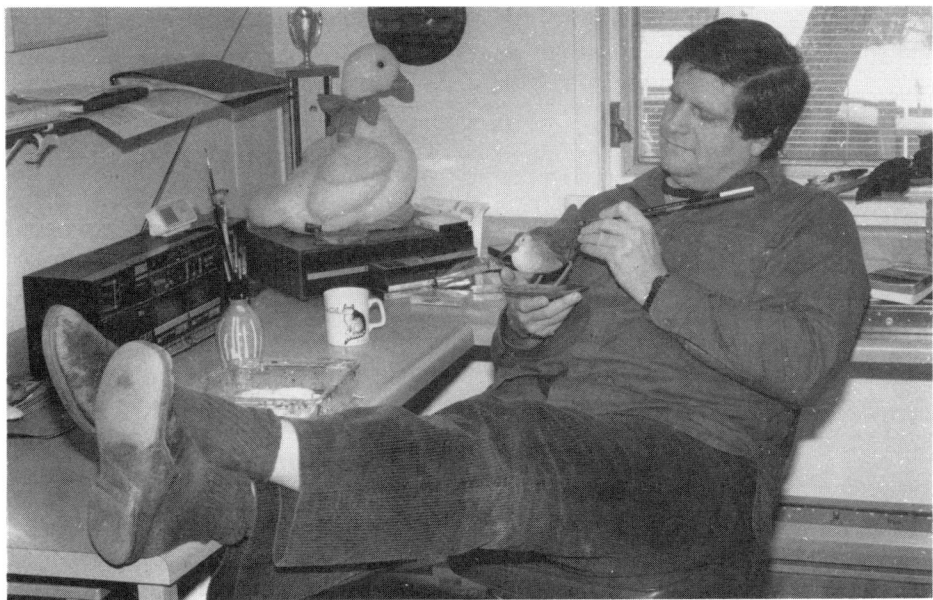

Mike Sykes

On June 23, 1976 just after one in the morning the St. Lawrence River fell from grace. Over the years the number of fish had dwindled and contaminants in the water increased, but the garden still seemed secure. Then, in a heavy fog, a tank barge hauling industrial fuel oil hit Comfort Shoal off Wellesley Island.

More than three hundred thousand gallons of thick, black, obliterating fluid leaked into the St. Lawrence River along the American channel. The barge, *NEPCO 140*, was pushed by its tugboat ten kilometres down the river to the first available anchorage at Mason's Point. The oil slick eventually stretched one hundred kilometres along the river. It took five hundred workers to clean up at a cost of $8.5 million in United States funds. The cost was charged to the owners of the barge.

The only traces of the disaster today are black rings on shoreline rocks around United States points such as Clayton, Alexandria Bay and Schooner Island and the memories of people like John Burt and Mike Sykes. Burt would eventually turn the disaster into a musical drama. Sykes, a reporter for the *Kingston Whig-Standard* at the time, would not forget the disaster despite the temptations of oblivion.

That morning in June all that was on Sykes' mind was the excitement of a hot story. He hired the fair-haired Gananoque fishing guide Tom Harrison and his boat, and moved as close to the spill as the United States Coast Guard would allow. The oil was bunker C, the worst type in a spill because it is too thick to dissipate.

"It was a very thick, gummy, molasseslike substance," Sykes recalls. "There was just so much filth. The shoreline was black scum.

"I found out where the oil barge had been holed, checked the chart, and realized we had the makings of a major maritime disaster, given the narrow channel and swift current.

"The U.S. coast guard warned us off about a mile from the mess. In fact, they got quite shitty and my rumblings about the public's right to know and all that fell on deaf ears. So Tom and I set course down river to follow the slick, about two or three inches thick by then.

"It was one of those calm summer days when winds are very light and from the southwest. Accordingly, we headed east. The wind had a negligible impact. We spent the next hour inhaling 'bunker C'— not a particularly aromatic substance.

"The marinas were scenes of frantic activity as booms were installed to keep the gummy oil from fouling boat hulls. The shoreline was marked with black, shiny oil marks that stayed for weeks."

Sykes produced some passionate prose for the *Whig-Standard* that week. In one story he wrote, "Upstream the stricken barge was bleeding her dark cargo into the St. Lawrence." He tracked down disgruntled refugees of the slick in a bar in Alexandria Bay. A fisherman told him with black humour, "You can walk on the water to Canada."

For Sykes, the oil spill would become one item in the catalogue of woes that the river suffered because of people. The channels had been changed, the fish disinherited, the land developed, the surface pestered with boats and then pollution --- a kind of industrial leukemia --- was the final insult.

Now Sykes has a home in Gananoque and makes his living as a wood lathe craftsman and duck decoy carver. Born in Montreal beside the St. Lawrence, Sykes was drawn to the water when he was young. He travelled to school by boat, hunted ducks and started whittling decoys at ten. The day that he turned seventeen he impulsively joined the Canadian Navy. He left the navy befuddled by bureaucracy, with tattoos on each arm and memories of Newfoundland fog. The unification of the Canadian Armed Forces in 1967 incensed him enough to take the offer of an honourable discharge in Kingston.

Sykes worked for the Kingston newspaper for five and a half years in the 1970s and again wanted out. His wife Pamela agreed. "One day inspiration struck. Why not escape to the river forever? Earn my keep out here?

"In cahoots with my wife a decision was made to launch a floating hot dog stand. We planned to convert a pontoon boat to a mobile dispenser of hot dogs, hamburgers, ice cream, assorted junk food and all the other necessary 'trappings' of civilization left behind by the great boating public.

"Alas, we were swamped before launch by insurance. No insurance company would touch us --- too high a risk. The scenario painted for our edification went like this: Sykes anchors off Gordon Island... Hungry kid dives into the water to swim out for a hot dog fix... Speeding boat minces kid... Bingo. Multimillion-dollar lawsuit --- and guess who's guilty as hell for providing the enticement?

"Somehow I feel our society has lost something...and I don't just mean my floating hot dog stand."

These days Sykes relies on the river as a soothing balm. Yet he says that the proliferation of powerboats makes it more difficult to find the river that he once knew. Boaters without common decency and manners foul the St. Lawrence like another kind of oil slick. The river has become a freeway obliterated by boats. "There's just far too many people. You've got the makings of anarchy."

Sykes likes the river, just as he likes carving ducks, because it means living "without a million rules."

"I've chosen a life with some distance between myself and other people because of the craziness. I go out there to indulge my solitariness. I've always felt at peace on the water. It wouldn't matter whether it was the St. Lawrence or a creek."

On Saturdays in the summer Sykes sells his wares in the open-air farmers' market across the street from the *Kingston Whig-Standard*. He says that he has no regrets. Carving ducks and staying close to the river is satisfying, he says. "I find what I do gives me sanity because I'm creating something."

During the time that he worked for a newspaper Sykes felt that he was struggling against the current of the prevailing wisdom.

There was the day in December of 1974 when the six-hundred-foot ore-trucking freighter *Roy A. Jodrey* hit Pullman Shoal near Grindstone Island. The ship "literally sank like a rock." Sykes sped to the scene. As a reporter he traced the survivors to a motel in Alexandria Bay. After a few moments he folded up his notebook and opened his heart to the men and women shivering in blankets from the cold water. They were stripped of dignity. The crew was humiliated for losing the ship without a fight, without a storm. Yet they also felt joy and relief at their own survival.

The ship's crew babbled with Newfoundland candour about the sinking, Sykes says. The ex-navy man knew how the third mate, the officer of the watch at the time, was trapped. "I remember thinking, you poor bugger. You're the one they're going to hang for this."

"I remember thinking, these people are hanging themselves. I knew if it got in print, they'd be beaten over the head with it."

Instead, Sykes wrote "the usual trite stuff" for his newspaper story. "My sympathies were usually with the victim."

Gananoque

Courtesy of the Kingston Whig-Standard

Oil spill, June 23, 1976

The River, the Goose and the Oil Slick

John Burt

One night while people in the Thousand Islands slept a black, obliterating flood of oil spread across the water like a bad dream. When the people woke, their world had been changed. They discovered that an oil spill had greater consequences than a mere petroleum mishap...

John Burt

"My first reaction, emotional reaction, was that something horrible had happened, like there had been a bombing. I felt like the air had somehow been spoiled and I didn't know why."

On his twentieth birthday John Burt woke to disaster on Choke Cherry Island. "It was very early in the morning, very hot and foggy, unusually hot for June. I remember being awakened by an unbelievable, pungent smell which I could not identify. I had no idea what it really was. I walked around to try and find what sort of evidence there was of this smell."

Burt's parents, Stuart and Ellen, woke up as well and smelled the mysterious odour. It was not until eight that morning that they learned from the radio of the giant oil spill on the river. The barge *Nepco 140* had run aground in the fog with the third mate in command and the captain sleeping. The industrial oil was floating down the river twenty-five kilometres from Wellesley Island to Choke Cherry Island, near Chippewa Bay.

The Burts braced themselves for the invasion. The island had been in the family since the years just before the Great Depression, when Ellen Burt's father, a Scotsman named Cuthbert, had bought the rock across the water from the family's sheep-farming homestead. The twin Scottish strands of the Burts and Cuthberts had lived in the river valley too many generations not to be outraged by the damage to the river.

"It was very calm, a glassy perfect river day and you could see the sun rays reflected off the oil slick about ten miles up river. We spent our whole day preparing for the arrival of the oil, taking out wooden boats. And there was a real rallying in the community. Everyone went from island to island helping pull all of these boats out. And you could see the oil coming down throughout the day. It didn't actually arrive at my parent's island until about five o'clock in the afternoon.

"Once the oil arrived, it was a massive, black, shiny curtain across the river, literally choking out the whole surface of the river. As soon as the wind arrived --- the next day became very windy --- all of the oil starting splashing up on the islands."

Booms were put out to contain the spill. The sickening goo, directed into Chippewa Bay for collection, was sucked up. But the disaster had also stunned the people as though they too had waded into the oil like the birds and found it sticking to their bodies. Having to wait for the oil to arrive did not help.

"There was a feeling of enormous helplessness. We knew we were sitting ducks. And I don't think I've really felt helpless before. It was my first memory of really feeling like a victim, of not having any choice in the matter.

"We spent our whole summer in oil. My mother was unbelievably devastated by it. She took it very hard. She really cherished the island and the river as the one place that was sacred. There's such a sacredness about the river. Suddenly that was truly destroyed. Not only physically, but by the number of people that came in and took charge of her paradise.

"I've never seen her so upset.

"She fortunately channeled that upset into action." Burt also felt roused to action, though it would be years before he found a unique way to respond to the pain and upheaval. "The river was calling for us to be involved in it."

Ten years later, on June 23, 1986 --- the anniversary date of the spill and a threshold for Burt, his thirtieth birthday --- the musical play *The Slick of '76* opened on a simple flatbed truck in the Thousand Islands. Burt had studied drama as a way to heal psychological wounds. The musical, which he commissioned David Schechter and Barry Keating to write, was his response to the hurt that he had seen the disaster cause. But bringing the calamity to the stage was not easy because the idea did not win automatic acceptance. At first Burt had to battle the resistance and skepticism of Clayton, where many thought it was folly to turn a badly acted disaster with amateurs for villains into a piece for the theatre. But Burt watched the reactions change as the charm of the play and the love of the river took hold.

The play treated the pain and sinister aspects of the disaster with warmth and humour. Feelings that were tricky to deal with, were made accessible through song and dialogue. *The Slick* began with a lyrical number called "The River Song." It chronicled with good humour the division between river people and summer residents, and then dipped into the oil slick with musical numbers like "River Run Black," "Slicklickin'" and "Mucker's Lament." A typical number had a mixture of comedy and suffering, such as the poor luckless goose who sings: "with my neck all covered with ticky tacky goo, smells like the leather of a stinky old shoe. Tell me what, what, can a poor goose do?" The goose could not change what had happened. The best it could do was to stir with its words compassion for the river and its creatures.

From a dark corner of the theatre Burt watched the hearts melt. He heard people cry in the audience when the oil rolled down the river again. The play was as infectious as the river, since the river was the image that people held in their souls. Some came time after time to see the play.

With that dramatic introduction to the community, Burt was back the next year. He was offered space in the 1903 opera hall on the main street of Clayton. The company, called River Barge Productions, produced three river pieces in its second year, *The Slick* again, with two new creations, a musical *Wind in the Willows* and *River Song Revue*.

Burt had combined two interests, the healing effect of drama based on events in a particular community, and his roots in the Thousand Islands. And *The Slick* had irresistible local appeal. Before long "The River Song" had been used as an anthem at a public school graduation and as a grade two number during a Christmas concert. If that was not gratitude enough, Burt was told, "Thank you for telling our story." One of his early critics came to him to apologize and added, "You've brought us together."

The play is "really about people's love of the river," Burt explains, which is why the story of the oil spill affects those who knew the disaster. If the oil spill had no more importance than dumping a load of gravel in the wrong spot, it would not have aroused such strong, lingering feeling.

Burt did not want to rest with the success of *The Slick*. He needed to grow as a producer and try new experiments, though the subject of rivers would stay with him.

Yet even on a hot August day Burt says that he still cannot escape the memory of the slick. His small niece climbs from the shore of Choke Cherry Island with tar on her feet. "What is this?" she asks Burt. "Oh, this is from the slick," he tells the girl, knowing she had not been born when the black witch of a barge, *Nepco 140*, hit the shoal. The lament of the singing goose stuck in the goo continues. There is still a ring around the family island. "It freezes and melts and freezes and melts and doesn't go away," sighs Burt.

Clayton

Pioneering Insights

Dr. John T. Omohundro

The oil spill was like the death of the river prefigured. It made people realize how much they had to lose. It also made an anthropologist realize that life on the river was a kind of living folk art...

John Omohundro

Behind the moonlike, wire-rim glasses the eyes are steady, unassuming. This is Dr. John T. Omohundro, anthropologist and professor of people. In the fall of 1976 he found himself exploring a frontier that he did not know existed, a culture in North America that had never been studied.

It was a group of people called river rats.

Omohundro was hired by the United States Coast Guard to study the way that the oil spill in June of 1976 affected people. The coast guard knew how to cope with disaster, but not with the disruption and upset that it has on peoples' lives. The coast guard needed to be prepared for the next oil spill.

The anthropologist talked to one hundred and thirty-eight people on the American side of the river. He walked along the shorelines of their islands with them. He looked where they pointed to reminders of the spill, such as rocks still stained with oil in the shadows of a dock.

The conversations stirred memories. "They were seriously sobered by the memory of their feelings. The most intense emotion was outrage and frustration. That was unbridled.

"People were shocked the most by the death of the animals because they would see them on the river or they would float ashore --- snakes, turtles, muskrats." The great blue heron sanctuary on Ironsides Island, east of Goose Bay, sat in the path of the oil spill. The sight of a baby heron dipped in oil was particularly devastating. "The symbol of animal death was the oiled heron because that is the bird that represents the river. That was the symbol that the river was oiled. When people saw the oiled bird, it made them fear that the river itself was in danger."

Omohundro was surprised by the talkative nature of the river folk. Usually, as an anthropologist, he found people hesitant to speak to strangers. But Omohundro was welcomed warmly, especially since he was asking questions about the river. These folk had their own brand of worldliness. They were not a tribe bred in isolation like natives of the Amazon. The river rats were accustomed to mixing with people from far-flung places like village traders at the crossroads of a caravan route.

The river folk are "fierce individualists and non-conformists and often self-promoting. They are not like your quiet and shy farmer," Omohundro says. "It's almost as though they were aware they were representing a certain style of life and they were going to defend it. It seemed like a conscious choice. They're all very self-consciously proud of being a member of that river rat sub-culture."

Life on the river is almost the same on both sides of the border, Omohundro says. National distinctions are not important in the islands. There was a change, however, when the St. Lawrence Seaway opened in 1959. Before the Seaway, Omohundro reflects, there was a great deal of traffic back and forth across the river. And during Prohibition the bootlegging brotherhood totally ignored the international boundary. Nevertheless the Seaway, the international bridge, and better roads changed the paths across the river and the way that life was lived in the area.

A decade after the study for the coast guard, Omohundro, a member of the faculty at the State University of New York, Potsdam, was still studying the Thousand Islands. He saw the river folk as a "disaster culture," a group that has suffered a catastrophe, such as an earthquake or volcanic eruption. And the upheaval of the oil spill helped the anthropologist understand how people along the St. Lawrence thought in their everyday lives.

Omohundro uses distinctions that are common in the Thousand Islands. He distinguishes between people who live and work on the river, or river rats, and summer residents, whose families may go back three or four generations in the islands. River folk are a separate class of people, a sub-culture, Omohundro says. What binds them together are "common values about the river, what it means in their lives."

Summer residents are "more or less cosmopolitan." They have more money than river people, whose income and chances for a job are as fickle in the winter as the changes of the wind. The summer people see the river affectionately as a playground, not as a business. Yet their worries about pollution and development come from the heart. And their ties to the area have the same sort of strength as a parent who loves an adopted child as much as a natural child. Although some wealthy folk build lavish houses, modesty is more common. "The houses along the river vary enormously and they say a great deal about peoples' orientation on the river. Some people try to build very small and inconspicuous places so they can blend in. They are so casual and unself-conscious you can walk in in dirty shoes."

Omohundro was surprised to learn that the summer residents had a deep emotional stake in the area. "I had no idea they saw this place as their home." He speculates that the summer residents change jobs and houses so often that the only stable home in their lives is a cottage in the islands, handed down by generation after generation as part of the family jewels. Thus, in the rat race of a city culture, roots in the Thousand Islands are cherished. The river community becomes a home town. It has the same face year after year and the summer residents absorb the local history. They are proud to see themselves as more than strangers or casual visitors. "What they like is the fact they know all the islands. They know all the people who live on the islands. They've grown up with these people. I think a lot of the Americans who live in the cities would probably envy them that sense of community."

The summer folk are often worried about the changes that development and commercialization will make in the Thousand Islands. Yet they can form their attitudes without the economic dilemmas of the river folk. Their incomes do not depend on the river and tourism. "I think the big difference lies in the sense that the river must remain a source of income for the river rat." Some summer residents enjoy the quixotic summer dream of a river freed from the shackles of commercialism. In that dream, the

Thousand Islands is a playground with no restrictions, a place to build castles --- as some wealthy people actually did. "And that would be death to the river rat culture."

"What would help the river rats' economic livelihood would be something that's not particularly good for tourism, like a factory --- which could very well hurt the river in some ways.

"But then, of course, you would also change the river rat culture."

Omohundro says that the differences between the two groups created tension in the reaction to the oil spill. In Alexandria Bay, the river folk, whose income depended on the St. Lawrence, needed to put the spill in the past. The residents who were financially independent refused to forget their anger and outrage. They needed to keep the oil spill alive so that the issue could be fought. Eventually, the tension subsided, the bonds of life along the river resumed.

The ties of the river community are powerful, partly because the frontier lingers. "It's a dangerous river and you may have to go out of your way to help somebody, even save a life," Omohundro says. The river folk stay in touch over the citizens' band radio. They may need help in a storm or a fire or an accident. In the city the government looks after emergencies. On the river it is different. "The ethics are, you stick together. You help each other."

Alexandria Bay

The Right Flutter for a Spoon

Dr. John Casselman

Among those who took a sip from the fountain of knowledge, like the Norse god Odin in exchange for an eye, was Dr. John Casselman, professor of pike. Casselman is blind in one eye, but that is not important. What matters is what he sees with the other eye...

Dr. John Casselman

As a boy John Casselman was taken across the water to the red-ochre star that Indians painted on Tar Island. It was his introduction to the river and it came through two Brockville men, Everett and Charlie Snider, who ran the family tour boat business. Everett Snider was better than a book. He spouted the lore of the islands like a hot-spring geyser. He showed Casselman the red star and explained that the original name of Tar Island was Star. The local tongues had dropped the letter "s" over time in a kind of linguistic erosion.

Casselman was taken to the pine tree on Cockburn Island to see the mark cut by a cable. There was a story behind the mark and Snider told it to the boy.

In 1930, thirty men died when lightning detonated the blast charges that had just been set from a barge. The barge had been tied to the pine tree. Ev Snider was there. He described the day. The boy listened.

"He talked about, after the boat blew up, the amount of debris and the dead fish."

Snider also told the boy about the changes on the river. He recalled blasting in the channel that stunned fish. He spoke of species of fish like pickerel brought to the surface in multitudes that turned the water white. Snider told the boy that the pickerel once brought up by the blasts had almost disappeared from the river.

For six summers, until he was seventeen, Casselman worked on the tour boat, absorbing lessons from Ev Snider, waving to people like Ed Senecal of the Grenadier Island clan. Senecal was a guide and one of the wise old men of the river. After a lifetime on the St. Lawrence he could see deeper into the shadows than others. Out on the water Casselman passed commercial fishermen like George Vanston, always garbed in the same cap with earflaps and oil skin pants. Senecal and Vanston were alike. They worked with calculated slowness and precision. Casselman noticed in both a curious freshness of skin, weathered, yet unwrinkled in middle age. Vanston explained to the boy how he applied his theory of "crop rotation" to the bays that he fished. He cast his lines in a spot for one year, then let it lie "fallow" two or three, depending on the breed of fish.

Everyday the boy on the tour boat passed men like these in his circuit around the river. He wondered about what he saw. The contact piqued his curiosity. "The river, all of the sudden, became an entity in my life. It had character."

When he was eighteen years old Casselman had to choose his course in college. He worked for the summer with a highway construction crew. The work was hot and he came home caked in grit and sand. In the evening he cleansed himself with a dip in the St. Lawrence. "That was the summer when I realized I wanted to be associated with the river."

As a subject for study, the river beckoned him. "It had more of a mystery. It had a dimension that you could not see."

Casselman learned from the observations of the river folk. He also realized that their facts were instinctively right, but that they did not know the reasons why. Casselman's analytic mind was stimulated. He wanted to know why a particular observation was right. There had to be an underlying reason.

Some of the guides' observations sounded like the babble of folklore. For instance, the guides said that if you lost the first smallmouth bass, you would never catch another in that spot that day.

Casselman recalls the time that he was casting at Haffie's Rock, a horseshoe-shape inlet. Nearby was the guide Joe Haffie with three customers.

"He baited up one of the ladies. He took his time and explained where to cast --- because there's never any rush. The guides are always confident that they will get the fish."

"She threw the line out and he got ready to bait the other lady. And all of the sudden a beautiful bass went right in the air."

The woman had not set the hook in the fish's mouth with a tug. The fish had jumped and dropped the hook.

"Joe didn't say one word. He turned around and he baited the other lady. He explained exactly the same thing to her.

"Bang, the same thing happened."

Haffie's misery was not complete yet. He still had to bait the third hook --- and to watch the third bass get loose. Then he could start burning.

"I could just see Joe's shoulders drop. And I heard him swear. He didn't say one more thing. He turned around and he slipped the anchor and took them back and put them on the dock.

"He told them he never wanted to fish with them again."

The incident was not only an insult to the guide, it stabbed him where it hurt, his reputation. "The guides knew they had to have a catch of fish, because the fish of today secure the party for tomorrow. So if a guide took out danglers, you often saw him fishing. That was a signal there was a problem. He wanted to put a few fish in the box to maintain his reputation for the next day."

There was another reason why Haffie dumped his three customers. After the triple disaster at the horseshoe inlet, he knew that Haffie's Rock had been violated. It would be impossible to catch any bass there that day. Casselman now knows why. "The first fish you catch is usually the dominant fish in the congregation or school. It's almost like cattle, where there's a pecking order. If the dominant fish moves out, the rest of the school moves with him.

"You could not hook the first fish and lose it."

While the young man was earning his first degree in biology --- he would eventually write both an M.A. thesis and a Ph.D. thesis on pike --- he spent the summers as a guide working out of Caiger's Lodge.

The work kept him in touch with the river and the people who could teach him. One of his instructors was the old guide Ed Senecal. Senecal knew the lore of the islands as well as he knew the currents and the shoals. He showed Casselman Indian relics that he had retrieved from the sand of Tar Island.

"He could tell you something about each one."

Casselman felt that much of the rich Indian lore had been forgotten, which was a loss to the islands. He was intrigued when Senecal told him that the Indians buried their dead on a sand hill that now has cottages on it.

"I said, 'Where did you get these beads?' He said they were on the top of the sand. The sand would blow off and the Indian beads would be there. And there were bones and everything over there."

Finding the relics made the islands come alive for Casselman. It was not dead history. The relics were a sign, like the flash of a fish's fins under the water, of the movement of life.

The same thing happened when Casselman looked closely at the people. There was a life flowing in them that was different from the life in other places. As Casselman watched he could see in Senecal the skills typical of a river man and yet unique. Senecal could fix a type of lure known as a spoon with the precision of a violinist tuning his strings. The old man knew exactly how he wanted the spoon to move in the water. "He preferred a black and white spoon. He used to take a pair of pliers and work and bend it until he got the right flutter."

Senecal had another lesson for Casselman. He decided that he had reached the end of his fishing days when his boat, made in the 1890s, was worn out. He had decided what his limits were on the river. There was also a wistful regret in the old man as he reflected about the dwindling number of fish.

"He had stopped fishing smallmouth bass. He said the smallmouth bass are gone --- he called them black bass --- the black bass are gone."

That was not true. There were still smallmouth bass, but not in the absolute numbers that Senecal remembered. The clear, flat, sandy banks where the bass used to collect around Indian and Goose Islands were no longer hospitable. They had filled with weeds.

"We knew that our best catches of smallmouth bass were on clear sand."

And the knowledge that the river had changed, that there were fewer fish, struck deep in Casselman. "I just knew, my gut feeling was, that the river could not stand that level of exploitation."

That feeling finally led to his decision thirty years ago to become a fish biologist. He would search for the meaning of things. Knowledge could make a difference. It could help to preserve the river and its living creatures. Casselman's role would be to bring into the light what the guides knew instinctively. He could make knowledge visible like the Indian relics exposed by the wind on the old sand hill.

Glenora research station

Sailing on the St. Lawrence

Keepers of the River

Muskie Musings: Time, the River and Evolution

Steve LaPan

The life out of doors can be a tiger or a lamb. It can be as tame and as harmless as a minnow. And it can be as fierce as a whale that swallows a man whole and does not spit him out until he has learned a lesson...

Steve LaPan

The best way to appreciate the life and vitality of the St. Lawrence River is through its great predator, the muskellunge, a kind of Viking lord over the common fish of the deep. As the muskie prospers, so does the river. Its strength is the pulse of St. Lawrence.

The muskie has been good for the men and women of the Thousand Islands. It has invigorated them like battle with a cunning and elusive adversary. The guides and anglers who like rough weather and a good fight on the end of the line are drawn to the beast.

For years the muskie, with its secrets hidden under the blue-green waves, seemed invincible. The river was a magical horn that bore its bounty endlessly. Then people started to notice changes. The numbers of the muskie seemed to be falling. Their size seemed to be dwindling. By the 1970s fishing guides like Clayton's James Brabant felt uneasy, disturbed.

If the muskie were declining, the river might as well be suffering a fatal wound. Anyone with a reverence for the life of the river felt the effect. Brabant and other guides were so worried about the fate of the muskie that they started releasing the creature live in the late 1970s. Brabant also warned a biologist named Dr. Don Osterberg of the State University of New York in Potsdam about the ill omens.

The muskie was feeling the effects of the disturbance caused by the construction of the St. Lawrence Seaway from 1954 to 1959 and by the growth of game fishing. In order to save the muskie from extinction --- Osterberg called the primitive fish an evolutionary Edsel --- studies were needed to understand the problem. Little was known about the muskie's spawning and eating habits. Science was a toddler that had to grow and learn.

In 1981 and 1982 Osterberg landed a grant to study the muskie at the College of Environmental Research and Forestry station on Governor's Island, near Clayton. Osterberg was a charismatic researcher and he impressed a young biologist from the Adirondack Mountains named Steve LaPan. LaPan, in turn, was inspired by his academic guru to undertake a master's thesis on pike and muskie in the St. Lawrence.

Before long, LaPan was hooked. He continued the research into the muskie on Governor's Island. The team wanted to know what the muskie did when it was hidden from sight. From 1983 to 1988 thirty-six radio transmitters were attached to muskie in the Thousand Islands. The fish, now broadcasting like aquatic radio stations, were tracked by aircraft and by boat.

Some of the findings were disheartening. One time a radio transmitter installed by the biologists became evidence used against a poacher who caught a fifty-two-inch muskie out of season. A determined United States game warden painstakingly gathered the facts that brought the man to court. The poacher received a two-hundred-dollar fine and lost his fishing licence for two years.

Yet most of the time the radio transmitters led to new information about the secretive fish. In the summer the muskie leaves its spawning grounds and ventures into deeper water to hunt fish. The biologists discovered that the St. Lawrence muskellunge could be a roamer at heart. Some ranged as much as forty kilometres in the summer from their spawning grounds. An occasionally adventuresome fish made a marathon one-hundred-and-twenty-kilometre voyage each way on the river.

LaPan also began to see through the cracks of an apparently dumb, brute existence. The muskie, LaPan realized, was crafty. It had the ability to remember. This led the biologist to believe that the fish had the spark of intelligence, a radical notion if followed to its logical conclusion. Lapan examined the evidence. Impressions of the muskie's mental ability were pieces that began to fit together.

The biologists never caught the same muskie twice in their nets. One lake muskie was observed backing out of a net after he foraged inside and boldly ate his fill of fish. The stories of muskies spitting out plugs disdainfully at anglers seemed less and less like tall tales. The muskie was not only a trophy for the angler, it was a prize for a scholar of fins and gills.

The new information also indicated that the muskie had been misunderstood and thus left unprotected by the fishing limits. In the 1970s thirty inches was a legal catch. But the biologists learned that muskies only start to breed after five years when they are about thirty-six inches long. The legal size for the catch meant that muskies could be caught before they had a chance to give birth. The muskie's ability to reproduce itself was in danger. Since the females grow faster and live longer, the muskie that was taken from the river as a trophy was the same one bearing the next generation. "Fishing parties would kill five or six muskie a day and there was no live release ethic," LaPan says, marvelling at the waste. With the low survival rate of muskie eggs and hatchlings, the savage ignorance of some anglers had put the strain under seige.

By 1988, the legal limit had been changed to forty-four inches on the American side and forty on the Canadian, giving the fish a few years grace to breed. However, that still left the problem of poaching. Anyone who wants to break the rules of the river has little to stop him but his own sense of ethics. LaPan thinks that the fines for poachers on the American side are too lenient. The Canadian side has stiffer fines and more game wardens.

The researchers led by LaPan were also able to locate the spawning grounds of the muskie in island bays. They wanted to know what the muskie needed to spawn, a step in trying to preserve the old underwater pirate of the St Lawrence. According to LaPan's reconstruction, the St. Lawrence Seaway and the dams changed the flow of the current and the level of the water. That, in turn, upset the balance. The situation was ripe for pollution and the careless destruction of the spawning grounds. The pike and walleye suffered the most. The numbers of muskie closer to the Seaway fell drastically.

However, in the Thousand Islands, LaPan thinks that the fish remained more or less stable.

LaPan sees a simple attitude in the relationship of human kind to wildlife. "We take, take, take, without giving a little back," the biologist says. And the muskie, which comes from a genetic strain developed solely in the faster flowing water of the St. Lawrence, can not be replaced. The river muskie is different, unique, LaPan argues. Its difference puts the stamp of creation on the muskie. "We would not want the genetic stock to be diluted with another strain because they could ruin the chances for survival of the muskie. If you ruin that pure St. Lawrence strain, you could crash the fishery."

The research into the muskie also had effects on LaPan. The rhythms of his life started to mesh with the seasons and the climate and the pace of existence on the river. The St. Lawrence gradually changed the biology of the biologist. By mid-winter in Syracuse, LaPan was "clawing" to get back to the river. As he spent half of the year on the St. Lawrence and studied the muskie, his purely rational credo began to crumble. The patterns of nature and evolution seemed wonderfully intricate. It was an emotional revelation.

Now LaPan lives in a world that feeds his life like it feeds the muskie. On evenings in the fall he watches the feverish, wing-flapping, horn-honking comedy of the geese and the ducks heading south with the tourists. The biologist rows a skiff into a marsh. He stops and listens to the heartfelt hum and croak and rustle of reeds. "That's religion to me. Instead of going to church I go and sit in Flynn Bay. I feel more in tune with the creator when I'm on the river than I do sitting in a brick building designated for worship."

The warmth of life flows over him like a current. Biology mixes with spiritual yearning. There is a sense of purpose.

At first science took him deeper into atheism, he says. Then a change came, an illogical, almost contradictory transformation, like gold made out of common lead.

"You start to believe more and more in some type of divine intervention, because it's just all too perfect. It's so amazing, so magnificent and so complex. There had to be some kind of master plan, some kind of guiding force, in evolution."

Governor's Island

Photo by Mike S. Kruse

Steve LaPan and muskie

Snakes and an Old Enmity in the Blood

Kathleen Burtch

Even people who scoff at the myths and legends of the snake, old father of chaos and deception, still feel queasy about the creature. There is something unnatural about the beast, as though it violates all the rules and conventions...

Kathleen Burtch

A rustle in the grass. A dark flash between rocks. A loose stick-shape in the water. Any of these could be a snake --- dread, unrestrained, uninhibited thing. In the Thousand Islands snakes --- usually the northern water snake, *Natrix sipedon sipedon* --- flow faster than the river. They flow against nature, uphill against gravity. They stream out of the water to sun their scaly, cold-blooded bodies on the warmth of island rocks. They hide in the islanders' mailboxes. They leap from docks to boats and have to be heaved back into the water. Ask Kathleen Burtch about snakes.

Born in Rockport into an old river family, Burtch works for the Canadian Parks Service in the Thousand Islands. She is a guide for school trips, a teacher in the woods, a sylvan schoolmarm. And she tries to cure children of their fear of snakes.

The children, she says, expect to see boa constrictors and pythons lurking in the woods by the river. Partly because of television, a small garter snake makes them think of the poisonous fangs of a rattlesnake, the kisses of a viper. Burtch knows the feeling. She had to conquer her own fear of snakes.

As a child Burtch had quiet brown eyes and an adventuresome spirit. She liked the forest trees, a coincidence, since her family name means birch tree and there are plenty of birches on the islands. One branch of the Burtch family, after a quarrel, split from their kin and defiantly called themselves Birches.

In fact, the birches came to the islands before the Burtches. The grey birch, a maritime *arbor*, made its trek to the area from the east coast. The tree hitchhiked as a wee seed to the Thousand Islands by riding by boat or storm wind or bird belly. "It just managed to creep along the shore and blow over to the islands," says Keith Dewar, Burtch's fellow park worker. The grey birch, however, made an abrupt and arbitrary stop in its westward passage at Mulcaster Island, near Landon's Bay, as good a spot as any to put down roots and settle.

The other Burtches were more daring. As a girl, Kathleen Burtch was a relentless explorer in a world defined by the river. She clambered across the islands with boy cousins who had the large, wheel-like ears of the Burtch clan. They built forts together in the woods and adopted small, rock caves as lairs. They made rafts from driftwood and fallen trees, which they sailed hugging the coast of a small island. They hunted painted turtles --- *Chrysemys picts marginata* --- and took them home for pets to sit humiliated in a small, dull basin of water. They drifted in marshes and gazed down through the water at the reeds where the red-backed salamander lives. "The roots were down so far you'd see pike swimming through."

Burtch baited her own hook in the boat, and dreaded the thrill of pulling a snakelike eel aboard by accident. The bountiful eels in the river had once made it good fishing grounds for the Iroquois, who had a fishing camp on Grenadier Island.

An eel "slithers through everything," Burtch says. "We were always catching eels on our hooks --- which is exciting. When you get an eel in the boat it upsets everything. The tackle box would be upset, the bait box. Or it would get under the boat and almost drag you out.

"When you're a kid, it's exciting."

The water snakes were worse. Burtch says that they will chase swimmers through the water --- their heads hoisted high like the periscope of a submarine --- when their territory is invaded. They will even nip at the skin.

When Burtch was six years old a clan of snakes turned a family picnic on an island rock into chaos. "We wanted to go down off the rock to swim. And the snakes came right up over the rocks after everyone. They were nesting there.

"I remember my father, my brother, standing there with big sticks trying to ward off the snakes.

"For years I was scared of snakes. It took me until I was thirty-five before I could pick up a snake.

"They feel strange to hold, but they won't hurt you."

Now Burtch teaches children to enjoy the plants and animals of the Thousand Islands. Not all snakes are poisonous, she tells them. And there is no reason to worry. There are no tropical lizards or wild boars or tigers in the bushes. The black rat snake has enough worries of its own, according to the park wardens. Loathed for its size --- over eight feet long --- its existence is threatened because so many are killed by cars, people and the development along the river.

How did the black rat snake get its Anglo-Saxon name? The name comes from the fact that the snake likes to dine on raw rat stew. Its menu includes everything from bats to small birds, and the snake often settles in a bird house or climbs trees to hunt for eggs.

Burtch helps the children understand the life of the black rat snake, the differences between the world of the river and the world of town. She takes them across the border of their everyday lives. Be quiet in the woods, she urges. Listen. Open yourself. She leads the children through a grove of maple or pine --- or birch, a tree of promise.

The birch, of the *Betulaceae* clan, is the first tree to bear a leaf in the spring. The first to make forest murmurs in the wind. Listen to the sounds, Burtch says. It's not the hiss of a television set, of electronic snow. Here is a richer, fuller sound. Rushing like the blood. Joyful, fearless. Here is the rustle of leaves, liquid and flowing like a brook through the forest.

Rockport

View from Grindstone Island

A Scrupulous Hunter

Ben Burley

It is an oddity of civilization. A special class of people had to be created such as biologists and naturalists and game wardens. Their job is to help preserve what should never have needed protection...

Ben Burley

It was a long, cold, futile night in February. A fresh snow had fallen. The snow lay idly over the warm carcasses of two does butchered on the ground. Ben Burley, a conservation officer with the Ontario Ministry of Natural Resources, kept watch all night. With him was a fellow game warden. The pair hoped to catch the poacher returning to finish carving the venison.

Burley had been warned that the deer had been killed out of season. He stalked the suspect with care. He stepped inside the snowy footprints of the poacher so that he would not leave any warning signs. But aside from the cold of the night that crept into the bones of the conservation officers nothing happened.

The next step was to gather evidence. The officers traced the trail of the bullet as it passed through one doe, dug a tiny tunnel in the snow and lodged in the root of a tree. They pried the slug out. Then, search warrant in hand, they knocked on the door of the poacher. In a freezer, almost empty of food --- although the man, in his mid-twenties, had a decent job --- was lying fresh venison. The officers seized a rifle for evidence. They collected a hunting knife stuck with blood and deer hair. A relative's vehicle was searched and deer hair gathered.

A conviction followed in court. The deer hair in the relative's car was incriminating. The slug that killed the deer was matched to the gun. For Burley, it was a successful conclusion to the case and he felt little sympathy for the poacher. The two does killed out of season were half-way through their six-month terms of pregnancy.

"One of the deer he took in his greed. He only took the hind quarters off, which was a waste," says Burley, who appreciates the scruples of the hunt.

Burley hunts duck and deer himself, not with a gun, but with a bow for the added challenge.

Burley is one of three conservation officers --- "when you say game warden, they know what you are" --- in the Thousand Islands section of the St. Lawrence River. The Brockville district office patrols the river, the islands and the inland stretch of the United Counties of Leeds and Grenville. Burley, a reserved, fair-haired man who likes to mingle with the country folk as part of his job, helps to enforce the game and wildlife laws. As a peace officer, he carries a loaded .38-calibre police special when he is in uniform.

Burley is more of a listener than a talker and does not romanticize the tales of a game warden. He has never fired his .38 revolver nor had to duck a bullet. He will admit only that there have been a few "scuffles" which he dismisses quickly. People breaking the game laws are not pleased to see a conservation officer, he says. They sometimes growl "idle threats in a moment of anger."

Still, Burley believes that the violation of game laws has declined in the Thousand Islands. He lays between forty and fifty charges a year, mostly over fishing, and gives three times as many warnings. In the mid-seventies the officers were laying thirty-five charges a day at the international bridge near Ivy Lea. The number of charges at the bridge dropped quickly when the Americans learned that the Canadian conservation officers were checking cars and trucks scrupulously.

The biggest problem with fishing in the area is anglers who catch and then release bass out of season. That may sound harmless enough. Yet bass in the St. Lawrence are precariously balanced for survival, compared to bass in warmer water to the south. In order for bass to grow large enough to survive their first St. Lawrence winter, the fry have to come from the first, early hatching. Anglers who take bass before the season opens --- even if they release the fish live again --- are damaging the breed. They are taking the fish that guards the eggs. When the guard fish is gone, predators can move in for the eggs. The out-of-season anglers may be harming the bass without realizing it.

Burley also believes that changes in the times have affected the violation of game laws. The poachers are dwindling along with dwindling numbers of ducks and fish. Better times economically and unemployment insurance have also made changes, he says. "People used to go out and poach as a way of survival, to put food on the table."

Most hunters and trappers obey the law, though they are more reluctant to talk these days because of the charges of cruelty to animals. People like Leonard Turner and Richard Senecal get their sense of ethics in the wild from the life they live. A big buck hanging from the barn rafters or a pile of muskrats skinned by a naked light bulb is part of the harvest. It is not canned meat.

But there is "a hard core that is incorrigible," says Mike Hart, the ministry's law enforcement co-ordinator in the district. The poachers, easily tempted, are encouraged by the sharp rise in the number of deer in the area. Yet even poachers live by a poacher's ethics. They believe in "honour among thieves" and want to protect the deer, Hart says. If outside poachers invade the territory of local poachers, the interlopers are in trouble. The local poachers will either give them a rough warning or turn them in to the game wardens.

As for duck hunters, the poachers among them have rationalizations to soothe the conscience, Hart says. A duck poacher will argue to himself that he is not exceeding his limit; he is merely shooting what he would have shot if he had been able to get out on the river during the week.

And so it goes. The river has its laws, the poachers have theirs, the ministry has a third set. And a man like Ben Burley straddles them all, ministering to the needs of the river, of the people.

While he chats on a Sunday afternoon in his truck by the St. Lawrence River seventy-four-year-old Leonard Turner spots the game warden. Turner pulls over in his station wagon. A big grin on his face, his chin white and prickled with day-old stubble, he is on the prowl for an excuse to talk. Turner asks about gun regulations and the two fall into a deep academic discussion on rifles. Burley enjoys the conversation on his sometimes lonely patrol.

Most of the conservation officer's time is spent on surveillance, ensuring that the still plentiful bass and pike are caught within the limits, that traps are set legally. Once in a while he is called in the middle of the night to help search for a drowned body. And he is careful of the unpredictable, the drunken man armed with a gun or a knife, the poacher with a criminal record.

One time the ministry was warned that three men were hunting Canada geese out of season. Burley searched the line of a fence near their property and found the bodies of two geese hidden in tall grass beside two guns. Carrying a search warrant and backed by the Ontario Provincial Police the conservation officers raided the home. The hunt was better than expected. The catch was bountiful.

The officers found a living room that had been transformed into "a marijuana garden" with pots everywhere. As they knocked on the door they also heard the frenzy of the poachers like muskrats in a cage trap. The men were desperately disposing of their drugs. "We could hear the toilet being flushed. We don't know what went down the toilet."

Brockville

An Easy Grace in the Underworld

Basil Gavin

It is an irony that a farm boy could appreciate. From the leaf of a harmless bush, the coca plant, comes cocaine, a drug which spills across the border like a dark, obliterating flood to ruin lives. And maybe a farm boy has to help clean up the mess...

Basil Gavin, undercover

Early in the morning on November 29, 1984 police in Canada and the United States made a quick, hawklike succession of raids. By the time they finished, twenty-three Canadians and thirty-nine Americans were charged with offences in the largest undercover drug investigation in the Thousand Islands. Of the sixty-two people charged, the sentences ranged from probation to fifteen years in prison for the drug lord who supplied the cocaine from Columbia, William Robert Allmond. The judge found three Canadians not guilty.

The Thousand Islands was a natural location for smuggling. The St. Lawrence River narrows here with only a few tantalizing kilometres of water between Canada and the United States. The labyrinth of islands and coves makes it easy for a boat to vanish in the shadows. Chasing a boat --- especially at night --- is dangerous because of the shoals and rocks. And strangers in the garb of fishermen pass unnoticed.

Mixing among the boaters and fishermen are drug runners, illegal aliens and sometimes even terrorists. In 1987, two members of the provisional wing of the Irish Republican Army rented a boat near Rockport on the Canadian side. They snuck across the water and thought that they had fooled the police. They were caught at the Watertown bus station in a joint police operation between Canada and the United States. The IRA members said that their organization had given them a free holiday in the United States. They were probably arranging to exchange guns and money.

The Thousand Islands has a long tradition of smuggling. Many of the river folk participated in the rum-running days of Prohibition. Rockport had a tough, professional rum-runner named Bill Circle, according to Claude William Hunt, who wrote a book about Ontario's bootleggers and rum-runners. Circle broke the ethics of the river --- but not by smuggling. His crime on the water was hijacking boats to do the work. Another local rum-runner interviewed by Hunt, Norm Conley of Wolfe Island, rowed the booze across the river when he was a teenager. The Americans saw the rum-runners as heroic, Hunt says, and farmers in the United States even sold landing rights on their property.

Yet if farmers and river rats helped in the smuggling, they also helped keep the law. One of the officers behind the 1984 drug bust --- called Operation Waterfall in the United States, Operation Waterworks in Canada --- was a friendly, middle-aged Ontario Provincial Police constable named Basil Gavin.

Like many of the officers at the Gananoque detachment of the OPP, Gavin has strong ties to the Thousand Islands. Born near the village of Lansdowne, Gavin shuns the sergeant's exam that would mean a promotion outside the area. The river, the lake region and the excitement of working in one of the OPP's busiest districts are a tempting combination for him.

Born on a dairy farm in 1934, Gavin looked for more worldly adventure than milking cows. At seventeen, like a brother before him, he joined a Canadian cargo ship company named Keystone Transport as a deck hand and wheelman on a two-hundred-and-fifty-foot lake freighter. The ships made runs from Montreal to Lake Erie carrying coal, wheat and iron ore, with the coal-fired engines throbbing monotonously all day long and spewing sooty smoke that the deck hands had to scrub from the sides. That was before the St. Lawrence Seaway opened the river and the Great Lakes to the giant, ocean-going cargo ships. In those days the smaller vessels avoided the Lachine Rapids by a dainty system of canals and locks.

The helm of a laker is different from other boats, says the sailor turned cop, because of the massive weight and momentum of the vessel. "It was a little frightening at first because of the size." The helmsman turns the wheel according to the skipper's instructions, but before the ship starts to turn, the helmsman spins the wheel back. He anticipates what the ship will eventually do.

Gavin remembers the difference a quarter load of iron ore made compared to wheat. "A load of iron ore makes the boat very sluggish, whereas a full cargo of wheat makes the ship handle much better." In those days the river traffic was much smaller and daredevils from Alexandria Bay came out in tiny boats to ride the great wakes of the lakers.

After three years Gavin quit the merchant marine and held a number of plant jobs, finally deciding in 1967, at thirty-four, to join the OPP in Gananoque. After five years on traffic and boat patrol for the local detachment, he joined the criminal investigations branch to track people smuggling cigarettes, electronic equipment and drugs.

One of his main tasks was gathering information. "When you are gathering information you don't get a big revelation all of a sudden. It's a lot of things that are put together that become important." Besides his insight, Gavin is fabled around the department for an almost perfect memory.

The Gananoque OPP and the New York State Police were central to Operation Waterworks because of their knowledge of the Thousand Islands. Operation Waterworks began in April of 1983 with Gavin directing the undercover operators on the Canadian side. He also worked as the backup in case of trouble, hanging back in the shadows, but packing a .38-calibre automatic. The operation consisted of painstakingly tracking down leads to the key drug dealers and traffickers in the area and making purchases which would be used as evidence in court.

The amounts were not large, perhaps an ounce of cocaine, speed or hashish. A deal would be struck either in person or by telephone, the drugs would be taken across the river in a high-speed boat to the drop point, where the undercover officers --- like New York State Police officer Tom Fenzel, who is also a fishing guide --- took the drugs like regular customers and bided their time until evidence could be collected against the entire ring. Gavin was too well known on the Canadian side to be used as an undercover drug buyer. As well, his age made him look suspicious. "I'm too old to buy drugs. No one would be interested in selling me drugs. They'd wonder what I would be doing," he says. Still, Gavin had a knack for sitting in a bar unobserved as the backup officer. There was no need for a disguise. He stayed "in a discreet position."

After the raids of Operation Waterworks and the court appearances, Gavin went back to his regular undercover work gathering information for convictions. He admits that being a cop in the Thousand Islands lets him see "the seedier side," but the river makes it easy to forget. "I wish it was different, but it doesn't take away the pleasure. That's part of being a policeman. You can separate the two things."

Gananoque

The Angler Undercover

Tom Fenzel

During the Prohibition era many of the river folk helped smuggle liquor across the water into the United States. But the current drug traffic is different in spirit. Some get their stimulus from drugs and money. Others get it from the river...

Tom Fenzel

Over a beer in a bar Tom Fenzel is an angler with a passion. He can talk about the thirty-seven-inch muskie that he landed after the boys in the boat had given up for the day. He can swap information about the best spots. Personally, he likes the "back of Grindstone Island," where the bass, pike, muskie and walleye are good. A likeable man with an explosive, boyish laugh, Fenzel makes friends easily. And that was the mistake that the drug dealers made.

For two years Fenzel, a New York State Police investigator, played a key role in the drug investigation called Operation Waterfall in the United States, Operation Waterworks in Canada. In the 1980s the police on both sides of the border believed that there was an organized drug smuggling ring operating through a pipeline in the Thousand Islands. Hash and chemically manufactured drugs like LSD were going south from Canada. Marijuana and cocaine were coming north from the United States.

The police in Canada and the United States decided that it was time to surprise the drug smugglers and work together on an investigation. Fenzel by then had developed a knack for drug work. He had been promoted into the New York State Police Bureau of Criminal Investigation in the Alexandria Bay area. Because of his knowledge of the river and smuggling he was given the rank of sergeant to help direct undercover operations. To extend his range, he was sworn in as a United States marshal and, a first in Canada, as an Ontario Provincial Police officer.

The work was long and often unrewarding --- much, Fenzel says, like hunting or fishing, and with the same need for patience. Fenzel and his operatives would come to the Canadian side, where they were strangers. They disappeared into the crowd on the streets and in the bars of Kingston and Gananoque. Then came the laborious work of putting out a line and trolling for drug traffickers.

Fenzel would chat about moose hunting and bass fishing and the Toronto Blue Jays in the bars. He listened to stories of big muskies. He fitted in well and the dealers trusted him, selling him marijuana at first. The buy finished, he might ask about another drug and that would lead to a new contact. The drug trade was based on a cold, feverish greed which made the traffickers easier to deceive.

The drugs were often transported in bags loaded with rocks so that the evidence could be thrown overboard if the boat were stopped. "Unknown to them we were controlling the situation," says Basil Gavin, a constable with the Ontario Provincial Police. "We didn't need to chase them because we knew where they were going."

Three boaters from Gananoque on the Canadian side and three on the American side worked for the drug network. The boaters were part-time criminals, Gavin says, who were proud of their boats and their knowledge of the river. "They thought of themselves as boaters. Their life was on the water."

Every once in a while the investigation would take an odd twist. Fenzel remembers the time that a man was paid $1,000 to smuggle a small amount of drugs across the river in his boat to Rockport. The trafficker, in turn, subcontracted the job to a friend for $100, pocketing $900 with no risk to himself.

Another time, at the end of winter, Fenzel, still undercover, sat in a car on Wellesley Island waiting for a drop. The smugglers wanted to avoid the border guards by crossing the ice from Hill Island on the Canadian side to Wellesley Island in the United States. But the river gave one foolhardy smuggler a taste of its winter codes. "He hopped from ice floe to ice floe. He scared the heck out of himself. It was in February or March when the ice was breaking up. He got in the car and said, 'I didn't know the ice was that bad.'"

The drug traffickers tried to cheat each other, even over the exchange rate on American funds. One of the dealers grumbled to an undercover officer that he had been cheated on the exchange rates. He should have been paid $100,000 American for drugs and was given a suitcase full of money. It was only later that he discovered that the top layer of $25,000 was American, with the rest in Canadian bills.

After a year of investigation, Operation Waterfall --- which also included the United States Drug Enforcement Administration, the Federal Bureau of Investigation, United States Immigration, United States Customs, Canada Customs and the Royal Canadian Mounted Police --- finally ended. Fenzel was commended for his work and in 1987 retired. He couldn't abandon his police work, though. He now works part time as an investigator for the Jefferson County District Attorney.

Fenzel also took a part-time job with the St. Lawrence Seaway Authority enforcing the speed limits for the large commercial ships. Armed with a radar gun he patrols the river in his boat. Sometimes at three in the morning with the rain falling he sits in a car on the shoreline watching for offenders. His biggest catch was a six-hundred-foot ocean-going cargo ship that was one and a half knots over the speed limit, a significant infraction in a sea lane.

These days Fenzel can be seen cruising the river in his sixteen-foot fishing boat *This Is It*. His laugh is still hearty and infectious. He has tips on the best fishing spots from the masters, such as the late Brendan Reid of Gananoque. But a big fish is a different kind of catch from a drug smuggler and inspires a different kind of ethic. "When there is a real wall-hanger, I don't keep the fish. I throw it back. I'm independent that way."

Alexandria Bay

A Confusion of Island Names

Anne "Blu" Mackintosh

A list of the names of islands in the river makes a whimsical sort of music. There is Potato and Popham, Codfish and The Punts. There is Heart and Habour, Idlewild, Spilsbury and Little Lehigh. Yet there is discord in the names, too. Mistakes and devilish confusion sometimes creep in...

Blu Mackintosh and her map

In 1535, the French explorer Jacques Cartier discovered the tail end of mighty serpent of a river, the 1,197-kilometre long stretch of the St. Lawrence River. It was a new, boundless land. And the river led straight into an unknown territory, if only the rock-fanged rapids could be wrestled into submission.

The new land also needed surveyors and cartographers. The geography of the Thousand Islands, with its wild proliferation of islands, was a cartographer's joy, a whole new galaxy of islands to draw on paper and name. The map makers would tame the chaos, give it a decorous shape, a comprehensible name. However, the task was heroic and larger than one person, since the number of islands was almost endless.

Coming up with a figure for the number of islands depends on the definition of an island. When does a rock poking through the water become an island? How big must it be? Should it have trees and plants? Is it still an island if it is submerged when the water is high? One definition of an island produces nine hundred and ninety-seven --- a niggardly three short of the magical one thousand. Keith Dewar of the St. Lawrence Islands National Park says that he gets "hung, drawn and quartered" if he quotes nine hundred and ninety-seven to river folk. There is another figure, 1,115, which includes "everything a boat can hit." However, Dewar says that purists insist that a shoal is not an island, that a genuine island "must have grass and a few trees." A third figure by river rat geologist Shannon McCune puts the number of islands at 1,865, plus an artificial island.

To add to the problems of fixing the number of islands, some islands with low spots have, within a relatively short period of time, split into two islands, and the construction of the Thousand Islands Parkway turned islands into peninsulas.

The difficulty of defining an island and then saying with authority that the number has been counted should be a warning. Life in the Thousand Islands sometimes refuses to be amenable and civilized. There is a built-in wiliness, like a beast that will not submit or be tamed.

Yet there is more. Not only is the sheer number of islands almost unconquerable for the heroic cartographer, the attempt to impose single names is doomed to defeat. Many of the islands these days have two or three names. So instead of a profusion of islands finally reduced to a simple order, there is more confusion. Even local people argue about the names, with variations that differ from one family to the next. Anyone who asks where an island such as Blueberry is, could get four or five answers.

Then came Anne Mackintosh, battler of chaos, restorer of order, like Adam in the garden, a kind of lexicographer or librarian sorting out the names of things.

As past president of the river watchdog group the Thousand Islands Area Residents Association (TIARA), Mackintosh decided it was time to tidy the records. With TIARA as the publisher, she produced a map covering the Canadian side of the river from Howe Island in the west to Mallorytown Landing in the east.

But many were the trials along the way.

Being a scholar of island names had its risks and dangers. For Mackintosh it was a long and arduous paper journey, tracing the names of islands through three hundred and fifty owners listed on the tax rolls. Cross-referencing the variations in names for the three-section map was a task that would have wearied anyone less hardy than Odysseus.

But the labours gave Mackintosh a fresh glimpse of the islands. The contradictions and confusion that she had to sort out gave her insight into life along the river.

Mackintosh worked through a series of island names that succeeded each other like one civilization built on top of another. Researching the map was an adventure in time and history and language, she says. "It was like an archeological dig."

The naming of the islands began with the Indians. Those names were part of an oral tradition largely forgotten now, though some islanders have tried to recreate the era of the Iroquois and the Mississaugua with exotic names like Sagistawika and Chinguacousie.

After the Indians the French came in the 1600s, followed by the British, who controlled the St. Lawrence after the defeat of France on the Plains of Abraham in 1759.

The British fought for possession of the area again in the War of 1812, and with that victory --- and the vindication of ownership --- came, not a flood of settlers, but a burst of island-naming. A British surveyor named Captain William Fitzwilliam Owen started naming the larger islands in a burst of industry.

Owen chose the names of naval officers and marine themes. For instance, in a cluster called the Lake Fleet Islands the bloodthirsty names Deathdealer and Bloodletter came from ships of the War of 1812, as did, oddly enough, the romantic Endymion and Camelot. Further along the river unseaworthy names like Cleopatra and Dromedary also came from ships. In the Navy Islands, Mulcaster and Downie and Bouchier were derived from officers in the war.

Probably desperate for names after a while because of the number of islands, Owen grabbed anything handy. There are islands named after nothing more inspired than boats --- Long Schooner, The Punts, Barge, Steamer, Scow.

After the British surveyors and the division of the river between Britain and the United States, the process of naming the smaller, more obscure islands fell to local people, who were free to follow their own inspiration.

River people were practical and down to earth, Mackintosh says. They named an island for its size or purpose or memories --- Burnt Island for a fire, Corn Island for crops, Hog Island for the hogs. Sensible enough.

Then, as islands were bought by summer residents and the local people worked as caretakers, the names followed different sociological channels. A summer resident would either adopt the traditional name or grasp for something more romantic. His local caretaker, thinking on another level, would be more pragmatic and refer to the island by the name of the owner.

Thus, for the people of Rockport the property once owned by United States Senator Himes --- he had no first name, as far as the local people remember --- is now listed officially on the charts as Himes Island. Previous names for Himes Island were Opawaka Lodge, Dashwood and Pine. Mackintosh says with a sigh that "official just means what the government is recognizing at the moment."

As one owner followed another, the names were piled on top, like an old stack of magazines, generation by generation. And an oral, rather than a written or recorded tradition was created. That brought more confusion, since people did not know how the names were spelled. Was it the island of Himes or Hime? Was it Birks or Burkes?

About the 1920s, as even smaller islands sprouted cottages, the pattern of the names began to change again. People from the cities, well read and romantic in their thinking, gave the islands elaborate, often dreamy names --- Atlantis, Fairyland, Lotus.

Since the name did not always fit the look or purpose of the island --- as did Flat, High, Lone Tree or Sheep --- it would be easy to forget names or accidentally transpose them.

Still, a river man would ignore the dreamy name of a rock, Mackintosh says. "He'd still be calling it Junk Island."

Sometimes it was a struggle to get the name accepted locally. For instance, Margaret Reid --- who appears later in *River Rats* --- changed the name of her island to the more romantic-sounding Chinguacousie. One day Reid phoned a local workman to come to the island, but trying to make him understand where she lived was like talking to a person with no ears. Reid battled valiantly for the honour of Chinguacousie and her right to rename an island, but she fell to defeat. "He didn't know what she was talking about," Mackintosh says. "Finally she had to say, 'Oh, all right, Potato Island.' "

There were moments of horror and frustration for Mackintosh, adrift in the chaos. The task seemed to grow unwieldy. The labyrinth of islands had spawned an even more vast labyrinth of names.

If others might have slipped beneath the waves of scholarship and drowned, Mackintosh, the heroic map-navigator, persevered. More insights came.

The older local residents, who prefer to use the name of the owner of the island, are "usually one or two names behind." This is because their tradition as caretakers on a certain island --- a heritage that makes them proud --- may go back several generations. "They love being involved with these families."

"And there's that curious relationship between local people and summer people. They've grown up with each other quite often --- for instance, Eric Truesdell and the Birks. The Truesdells have always looked after that island."

According to Mackintosh, the summer residents and the river folk have an affection for each other, having spent years together. Yet they are not blind to the sharp differences between themselves. "Each of them has an admiration for what the other does and probably each of them, by themselves, would make fun of the other, such as 'city dwellers don't know beans' and 'country dwellers aren't sophisticated.' "

"It's a wonderful relationship.

"And you have layers and layers of it as families grow up together."

Trying to fix the official name of an island was often a nightmare for Mackintosh, as though the more orderly she wanted to be, the more chaotic things became. Some of the islands were real puzzles, especially when people gave different locations to an island with the same name.

Before long Mackintosh realized that there could be two or three different islands with the same name. "Until you recognize that that's happened, you think, 'What is wrong with me?' "

For instance, when Mackintosh sent letters to the residents of one numbered island she got two names, Alnwick and Sunset, sometimes from the same person. She learned later that the confusion came from her own assumptions, from not asking the right question.

In the case of Alnwick and Sunset, a low bridge of land became a channel over time, creating two islands. Yet both islands were known by the same official number and were drawn as one island on the chart.

There is also a lot of duplication of names, which multiplied the confusion. "People kept saying this is Red Horse. I finally had to admit there were two Red Horses."

"So someone would say to you, 'Do you know Blueberry Island was also called something else?' And you'd say, 'Which Blueberry Island?' "

Mackintosh was able to find five Blueberries, four Huckleberries, not to mention inspired name-spawning, as one island becomes the little version of another. So White Calf has Little White Calf, and Tar keeps company with the tongue-twisting twins, Baby Tar and Tar Baby. What else would the smaller version of Pine be but Pine Cone? The word game could be elaborate, Mackintosh discovered, with Belabourer followed by Belittler.

Another typical piece of devilry for Mackintosh was the confusion between Ash and Lyndoch, which still frustrates island owner Bill Browning. Browning --- described later in the section "The Man Who Gave an Island to the Birds" --- wails against the official government maps that designate his island as Ash. Browning says that Ash is really Lyndoch, the name which appears on the charts as a small island under the spurious Ash. Mackintosh agrees that Lyndoch is the original name of Ash and says that the Lyndoch on the charts is a misspelling of Lyndoe.

Keeping the islands straight is not easy.

A husband and wife interviewed by Mackintosh each thought their island had a different name. And both were right. That island had two traditional names. The harmony of the marriage was restored.

Mackintosh discovered that river people, like the islands, fell into different clusters, decided mainly by the logic of the river. "The people in Gananoque did not know Rockport, and I had to get another source for the islands near Mallorytown Landing." Gananoque is only twenty kilometres from Rockport.

Yet the same people from Rockport who did not know the Gananoque stretch would know the islands across to Alexandria Bay on the American side. Mackintosh saw logic in this, especially for the older folk. "They rowed places. They didn't go by motor boat. They knew across the river.

"They would be talking about their youth and they'd say, 'Oh, when we were young we went over to the Bay for dances.'"

Mackintosh thinks that the nature of the river and its currents was part of the reason for this behaviour. It would be easier to row across the river to Alexandria Bay than strain against the current to Gananoque. Thus the river may have done more to shape social groups than the political differences between Canada and the United States.

Naming the islands followed similar patterns. The river folk would name an island inside the natural geographic boundaries of the river and would not know the islands outside their area. Thus the same name --- such as Pine or Corn or Blackberry --- would be repeated in two or three locations.

Part of the fun of naming an island was the ingenuity involved. It took humour to come up with a name for tiny islands, such as Toothpick and Flea Bite. Paradoxes abound, such as Upper Twin with no Lower Twin, since Lower Twin was inexplicably changed to Dock or Submarine Island. And looking over the map bizarre and out-of-place names leap out, such as a Wyoming and Cuba in the middle of the St. Lawrence.

Among the wittiest was the family who came up with the ultimate name for a small nameless island. They were tired of being asked, "What is the name of that island?" The question was repeated so many times it was irritating.

Finally they gave the rock the name that answered the question. What is the name of that island now? Why, it's That Island.

Shipman's Point

Rugged shoreline

River Rats

With Peace and Calm of Mind, All Passion Spent

Walter Dowd

There are borders that separate countries. There are borders that separate times and ages. And there are borders that separate types of people. Crossing the border between river rat and landlubber, between the man of independence and the man of convention, are the Walt Dowds ...

Walter Dowd

The Thousand Islands is still a frontier, a border area. There is the political border between Canada and the United States. It runs down the St. Lawrence River snaking and dodging wildly between the islands like a beast that refuses to be shackled. And then there is the mental border between different ways of life.

Some people, like Walter Dowd, cross back and forth between town and river, between one way of life and another. During the winter the town of Gananoque is Dowd's fortification. He lives on an obscure back lane that looks like a driveway between houses. In the summer, Dowd leaves the town and makes raids on the fertile country of the spirit, the river. In his own cautious and reverent words he is a "part-time" river rat.

Dowd came to Gananoque and the river in 1935. He was thirteen, on the threshold of puberty, a time of change and experiment. During that period the lure of the river mixed with his hormones and concocted a rich and heady brew. It was the beginning of a lifelong fascination with the water and the islands. Dowd does not quite understand what moves him, but he knows he is part of a crowd.

"For some it's an attraction. For some it's a compulsion. There are times when the water just takes precedence over everything. I may have lots of things to do around the house, but the river gets first call. I don't know whether you'd call that a compulsion or not, but it's the river that I go to. It's just like a magnet."

The need for the river can be absolute, Dowd says. He jokingly calls the seduction a fatal attraction, a bond that can only be broken by death.

Dowd recalls an islander who died the previous year. "He had a home on Hay Island and --- he wasn't a local person --- but even though he was deathly ill, and even though he could only be up for twenty minutes a day --- he had to spend the rest of his time in bed --- he insisted on being on that island every summer." The man was forty-eight when he died.

"Many, many, many people have that same attraction."

Some are tempted by the river. They forget their duties and responsibilities, like a flirtation in a distant foreign land. But the relationship does not last. In the end the harshness of the winter breaks the romance. "Sooner or later fall comes. You can't stay there anyway.

"But there are people, the Orrs for instance, who come up here as soon as the ice is out. It is just absolutely miserable and they're there every chance they get."

Dowd launches his boat in the water soon after the spring break-up of the ice, the true equinox and sign of the new season for the boaters and islanders. He recalls the marks left in the woodwork of the weekly newspaper office in Gananoque, where he worked for fifty years beginning as a printer's devil, or apprentice. Going down the staircase into the basement someone, a kindred spirit of the water, had written on the wood the times of the spring break-up. The moment that the ice broke up was as important as the phases of the moon are to an astrologer.

Dowd is a man who keeps his thoughts private, unlike forceful, blunt river rats such as Harold Herrick and Bruce Woodman. The town-bred moral censor is always working in him. He refuses to divulge the wild tales he knows about river folk. He prefers to keep the peace instead. Unlike the river rat, his caution and morality leave him with a storm of pent-up energy.

Yet Dowd has a form of release. He goes to the river to ease the problems of the day. "If there are any frustrations, I get wound up very tight." Dowd's old-time elixir and prescription for good health was to cross the border on the water twice, cut under the international bridge at Ivy Lea and then circle back. It seemed to work. "If I was really wound up, I'd jump in the boat and run from Gananoque to Clayton to Alexandria Bay to Rockport, do the fifty-mile trip, be back before dark. I beat out my frustrations by pounding the hell out of the boat."

By coincidence, Dowd was using the river as it had been hundreds of years ago. The passage from turmoil to peace was once recognized in the same spot in the St. Lawrence by a rite of baptism and initiation. Researcher Christina Bates says that the rite took place at the Lost Channel, which the Canadian span of the Thousand Islands International Bridge now crosses. Bates quotes a British officer who described the ceremony in 1785. After rough treatment from the rapids on the river, the Lost Channel (also called by its French name, the Petit Detroit) signalled the beginning of gentler water. "At the Petit Detroit they perform the ceremony of baptising those who have never gone up the river before," the British officer said. The initiates were sprinkled with water from a branch of leaves dipped in the river. "The whole [ceremony] finishes by you making them a present of a bottle of rum."

Now that Dowd is retired and can enjoy the river as much as he wants he faces the curse of the area, the unrepressed boat traffic in July and August. It is not the same river that the longtime residents remember. At least Dowd's island, Juniper --- one or two vacationing deer swim there every season from the larger Leek Island --- is still a quiet refuge. There he does the ritual chores --- "a little painting, a little cutting grass" --- and fishes for pike, the lazy man's fish, not bass.

Yet for all the pike fishing, Dowd says that he can not compete with the deep-current souls of the Thousand Islands. They are different. They have had the river "inbred" in them for generations. "The water, for me, has been a sideline. They're much more relaxed and devil-may-care than a part-time person like myself."

Dowd marvels at the cool abandon of a man like Clarence Huntley. "He's a very efficient man on the water. He does his work well and he does it economically."

Dowd remembers one stormy day when Huntley braved the windy, open water of the Forty Acres at the mouth of the river. Huntley was towing two barges and a small boat using only his half-cabin launch as a tug. "I was just amazed that he started out."

"Rolly McIntosh is a river rat. He makes his living from the river. He probably had choices. He chose the river.

"I think he's very inventive, original. How many boats do you see around with windmills on them? He is unique in many ways. He makes the river adapt to him. He doesn't adapt to the river. Most everybody else, we adapt to the river."

Gananoque

Gananoque

The Barefooted Old Boy of the River

Rolly McIntosh

If the marshes and the sly, ingenious, hidden channels of the river could talk, they'd have the voice of one man. His image is legend along the river, compounded of bare feet, a windmill luxuriating in the wind, an occasional brawl ...

Rolly McIntosh and Rita Cirtwill on the houseboat

The blue eyes are flecked with a milky white. They have the untouched, faraway look of a dreamer. In summer and in winter the bare soles pad easily, softly, over the decks of boats and barges like the feet of a human panther, a seafaring gypsy. This is Rolly McIntosh, a man apart from others, the closest anyone can get to being spawned and bred and shaped by a river.

It is easy to catch sight of McIntosh's home in the Thousand Islands. Just look for the outlandish red-tipped blades of a windmill on a houseboat. Sometimes, if the houseboat is moored beside barge and crane, the assembly looks like a tiny nation, like the Grand Duchy of Luxembourg afloat.

McIntosh has built for himself a way of life that follows his own star. If he wants to move his home, he pulls the anchor and starts the engine of the houseboat. Two waterwheels powered by a one-hundred-and-forty horsepower diesel engine churn the water. McIntosh steers the ungainly square block from a small wheelhouse.

Catching McIntosh, the owner of a marine construction business, for an hour or two is another matter. He loves to chat, but he also fidgets, uncomfortable with the chains of clock time and the compulsion to reflect. He follows his own dates and deadlines and schedules. He is good-naturedly late at times, but the mixture of strength and vulnerability is alluring. Friends can be forgiving. And it would be a shame to have the free-spirited McIntosh bound by conventions.

One of the first memories McIntosh has is "bouncing around through the big waves" of Lake Ontario at five. McIntosh was born in 1933. His father was a commercial fisherman living near the water in Picton. Details about the family are obscure, though the father, Clayton, was a Canadian-American hybrid. Was Clayton an American? "In a way he was," answers McIntosh. "I think he was born in the States."

At fifteen, McIntosh announced to his mother, "I'm going to go sailing if I have to sail a barge." A year later he quit school and started a salvage business with a friend modelled after work he had done for his father. The two boys salvaged the shells that the wartime Royal Canadian Air Force dropped in the water near Picton for target practice. Some of the shells were live when recovered, McIntosh says, and he had to defuse them. Then the lead was sold as scrap.

By the late 1950s McIntosh, nearing thirty, was driving a tug boat for the construction of the St. Lawrence Seaway. He slept on one of the large crew barges and avoided disasters like the time the boat his brother was piloting stalled and slipped over the edge of a twenty-foot dam. The boat was smashed to pieces. The brother was unharmed and swam to shore.

Next McIntosh joined the dredging company of Douglas Mackintosh --- called Black Douglas after Mackintosh's Scottish ancestry --- and started hauling sand from Grenadier Island to Brockville for cement. It was a rough river enterprise that ended in fist fights and court actions over territory. The sand was a humble mineral, dredged from the bottom with a suction machine and washed. And the result was "a beautiful sand, a good, sharp sand," McIntosh says.

But the Black Douglas crew ran afoul of a man who had been dredging the Grenadier Island sand for years. A dispute erupted over a bay and the work crew found its way barred deliberately by a boat. The man refused to budge. Black Douglas retaliated by towing the boat away, which added fuel to the feud. "He hired a bunch of thugs because he knew we were going to pull him out of the way," McIntosh says. The river man brawled with the man's two sons, claiming victory in at least one round.

McIntosh remembers a moment that came sweet with revenge. The ornery contractor had parked his boat in the way and had his deck loaded with men itching for a fight. McIntosh came prepared with one of the high-pressure hoses used in the river work. "I grabbed the hose," McIntosh says, "and I washed all his crew off the deck. The old man hung on as long as he could and finally skidded across the deck." The man got even by taking McIntosh to court for assault with the hose and won his case. But the contractor was also taken to court over water rights and damaged income and lost the case to Black Douglas.

McIntosh and Mackintosh became partners when Mackintosh bought forty acres of waterfront property west of Ivy Lea and set up a permanent marine construction and salvaging business. A channel was dredged, which over the years has collected a few backwater castoffs, like the small, half-sunken trailer McIntosh once called home. In 1967 the partners split, though they are still neighbours.

The river is not as dangerous as Lake Ontario --- where McIntosh once lost a boat in a storm --- but there have been some close calls on the St. Lawrence. One time McIntosh and a crew were towing a barge that they had salvaged in Quebec with a fifty-foot tug boat. The snow was flying as they entered the narrows near Brockville after dark.

"We didn't see the ship coming. We didn't have a quarter enough light." McIntosh saw a seven-hundred-foot laker loom ahead out of the snow and grabbed the wheel to turn tug and barge hard to starboard. The crew on the barge got as close a view of a laker as anyone could want. "They claim they could see every rivet going along the ship's side."

Over the years McIntosh has seen almost as much of life on the river as the fish. One time he salvaged a boat from Gananoque that had run up on Crossover Island two hundred feet into the woods. The boat knocked small trees out of the way as it ran ashore. The boat engine "must have been wide open," McIntosh says. When he found the craft the next morning the party was still aboard, "half plastered." The boat took a vicious scraping, though McIntosh was surprised the damage wasn't worse. "It was amazing the whole bottom wasn't gone off." In the late sixties McIntosh also lifted from the bottom of the river a car that had rolled off a dock while the people were still inside. The doors on the car stuck,

Rolly McIntosh's houseboat

but the people escaped in the water by cutting the canvas top of the convertible.

Yet whatever bizarre things happen on the river, nothing could match the sight of the houseboat McIntosh built himself in 1981. Working without plans from a design in his head --- as he did for the countless barges and four tugs he also built himself --- he first constructed a twenty by forty-five-foot steel barge, then lifted a flat-roofed bungalow on top by crane.

McIntosh cut a hole in the floor in the middle of the living room. Over the hole was fixed a table, hollow in the centre like a donut. A fishing line was tied to a ship's wheel on the ceiling and dangled through the hole in the table into the water below. When a fish grabs the hook a bell on the line jingles. "It's nice for the winter. You can sit right here and fish and play cards."

The roof of the houseboat is laid with green outdoor carpet, what McIntosh calls his "front lawn." It has a picnic table with a Coca-cola umbrella, a child's wading pool and flower boxes growing tomatoes, carrots, peas and lettuce. The windmill turns in the air currents storing electricity for the generators. And, says the cunning McIntosh, there is no tax bill for a house that floats on water.

On a summer's day you can sometimes see the houseboat fixed in the clothlike haze of river heat like a mirage. McIntosh may be out there somewhere, if you can find him. The hook hasn't been made that can catch and hold him for long. And there is only one thing that can get him off the river. "I'm going to have to give it up some day --- I'll be dead."

Near Ivy Lea

Rolly McIntosh's houseboat

The One-Eyed Rabbit Comes to Dinner

Martha Service Grimes

Too much solitude on the river can drive a person insane, says Martin Copp, a man reserved for a later appearance in River Rats. For the moment, the corollary according to Copp is that the men who keep their sanity as river rats need a wife and a family ...

Martha Grimes

A river rat can be a seductive creature.

When Martha Service was fifteen she was drawn to an unusually quiet boy on the rim of the high school's social life. He spent his school days dreaming of freedom and independence on the river, and played hooky to go hunting or fishing.

The girl was also quiet, but responsible, without the same abandon and streak of rebelliousness. She admired the boy's daring and was intrigued to be stalking a hermit creature who eluded others. "I was looking for a boyfriend who was different. My friends thought I was crazy."

"Nobody knew him. Nobody had taken the time to find out about him. He was standoffish. He was very much an individual. His conversation -- if you got conversation out of him was not playful bantering between boys and girls. He wouldn't have said anything voluntarily."

Martha Service had little choice if she wanted to spend time with Hunter Grimes. He did not go to dances. She would have to go fishing.

That was not a great concession, she felt, since she loved the memories of bullhead fishing with her grandfather. In the evenings the Service children would dig up nightcrawlers in the garden, then, sitting on the shore of Cranberry Creek, dangle the lines from cane poles under the humble glare of a kerosene lamp.

Fishing with Grimes was "a ritual," she says. "He would tell me what we had to do, what time we had to be there.

"I remember one time --- we were probably sixteen --- we went fishing in the summer during bass season and I caught a really good-sized bass, which he cleaned for me. I took it home and my mother cooked it for dinner. I was quite proud of that."

"As we got older, he took me deer hunting with him and was trying to teach me to enjoy the woods as much as he did, which I did, but for different reasons.

"I wasn't there to pursue the deer. I was there because it was quiet. I went to be with him."

The romance with the river rat deepened. In spite of Grimes' absolute and uncompromising nature, Martha did not feel dominated. Her mind was her own and she admitted that she liked tasting another side of life, one that might have been denied to her. When Grimes came back from his tour of duty in Vietnam --- for special service work he could not discuss with her --- the allure was intensified.

The two married in 1970 when both were twenty-four. Martha Grimes had won her Rhinegold, a bright wedding band, and committed herself to pursuing the intoxicating impulses of Grimes the adventurer. The penniless newlyweds headed north. Six weeks into the marriage found them in Alaska, where a September snow had fallen on the cold ground. Martha Grimes, who had never fired a gun before, was carrying a double-barrelled shotgun to hunt small game for dinner. After a long wait a rabbit shook the bushes politely, hopped trustingly into the open. Martha Grimes fired. The unexpected kick of the gun knocked her head over heels. The rabbit escaped. Grimes took the shotgun and handed his wife a more domestic instrument, a pistol.

"Sure enough, another rabbit comes hopping along. He's yelling, 'Shoot, shoot.' I turned my head the other way and shot. And," she says with a burst of shy, amazed, exultant laughter, "I shot the rabbit through the eye."

Alaska was part of the adventure of marriage for Martha Grimes. Her husband was changing, becoming more outspoken and sociable, with a charm that later would be contagious, and the lure of his bold, unconventional nature still set him apart.

Alaska was a magic kingdom for a couple starting life together.

"We were so dependent on each other --- because we were so far from home. We knew no one when we got there.

"And it was like neither one of us could exist without the other."

The two returned to Alexandria Bay. They hunted and fished together and Grimes brought to the marriage, to the dominion of romance which was Martha Grime's river, different kinds of game. In the chili, wild moose meat was substituted for grocery store hamburger. Grimes shared the duties at the stove, taking control if the lean, easily dried game needed to be kept raw and cooked with no waste.

Martha Grimes had a university degree which would allow her to teach and the pair were about to start a family of two. But the parent and a teacher in her now saw the river through changed eyes.

As a teacher Martha Grimes felt more deeply the social problems of isolation on the river. One family, she remembers, lived in a swamp without electricity. Adapting to the school and social life was difficult for their children, who sometimes had the forlorn look of teddy bears with an eye torn out.

As her own children became teenagers, the lure of the river sounded again, creating a new dilemma for Martha Grimes. Her son wanted a boat of his own and freedom on the river. He was declaring the same independent spirit that had drawn her to Hunter Grimes.

Yet a mother thinks differently. There would have to be restrictions for the children on the river. Her son would not be allowed the same rebellious freedom as his father. Yes, it is a contradiction, she says.

"I hope he learns from his father all the skills he needs to be a river rat," she says laughing. "I know he's caught the bug."

Alexandria Bay

Temptations of a River Rat

Hunter Grimes

The man who Martha Grimes married is a remarkable creation who tested all her resources and proved that she had the resolution of mind and the independence of spirit to resist being swallowed by the strength of his personality ...

Hunter Grimes and his set of wings

In the eyes of a ten-year-old river boy a river rat was common stuff. And near Alexandria Bay on a tiny island in Otter Creek was an old river rat.

"He was gnarled, compact, very muscular for an old man. He was always an old man when I knew him, typically weather beaten from squintin' into the sun --- You get a lot of sun off the water. It does that to you --- dishevelled and unkempt. I never saw him really filthy, though. He never seemed to smell real bad. He smelled rich, earthy --- which I don't mind at all."

The old man would let the stubble on his chin grow till it irritated him, then shave, Hunter Grimes recalls.

"He had a one-room cabin. It was always dark. When we were kids we'd row up the crick to go fishin'. He had his door open and nine times out of ten he'd be standin' outside somewhere, but you couldn't see into his shack. It was always dark in there. There wasn't a lot of windows.

"I don't think he looked on it as an invasion of his privacy, to paddle up his Otter Crick. He just was an observer.

"He trapped and fished and probably had nightlines --- there are lots of bullheads and pan fish in that crick --- and there was no way he was going to go hungry.

"I remember he had a St. Lawrence skiff that he would row all over the river. And you'd see him pickin' up little bundles of driftwood here and there for firewood. And I really don't know what else he did. He was just there."

For the boy, the old river rat was part of the scenery, like a muskrat or great blue heron. It was part of the life that drew him, like the songs of the half-female sirens that once lured sailors on the sea. He sat daydreaming behind a small, dull school desk.

A lot has happened to Grimes since then. He is now a successful marine contractor and an executive member of both Ducks Unlimited and the conservation group Save The River. He has two bronze stars from his tour in Vietnam, a wife and two children, and a red and white seaplane to give him freedom in the air over the river.

But Grimes is also a river rat with the radical streak of independence, the strong will and the bond to the river that make his breed. And he admits to some irresponsibility.

Grimes' father was an aristocratic tugboat captain from Virginia who moved north to the river. He was a strict man who stayed apart from the community around him. The father was a harsh disciplinarian. His son, born in 1946, was polite and quiet and withdrawn. The son loved to hunt and fish on the river, the only place his father gave him absolute freedom. In the father's eyes, the river did not have the risks of the town. His son was safe from moral contamination there.

The life on the river fascinated Grimes. "I had a rowboat before I had a bicycle. I was gone all the time.

"Little kids could find a million and one things to do on the river and up in the little swamp holes and back waters and cricks. You just never got bored and you only went home when you were hungry."

When others ate turkey, the family of seven ate muskrat meat after the animal had been skinned by a trapper.

"I was a typical little barefoot river rat."

The difference was --- though he skipped high school classes in the fall to go duck hunting --- that Grimes was not a bold and reckless lad. He was also a sensitive and highly intelligent introvert.

"A little kid starin' down into that water for hours on end watchin' things that happen under the water. It's mesmerizing. And it becomes a habitual mesmerizing that becomes deeply ingrained in you.

"I'm not ashamed to say different moods of the river affect me different ways. It's something that you crave. You look for it.

"You can't wipe all that slate clean because all of a sudden somebody says, 'Hey, you are an adult now and you have to be responsible for your actions and make your way in the world and contribute to society.' There's too much back there."

In the period between the time when Grimes left Alexandria Bay to attend college and eventually returned, from Vietnam, his personality changed. The introvert who could not deal with people was transformed. In 1966, Grimes was called to serve with the United States army in Vietnam. To avoid the discipline of the army, he joined the navy for four years. Then he volunteered for the elite and secret Seals team, a special forces branch of the navy which did "dirty stuff" such as assassinations and ambushes. In 1969, Grimes and his unit performed one hundred and twenty-three missions in Vietnam. Some of the work involved bringing back special targets for interrogation.

Joining the navy and being sent to the Vietnam war were part of the river boy testing himself, Grimes says. "Boy kids growing up --- this is part of fumbling into manhood. You find ways of testing yourself. I don't care how timid a person you are, you will always find ways to test yourself and evaluate yourself.

"And I've done that repeatedly --- the service and everything else. I see others continually using that river as a way to test themselves and judge themselves. There's a certain lure to a nasty day on the river.

"It can be dangerous, if you're stupid, especially dangerous and unforgiving. You perish so fast in that water. And yet these characters around here, that's when they want to use the river."

Hunter Grimes

Vietnam was the final test and the change was radical. "It was like finishing school. It turned me into an extrovert from an introvert."

Or at least into Grimes' model of a river rat, "a subdued extrovert."

A true introvert would not be a river rat, he explains. An introvert turns inward to his own mental world, finding nourishment there, not in the outer world of the river. A river rat can be quiet with strangers, Grimes says, which makes him seem withdrawn. But if he feels comfortable with you, he can weave an extravagant mental tapestry of observations.

"The way my mind works is a little bit more complicated than some of these guys that are river rats in the traditional sense. They don't need interaction with other people. I don't think you need that to be a river rat. There's different ways you can function in society and still maintain that bond with the river."

Grimes --- veteran of four universities and no degree --- is unnaturally perceptive, uncannily clear minded, like someone with the advantage of an extra eye.

"There's a big void in your psyche if you don't have somethin' that you can fall back on."

Driving his dusty pickup truck Grimes picks up a wooden cylinder on the dashboard, his duck call. He has a reputation as a wild driver. Both hands leave the wheel for a moment. A throaty whistle fills the air. It is not hard to fool the birds, Grimes says. And fooling the ducks with a duck call makes a difference. It proves you are part of them, of the river.

"You start to find things that make sense. And that's what you need in the back of your mind. You need something to have faith in."

Alexandria Bay

Making a Choice of Sinking or Sailing

Harold Herrick

In the Thousand Islands some people treasure the sleek, cedar-strip St. Lawrence skiff as though it were a living creature like a muskie or a great blue heron. The St. Lawrence skiff is unique to the river and it takes a unique individual to understand its ways ...

Harold Herrick and the book of his heart

Harold Herrick's cluttered home looks like a museum of the St. Lawrence River. In the kitchen, four rows of miniature duck decoys stare from shelves. Their wooden eyes have the same undeviating assurance as the man. From the ceiling dangles a wooden black bass, one of the distinct natives of the river along with the muskie. The walls of the rooms are crowded with river paintings, wild ducks in flight and a duck stamp collection.

From his Cape Vincent home Herrick has run his national animal show insurance business for twenty years. He believes in self-reliance, both in business and on the river.

"When you are in business for yourself, you have to be self-reliant. If you make mistakes, you pay for it."

Herrick pushes his glasses up on the tip of his head and gestures with his hands. His booming voice needs no amplification. He follows his own inspiration with absolute confidence. "Not everybody can do it. They want security."

Herrick first shook himself free from security during summers at the family cottage on Grindstone Island. His grandmother, Pauline Post Bacon, had owned property on the island since the 1890s. Unconventional for the time, Bacon was a great sportswoman and loved to fish from a twenty-two-foot St. Lawrence skiff with her fishing companion, Mrs. Morgan of Papoose Island. A local guide rowed the skiff, with the two women fishing from wicker-back chairs. With graceful formality they wore broad-rimmed hats, vests, jackets and neatly tied white cravats. In August of 1904, after a forty-minute battle, Pauline Bacon landed a forty-pound muskie off Wolfe Island. To signal the muskie catch in the traditional manner, a white flag was raised on an oar jammed into the bottom of the boat.

In this gamesome atmosphere Herrick was brought to the river practically from the day he was born in 1919. "I grew up in the summers here on Grindstone," he says. "It showed me the magnetism of the river. Some people are attached to mountains. Some people are attached to rivers."

The young Herrick swam, fished and learned to sail. He was particularly drawn by the challenge of the rudderless St. Lawrence skiff. The genuine skiff --- which, according to Herrick, evolved out of Kingston and spread along the Canadian shoreline to Rockport, Gananoque and Brockville --- is balanced so precisely that it can be steered by shifting your weight and moving the sails. The slender, pointed boat will never sink because of the buoyancy of the cedar. "If you want to be in a storm on the river, you better be in a skiff," Herrick advises. Yet the boat can be swamped easily.

Herrick says that he sailed the skiff in stormy winds hitting sixty-five to eighty kilometres an hour to test the limits of himself and the boat. "I capsized all the time," he admits. "The water would come over the bow. You go to land, bail out and start all over again." And that was the point. Herrick wanted to know how much it took to tip the skiff. He couldn't know the boat and himself thoroughly without finding the outer limit. Why would anyone want to sail with timidity? Certainly not Herrick. "You capsize and you experiment. You and the boat became part of each other. It's instinct."

By sailing the skiff, Herrick was forging a link with the past, the era when the skiff evolved naturally on the St. Lawrence. The skiff was a sturdy work boat and yet swift in a race. "It's well adapted for the choppy waters on the lake or the river."

Herrick also discovered that in the city he was like a skiff out of the water. While living in the Long Beach area in New York, he kept his ties with the Thousand Islands. Finally he could no longer bear the drudgery. The family moved to Cape Vincent in 1974 "to get out of the jungle of New York City" and the small house began to fill with Herrick's collection of river curios. Herrick also became a preserver and defender of the river's heritage in the shape he understood best, the St. Lawrence skiff.

The St. Lawrence skiff evolved in the middle of the nineteenth century because of the needs of the people in the area. The river guides required a hardy, stable skiff that could handle the currents, the rougher open stretches of water and the abrupt squalls. It was a practical boat, and yet, in spite of its weight, its sleek lines made the St. Lawrence skiff a challenge to sail. In the summer, bat-wing sails were hoisted and the skiffs were raced across the water. Eventually the skiff, a creation of the area, stood as an emblem of the Thousand Islands beside the muskie and the great blue heron. And yet the time of the skiff had passed. In an era of motorboats and sailboats that never had to earn a living, the skiff no longer had a practical purpose.

Herrick was worried that the lore of the skiff would disappear. He hunted down the boats in barns, oversaw their restoration, publicized their character across the continent. But in spite of his devotion, he had trouble finding a publisher for a book of paintings and photographs of the skiff, with the text by river resident John Keats. Finally Herrick and his son, also named Harold, put up $35,000 to publish a deluxe paperback in 1988 called *The Skiff And The River*. Beautifully illustrated with colour plates of river paintings, some by Michael Ringer, the book charted the evolution of the St. Lawrence skiff. It was a book rejected by publishers who said it would not make money, especially with the extravagance of colour reproductions. Herrick's press run of two thousand copies was virtually sold out the first summer.

Characteristically defiant and extreme, Herrick --- who calls himself "a radical publisher" --- vowed there would be no reprint. He broke even on costs and made his point about the heritage of the skiff. The book was intended as a monument to the skiff that would withstand time, "a primer of the river" for the next generation. Although the practical, tough-minded Herrick sounds as though he were hatched from the granite cliffs of the river, he insists that he doesn't deserve the distinction of river person. "I'm not a native. I'm a transplant," he declares. Yet in spite of all his bluster, his affection for the heritage of the river betrays him. His feelings run deep. Herrick pushes himself to the edge like a skiff in a storm. He would probably sink if it weren't for the buoyancy of the river in his soul.

Cape Vincent

Herrick was interviewed in the summer of 1988. He died on October 4 of the same year from cancer and was buried in Riverside Cemetery, Cape Vincent. His wife of forty-four years, Mary, remembers a selfless man "who filled the house" with energy. In an obituary, New York Times *columnist Nelson Bryant remembered a man who "had no truck with sham or whimpering." Herrick, Bryant said, lived with a boldness that left "more cautious mortals ... pleading for time to cogitate."*

Photo courtesy of Pieter Bergen and the Museum of the Great Lakes, Kingston

St. Lawrence skiff with bat-wing sail

Flippers and a Fresh Supply of Oxygen

Donald "Moe" Hunt

Most people are content to stay on the surface of existence. Others want to dip beneath and search for the secrets of people and time and the river lying hidden on the bottom ...

Moe Hunt

In 1764, a schooner named *Le Blanc Henry* carrying gold and silver was lost off Wolfe Island and sank to the bottom of the St. Lawrence River. In 1877, the two-masted schooner *Lilly Powers* sank on the northwest corner of Sparrow Island with a cargo of coal. In 1909, the *Islander*, a side-wheel steamer, burned and sank near Alexandria Bay.

Ever since ships started navigating the St. Lawrence, the bottom of the river has been a connoisseur of shards and broken bits. Ships were lost in storms or hit shoals. A drilling and blasting barge named the *J.B. King and Company* was hit by lightning in 1930, producing a crop of thirty corpses for the river. The lightning detonated the dynamite set to blast the channel below the barge. An old, feeble British troop carrier was weighed down with stones and used as a wharf at Fort Haldimand, Carleton Island, until it settled into the mud. As inevitably as men designed and built and sailed the ships, the river collected the wood and steel.

And no one knows the wrecks and the lower depths of the river better than one of the pioneers of diving, a restless man with a cleft chin and rugged good looks, Moe Hunt. For thirty-five years, since he built a homemade scuba tank out of an inner tube filled with compressed air from a gas station, Hunt has been exploring the bottom of the river, either as a marine construction contractor or a diver hoping to discover an ancient ship. In the summer Hunt and his wife Irene operate a tiny diving shop at the end of Fisherman's Wharf in Clayton. Hunt also trains and certifies amateur divers.

At times the diving has been gruesome. Hunt, also known as a body hunter, has been called over the years to retrieve the bodies of sixty people lost in the river. Ferrying the dead to the surface is the most dismal part of his work, he admits. But his blood no longer chills. Like a doctor or ambulance attendant he has grown accustomed to death. And he can not change destiny. There is no way to bargain in the deep and bring the body back to life. "It is just a body with no life to it," he says. Sometimes Hunt is called in the winter when a snowmobiler falls through a hole in the ice. Sometimes a fisherman or a boater drinks too much and drowns. There are a few suicides.

Once Hunt had to bring up the corpse of a diver who tangled himself in his anchor line as the oxygen ran out. He also recalls the time a woman flying a seaplane in a fog "drove head first into the river" off Cape Vincent, near the old British fortification at Carleton Island. Hunt dove to recover two bodies from the plane. Under the water he found the corpses with two sets of eyes gaping open and mysterious holes lurking behind the ears.

Hunt says that he has never suffered nightmares from body hunting, though years ago, when he was a United States army paratrooper in Korea, he dreamed of falling without a parachute. Under the water you cannot fall to your death, but Hunt has had several close escapes.

Once he was being towed underwater to look for a sunken outboard motor. The surface boat turned and the rope caught around his regulator. Near the point of exhaustion, he fought free at the last moment. Another time Hunt and a fellow diver were photographing the underwater damage to a large Russian fishing trawler when two ships passed at the same time. The combination of the two churning propellers created a destructive current. "We thought we were goners," he says. "The suction between the two ships, it sucked us downstream. It turned totally dark. We were holding onto the rocks to save ourselves." Twice Hunt has used the decompression chamber on his barge to save himself from dying of the bends when the change of pressure came too swiftly.

The decompression chamber is a good symbol of Hunt's hasty life. He has always been in a hurry to do things his way. Born in 1930 in Watertown, New York, his father was Canadian and his mother American. His father died when he was five, leaving his mother to raise six sons and one daughter in the Great Depression.

In 1951, Hunt joined the 187th airborne regimental combat team in Korea under the command of Colonel William C. Westmoreland, who later commanded the United States army in Vietnam. Hunt was a paratrooper stationed in an outpost three miles ahead of the lines. He carried a Browning automatic and was also a demolition man. One day on a dare he and an army diver switched roles and Hunt got a taste of diving. In 1953, he left the service.

Hunt took design drafting in college, but the lure of scuba diving remained strong. Office work seemed like drudgery. "Life's too short to be a machine," he says. "Behind a desk you become a machine." By the time Hunt got out of the service, scuba diving was still new. It was only in 1943 that Jacques Cousteau and Emil Gagnan invented the scuba tank to open up underwater exploration.

In the beginning, Hunt had to be content with his primitive, makeshift tanks. The inner tube experiment filled his lungs with thin, musty air from the inside of a car tire. Hunt was undeterred. His knowledge of diving in the early years gave him an advantage in a business which had risk and excitement.

Chasing dreams of adventure by diving for old ships is the most romantic side of Hunt. There are more than thirty recognizable ship wrecks in the St. Lawrence, on top of fragments obscured by the mud and weeds. Hunt has visited twenty of the wrecks, watching the ravages over the years of time and souvenir hunters. He brought up the paddle wheel of the wood steamer *Arizona*, which burned and sank off Cape Vincent in 1922 in twenty-five feet of water.

Hunt was one of the first to dive to a three-masted schooner, the *Victory*. The one-hundred-and-twenty-foot ship from the eighteenth century sank to hang partly over an underwater cliff at the Rock Island lighthouse near Clayton. Hunt and his brother-in-law donned flippers, masks and tanks to make the dive through sunless water and swift current. The water shut off the upper world. It muffled noise. At the same time it amplified underwater sounds in the stillness, like a world newly created with strange, wayward rules.

The divers didn't know what they would find. "We swam along the cliff," Hunt says in a deep bass voice that rolls relentlessly forward. "We saw this big dark shadow, darker than the river. We stared in disbelief." The masts and the rigging of the *Victory* were still intact. The divers could see the deadeyes, the round wooden disks used to tightened and control the rigging lines on masts that now had sheets of water for sails. The ship acted as a break against the current and hundreds of bass swam in and out the holes.

The memories are great, and Hunt loves to chat, but he keeps glancing at the diver's watch on his wrist. He says that he is timing some divers near by, but like the flux and weaving of currents in the river, other parts of him press to move on. Hunt's mind jumps from subject to subject like a fidgety mountain goat. "Everything moves too slow for me," he apologizes. "There's only twenty-four hours in the day. That's not enough to do what I want to do."

Clayton

Not One to Be Shamed by a Shoal

Lawrence Balcom

Some people pride themselves on their education, on the use they make of their minds through books and libraries. Others take knowledge directly, in small sips from the river over a lifetime ...

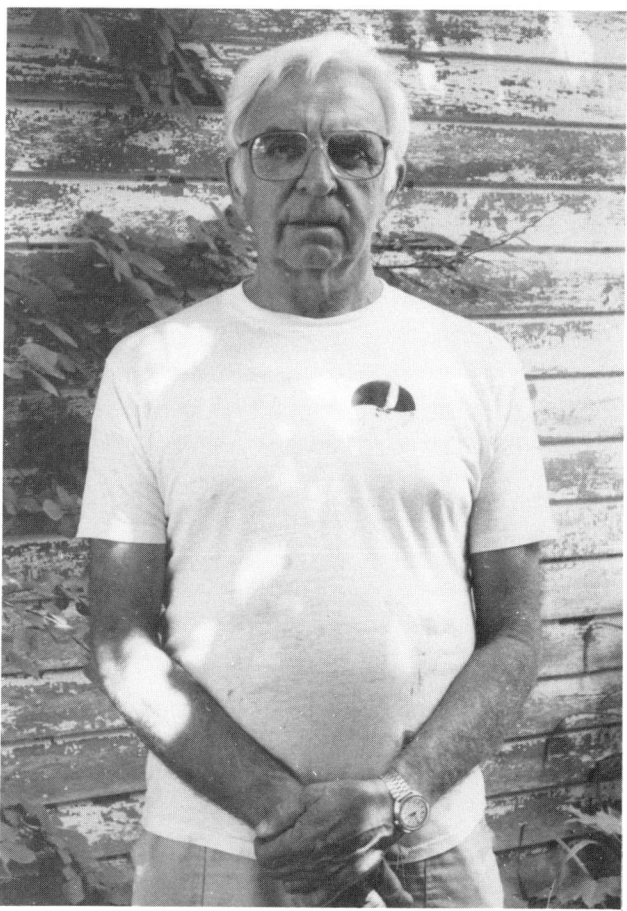

Lawrence Balcom

"I never lost a passenger and I never hit a shoal," says Lawrence Balcom, prouder than a fishing guide bringing home a prize muskie. "I learned the river by being with the captains. And every opportunity I had, I went on the river alone and explored all the channels.

"I was announcing the river when I was nine years old," he says. Years ago children hired by tour boats could recite the lore of the islands with authority. With the help of men like Captain Fred Cuppernal, Balcom got his captain's licence at fifteen and took passengers out on the river in Cuppernal's *Spray Six*, a fifty-two-foot boat that carried forty-nine people.

Balcom learned to navigate the tricky "whirlpool" channel just west of Georgina Island. In the same spot he saw the constellation of small but powerful eddies toss the boats of careless captains on to the island. He remembers the story of Captain Will Charlebois of Grindstone Island who put the side-wheel steamer the *St. Lawrence* "up on a shoal with a full load of passengers in front of the farm where he lived." With a chuckle, Balcom comments, "I guess he was waving to his wife."

Narrow channels, swift currents and shoals as sharp as harrow blades put other river captains to disgrace. But in forty-five years they never caught Lawrence Clayton Balcom napping.

Balcom --- nicknamed Lawrence St. Lawrence for his affinity with the river --- has seen it all: the captain who blew booze-laden passengers skyward when he turned on the ignition; the storms and "thunder squalls" that only a "damn fool" like himself would try to navigate; the dry Prohibition throats athirst for liquor on the liberal Canadian side. And Balcom, making five three-hour trips every day, seven days a week, never tired of the sights.

"I'm tickled to death I saw the best part of the river," says the white-haired mariner. "It was never dull or repetitious. I was very observant. I noticed little changes.

"One time I was going down in the Horseshoe Channel and I saw these little ducks scurrying, and they were just a scurrying, trying to fly, but they couldn't fly. Then I saw this big muskie swimming underneath them. Then all of the sudden I saw one of the ducks go down. And the water was clear enough and I was close enough I could see the muskie grab that duck.

"I used to see animals, birds, vegetation, something different every time."

From the time he was a boy the river was a place the family could explore together. They rode to the islands with a modest one-cylinder engine pushing their St. Lawrence skiff. "We would go picking blueberries, huckleberries in the islands --- raspberries were plentiful. In the fall we would gather hickory nuts, butternuts. These were great outings for the family."

Balcom was born in a Clayton boathouse in 1920. The family, French on his mother's side, went back three generations to businessmen in the profitable timbering industry on the American shore. "We're all extractions from the French," he says. The deep bass voice rolls like a current through an underground cavern. Behind him, the severe face of his Canadian grandmother watches from a kitchen wall in his Clayton home --- "You look at her long enough and she can look through you."

Balcom's great-great-grandfather, Napoleon Bonaparte La Paige, came to French Creek to start his own logging business. Logging along the St. Lawrence was for rugged, seafaring lumberjacks. The timber rafts were bound together at the edge of the river and floated downstream with the men camping on top. The most adventuresome part of the voyage was shooting the rapids at Lachine and Long Sault.

Balcom's great-grandfather, Edward "Buck" La Paige, was one of the first men to own a schooner on Lake Ontario. He built the one-hundred-sixty-five-foot commercial sailing ship the *Blue Gill*, which weighed thirty-two tons and carted lumber and coal around the lakes. Balcom's grandfather, also Edward La Paige --- the French priests insisted that the names not be anglicized --- owned the one-hundred-seventy-eight-foot *Black Duck*. The ship sank in a storm in 1872 near --- "it's a long, staggering name" --- the Galloo Islands with a load of whiskey and coins aboard.

La Paige also helped build schooners and steamers and tugs in the Clayton shipyards. With his seafaring ancestry, the young Balcom wandered through the buildings looking for his grandfather among the smell of clean, freshly cut timber and the pockets of fires where the ship blacksmiths hammered. "I hung around a little machine shop on the river. It belonged to Ralph Denny. He took me under his wing. I was his protégé." For the shipyards, he realizes now, "It was the end of the era. They weren't in full bloom."

Balcom says that the exuberant days of the river were around 1929, the Prohibition years before the devastation of the Great Depression hit home. "I think Prohibition made it busy," he says. The visitors "came to see the islands and stop in Canada for a drink." The American river captains took boatload after boatload of parched American gills to King's Landing, near Ivy Lea, for a twenty-minute stop at the riverside tavern. The boats came so thickly to the small dock that they sometimes parked three abreast.

Balcom remembers a captain who herded his passengers tamely on board only to blow them out of the boat a few moments later. A spark ignited the gas fumes. "The captain hit the starter and the boat blew up. This blew the passengers into the river and over onto the other boat --- and not one passenger was seriously injured." Balcom admits that the liquor may have dulled the effect of the explosion for a few. "They were probably well relaxed."

The passengers also bought bottles of liquor, which were confiscated at the customs stop at Boldt Castle. In a back room, while the captains waited and played cards, the glasses were filled and the bottles tipped back. The Canadian captains were the best drinkers, Balcom insists, rhyming the names of some legendary Gananoque navigators. One captain from Gananoque made four trips a day, says Balcom, which meant four sessions in the back room, and by the end of the day he was "hammered." But he always sailed his boat home in one piece to moor safely beside his wife in bed. That takes some skill. "You might of called it sixth sense."

Clayton

A peaceful riverside scene

The Sailor Who Came Home from the Sea

Lawrence R. Hickey

As long as there have been rivers and seas there have been those who used them to satisfy the urge to roam. Sailing to faraway places takes daring and initiative, but so does coming home again ...

Lawrence Hickey

It's obligatory. Every ocean-going freighter plowing down the St. Lawrence River must past the tiny Buccaneer Motel in Cape Vincent where the guests fish with modest poles from the bright-red dock. The motel has a mere ten rooms and will never make the owner a millionaire. But that's fine, because Lawrence Hickey can watch the ships that make his world larger and enjoy life in a small town at the same time.

Hickey knows the freighters as intimately as he knows the islands and shoals of the river. He is a licenced pilot for the river who bought the motel as a home away from the sea.

For a man who has sailed the world, ridden waves churned by hurricanes and ducked bullets in Vietnam while delivering military cargo by ship, Cape Vincent might seem tame. But Hickey says there is no contradiction in a rover wanting to settle in the village. Here the wanderer in him found the warmth and friendliness he needed.

It's good to live in a community where everyone knows your name, where, at the shriek of the fire siren, Hickey jumps into the boots of a volunteer firefighter to help his neighbours. A man needs adventure and he also needs a community and a family, according to the river pilot. A small town is not that different from an ocean freighter, he muses. The crew lives together in a small space and depends on each other.

Hickey was licenced as a river pilot --- one of about thirty Canadians and Americans certified for this stretch of the St. Lawrence --- after climbing through the ranks of ship officers and passing an arduous series of tests. The effort was worth it, he says, because the St. Lawrence and Thousand Islands are among the most interesting parts of the world to navigate.

Most of the time an ocean freighter sails through nothing but open space. And open space can be boring. In the Thousand Islands the giant seven-hundred-foot freighters have to squeeze through a narrow channel like a truck through a back alley. The foreign crews "stand in absolute awe that you come so close," Hickey says. "If you had a baseball, you could throw it and hit one of the islands."

In the wheelhouse of the ships Hickey recites the names of islands and their residents to the foreign captains. From the deck he hails the familiar faces across the water. "There's Mr. Laidlaw at Point Vivian. Always I come down and blow two little short whistles and he comes out and waves. He flicks his lights at night."

Every year freighters from countries as diverse as Greece, Yugoslavia, Peru, Iceland and the Soviet Union use the main channel of the St. Lawrence, which winds back and forth across the border from Canada to the United States. Between three and four thousand cargo ships use the channel yearly, a sharp decline from the 1960s when there were seven thousand a year.

For river pilots like Hickey, who came to Cape Vincent in 1967, the foreign ships are a chance to recall foreign sights again or to meet old comrades. Hickey recalls with pride the warm words of a Russian captain. As Hickey came aboard to guide the ship down the river the captain said, "Oh, I came here fifteen years ago as a second mate and I remember you." Foreign sailors get along well, Hickey explains. "Politics never enters in. Seamanship is above and beyond politics."

Hickey got an unlikely start for a river pilot. He was born in the New York City Bronx in 1939 and his father was a dispatcher on the subway. "I had never been on salt water," Hickey says. "I had made one trip on the Staten Island ferry." But New York was a world in miniature, a port that filtered the flood of immigrants into the United States. Hickey grew up among the sons and daughters of the Irish, German, Polish and Jewish families who came to America by ship. His taste for travel was sharpened by the trips he and his father made together. Then, as a young man, lured by the promise of a world cruise every summer as a cadet, Hickey entered a maritime college. He graduated as a third mate and joined a New Orleans shipping company which sent him around the world from 1962 to 1967. During that period Hickey delivered cargo to the United States army in Vietnam and saw the war develop from the deck of a ship. The ships delivered ammunition and military equipment and once Hickey recalls running a deadly barrage of enemy fire while sailing the Saigon River.

There is a seductive excitement in the danger of being at sea even without a war, Hickey says. "I was in three or four hurricanes. You heave to. The ship's rolling thirty degrees. You're worried that the cargo is secured so that it doesn't start crashing around. The ship is diving and pitching and climbing up tall fifty, sixty-foot seas. You climb up to the top and slide down the other side of a massive wave," Hickey says. "It's a great life."

While Hickey advanced to chief mate, he also married, had a daughter, and found that it was difficult to be away from his family for months at a time. The opportunity to be a pilot on the St. Lawrence River meant he could satisfy both sides of his personality --- the longing for the intimacy of a family, the desire for the freedom of sailing on a ship.

The St. Lawrence is not the Saigon River and hurricanes are unlikely here, but Hickey is worried by one danger, human ineptness. Navigating the St. Lawrence requires very skillful pilots, Hickey says. He believes that in spite of disasters like the oil spill of 1976, the pilots have kept the risks to a minimum. But the river is fragile and danger always near, he warns. Hickey is particularly worried because the Canadian government, through a "loophole" in its regulations, allows less stringent licensing of foreign-born pilots which the United States government has to honour under a treaty.

Hickey thinks back to the giant oil spill when the *Nepco 140* barge broke open like a rotten egg and oil oozed out. He was sitting up river in the first ship which had to cut through the oil. "I guess we always expected something like that to happen," he says.

Thousand Islands bridge and freighter

"What a holy hell of a mess it was." He remembers the crude oil spread out on the water looking almost solid, like a black ledge of smooth lava rock which pushed the water aside. "It was like you could walk ashore on crude."

That was years ago, though Hickey is still wary of the risks on the river. He is proud of his years at sea and the licence that he earned as a pilot on the St. Lawrence. And yet in spite of his sense of honour, of having passed year after year of gruelling exams, of having earned his ascension from third mate to chief mate to pilot, the wanderer in him has changed. The chain of an anchor rattles mentally through the eye-hole and plunges to the bottom. The feet steady against the unyielding earth. Thus says the owner of the wee Buccaneer Motel: "I think sailing is a life for an unmarried man."

Cape Vincent

A Boy Among the Bootleggers

Clark McCready

Restlessness is like a spark, a seed. It spurs people to action and propels them onward. There are people who need movement like the river needs a channel...

Clark and Florence McCready, dockside at their home

The Thousand Islands is a popular corridor for smuggling drugs and contraband back and forth across the Canada-United States border. But smuggling never saw as much vigour and enthusiasm as during the American Prohibition years of 1920 to 1933. During that era running booze across the river was a profitable local industry. The same rocky countryside and bewildering maze of islands and channels which had been a frustration to soldiers and settlers and farmers was a blessing to smugglers. Where others could get lost or hit a shoal, the river people were adept at finding their way across the water.

In the late 1920s a farm boy raised on the sixth concession of the Township of the Front of Leeds and Lansdowne was a witness and participant, serving beer in an impromptu tavern on the river near Ivy Lea and driving trucks from Montreal to the Thousand Islands loaded with illegal booze.

The years have not dampened the adventuresome spirit of Clark McCready. He is a wily, alert man who lives these days with his wife Florence in a converted boathouse in Ivy Lea. The front windows of the McCready home have a wide view of thirty-seven islands --- "I've counted forty-two from the dock," Florence McCready adds. Once a boat racer, after he retired in his fifties McCready continued to wear out motorcycles and snowmobiles as fast as he could.

In 1988, when McCready was turning seventy-eight, he and his wife rode a motorcycle nine thousand kilometres cross-country to Kamloops, British Columbia and back.

"He's kind of wild," McCready's wife says, her mind travelling back to her first impressions. "He was kind of devilish. I guess I thought he was a smart aleck." On their first date McCready took the young woman on a boat ride through the islands. "I suppose you know all the shoals?" the woman asked, looking for reassurance. "Sure, I know every one of them," he boasted. A few moments later the boat struck a shoal at Georgina Island. "And that's one of them," he said.

The couple had only been married a few days when McCready flipped his ninety-five-pound Seaflea, which reached ninety-eight kilometres an hour at full throttle, during a boat race at Gananoque. It looked as though he had bought a ticket to the next world when a boat ripped over his submerged head. But, as his wife watched, McCready bobbed to the surface unhurt, undaunted.

McCready was born in 1910 in a two-storey farm log house with no running water. One image --- important only as a link to long-gone days --- stays lodged in his memory. He remembers that the large, thick planks of the basswood floor in the kitchen were painted bright yellow. His father died when he was ten, leaving his mother to earn as much as she could as a seamstress. The family was "destitute."

In contrast, the river was full of opportunity. It was ready to inspire a lively spirit of enterprise during Prohibition. Canada and the United States took different directions in banning alcohol. In Canada the ebb and flow of prohibition was erratic. During the First World War most of the provinces passed temperance acts to close their drinking spots before Prohibition in the United States. This created a typically Canadian confederation of scattered rules. Each province went its own way. Quebec, next to Ontario, ended its experiment with prohibition in 1919, but Ontario dallied till 1927.

McCready started to work young during his family's time of hardship. He began driving a two-ton Ford transport truck when he was thirteen years old. By fifteen, he was driving an even larger truck back and forth to Montreal, where he was introduced to the speakeasies in the back rooms.

When he was a teenager McCready poured beer for Americans in a Prohibition-era tavern on the waterfront at Swift Water Point next to Ivy Lea. The tavern, in a small renovated house, was run by a man named Mark Cane. The area is now known as Smuggler's Cove and is still popular with outlaws on the river. A few years ago during the undercover drug investigation called Operation Waterworks the police discovered that Smuggler's Cove was one of the drop points for drugs. Another drop point, not far from Ivy Lea, was the foot of the one of pylons of the Thousand Islands bridge.

During Prohibition, Cane's Swift Water tavern was a well-known fountain of liquor. Once an hour it drew its capacity of Americans on the boat tours from Alexandria Bay and Clayton. "We had a saloon. We'd sell four-four beer, watered down a little bit. And then upstairs we had a room for the captains and important Americans that would be introduced to the boss and they'd get hard liquor."

McCready also worked for a wild and handsome American bootlegger named Pearson, who had a slight build for his six-foot frame and constantly changed his appearance by growing a beard and shaving it off. Pearson had trucks cart the booze to the Thousand Islands, where it was loaded from docks in Ivy Lea to his small fleet of bulletproof boats and run across the river.

McCready remembers seeing a bullet hole in the window of one boat after a shootout on the river. "I thought it was exciting." He says that the smugglers stashed the contraband bottles in sacks of salt. If the revenue agents chased them on the river, the sack went overboard, the weight of the salt pulling the load down to the bottom of the river. When the salt dissolved in a few days, the bottles floated back to the surface, and the smugglers collected their wares.

Hiding the alcohol inspired ingenious devices. McCready watched thirty-pound rolls of cheese being hollowed in the centre. Then the alcohol was poured into the empty space. "And then we'd drive it right straight through the police lineups," he says.

Smuggling was well rooted in the area, where local people helped load and transport the contraband and kept their mouths shut. "We all had a hand in it. It was exciting. I enjoyed it." McCready adds, "I think police on both sides of the border were in on the profits."

As for Pearson, even if he was a "hoodlum," he was "very straight" with the two or three boys that he employed. "He adamantly refused to let us have a drink of beer."

McCready was there the day that a smuggler loaded his boat only to find he was surrounded by the Royal Canadian Mounted Police. He roared away in his boat with the Mounties firing their guns, but the river reached out and snagged him like a small, wayward fish. The smuggler had not gone far before he hit the shoal at Swift Water Point and was captured.

One time a large cruiser pulled into the dock at the tavern blocking a small antique boat. The captain refused to move the boat for the owner, a woman, saying with a smug grin that she was in no hurry. "If you don't move it, I'll put a hole through it," the woman blasted back. The captain laughed and shrugged her off. The woman started the two-cylinder engine and "rammed the bow of her little boat into the front end of this great big cruiser and put a hole right through it. It didn't take very long then to get out and back the boat out of her road."

After the excitement of Prohibition and the river as he was growing up, McCready left Canada during the Second World War. He was a Royal Canadian Air Force flight engineer for the Lancaster bombers stationed in England. He returned to Kingston, met and married Florence, and in 1953 the couple bought Mooney's river store and gas pumps in Ivy Lea. Typically they catered to a colourful type known by river folk as "millionaire Americans."

The McCready's kept their independence and refused to fawn over the wealthy. McCready remembers a rich man named Hecker who had a summer home on Halstead's Bay. "He wouldn't let anybody put gas in his boat but me." One day McCready was gone. Hecker, refusing to let anyone touch his boat, decided to do the job himself. "He took the wrong cap off and poured gas in and come to find out it was just a vent. He had about fifty gallons of gas in the bilge of his boat."

Another wealthy American typically crossed the water from Ash Island in a drunken stupor unable to land his boat at the dock. McCready would have to go out and haul him in with a pike pole. The man was sometimes wearing only "the top of his underwear," with everything else "bare naked" below. "We got used to him."

"The river's been so exciting," McCready says. He vows to keep his vista of the river in Ivy Lea and never surrender his independence. "When we had that marina I don't believe there wasn't a day that some little thing happened that would either make you madder than a wet hen or make you laugh your head off."

Ivy Lea

Where the River Never Freezes

Helen Truesdell

Before there was a Muskie Jake there was Sturgeon Truesdell. In old age he landed a whale of a fish and proved by example that the life's work of a man, his corpus, is equally hard to catch...

Helen Truesdell

"He was many years older than I was, but I was the boss," Helen Truesdell says with a bold, unflinching laugh. Her husband Fred Truesdell was a small, quiet man, born eighteen years before her in 1882. But he had inner strength and his seventy-year-old muscles could still haul giant sturgeons out of the river.

In 1920, the pair married and moved to Ivy Lea. Helen, an American from Alexandria Bay, was a lively twenty-year-old woman with reddish-brown hair and green eyes. She loved the open water and was happy to move to a rented cottage by the river with her new husband. "We didn't have hydro. We didn't have any faculties at all."

Four years later the Truesdells bought land in the settlement. Fred Truesdell, by temperament a kind of shepherd, set to work in gentle occupations --- raising sheep, fishing commercially on the river, working as a builder on the islands. He built a house next to the water from large cement blocks that he made himself. The home had thirty-two double windows, says Helen, who cleaned every one. "It was too much."

"I think my husband was the best Truesdell that ever was." He died thirteen days short of the couple's fiftieth wedding anniversary. "He was mild and gentle. He never smoked or drank. He wouldn't even take liquor for a cold."

Ironically, during Prohibition, the abstainer could not escape the stealthy night sounds of wagons rolling down the muddy path by his home. The liquor was smuggled across the water into the United States. He never said a word.

"Everybody knew about --- what did they call it --- bootlegging ... *bootlegging*. Most of this bootlegging was done with horse and wagon. You'd hear the boats coming in and out."

Truesdell had been born on a farm near Lyn. His father was once a champion baker who "won a barrel of flour as a prize." One of the brothers, Andrew, came to Ivy Lea and fished commercially, and Peter --- "I think he had an icing business" --- moved to Gananoque to start an ice house. Peter Truesdell's sons continued as the sturdy billy-goats of the river.

In Ivy Lea, Fred and Helen Truesdell raised two children, a son and a daughter. The daughter went to school in the village of Lansdowne and was called a "river rat" by the other children. The girl resented the name. Helen Truesdell says the girl was teased because the others envied a home on the river.

"You can go down to my dock and see half a dozen islands," she says with pride.

She points to Moser's Island across the bright stretch of water. "We caretook there, too. We caretook for that island. He was a nice man. He's dead. She's livin' yet. And their two sons are doctors, both of 'em. Her people were the Finlays, out on the highway. The island was the Finlay Island. And that's one of the oldest cottages on the river. Moser's."

"Fred always worked on the river. He knew the river from ay to zee. He could go out in the darkest night."

In the summer the Truesdells pastured their forty sheep on land rented on Ash Island. The river man sold the island-fed mutton in the summer to the island residents on both sides of the border.

The whole river was accessible by boat, which made it easy for the farmers to sell their meat and vegetables across the water. But the river also made it easy for the poachers to slip back and forth unseen. Anglers from Alexandria Bay used to raid Truesdell's lines and steal the fish, his wife says. They knew who the Yankee pirates were and set the game warden after them.

In the days when the giant sturgeon could still be fished from the river, Truesdell would lay a thousand-foot nightline and haul it up in the morning. In a good season Truesdell might land eight or ten sturgeons weighing between eighty-five and a hundred pounds. He shipped them to New York City, though the family also kept the smaller ones to eat. "It's delicious any way. It's white and it's tender. There's no fat on it. You roll it in batter and fry it in butter. Bass is nice, but sturgeon is special."

Ironically, in the nineteenth century the sturgeon was thought a nuisance. It was used as fertilizer, a sad end to a long and dignified career. The sturgeon, which can live over forty years, has an ancient lineage. It traces its ancestry back seventy million years. So there was Truesdell, the mild man of the river, against a breed of fish far older than the pharaohs of Egypt.

"He was a little man, but he was very strong." When Truesdell was seventy-nine he caught and pulled aboard by himself a one-hundred-and-sixty-five-pound sturgeon. No one told him he was too old to be hauling monstrous fish out of the deep. Still, the one-hundred-and-sixty-five-pound sturgeon was not Truesdell's record. On December 15, 1949 when ice was floating in the river, Truesdell, then sixty-seven years old, caught a two-hundred-and-thirty-seven-pound sturgeon off Sheep Island. He only weighed one hundred and sixty pounds himself.

Helen Truesdell does not brag, however --- not even on behalf of her modest husband. "Jim Peck from the Bay caught one, three hundred and ten pounds. But he used a net, not a line."

A picture from the time shows Truesdell in a small boat. He is holding the two-hundred-and-thirty-seven-pound leviathan of the St. Lawrence with its white belly half out of the water.

It was a heroic battle --- "he said he let it up and down twelve times to tire it out" --- yet Truesdell was not the type to spin tales about the escapade later. "He never was expressive like that. I did more talking than he did.

"He said he just caught it and he was so glad when it was gone because they come for a week. He had it in a cage and the people come from all over when they heard he had that fish. And we got so tired. At the time there was no electricity. You'd have to light a lamp and go down to the dock and show them the fish."

Fred Truesdell died in 1970 at eighty-seven, long after the mighty sturgeon made its exit from the river. His wife, as alert as a cold, crisp day on the river, still lives in a house overlooking the water in Ivy Lea. She likes the open space of the water.

She remembers the day in 1938 that the Thousand Islands International Bridge was officially opened within sight of her home. She and her husband went to the ceremony, but the crush of the crowd made her stiffen and freeze. "I have a bit of claustrophobia," she explains. She stayed in the car and watched. "I don't like to be in a big crowd. I don't like to be in a room shut up." A city is no better after a lifetime by the river. "Who'd want to live in the city. It's a clutter --- and the confusion..."

Helen Truesdell keeps a strip of land by the water, and her dock, like a gaff hook clamped onto the side of the river.

"There's places that never freeze, because we're right in the swift water part. Right out here is a spot that never freezes, between us and Moser's Island."

Ivy Lea

'We Used to Dig Out Skunks in the Fall'

Leonard Turner

Some people pass through life like scarecrows. They are stiff, unyielding, paralysed --- fit only to scare a few birds. Then there are those who have not bartered their souls to a life of solemn bonds...

Leonard Turner

An early, wet snow had fallen from an October sky. It clung damply to the rock like white moss, smooth, trackless. On the rock ledge was the cabin of Leonard Turner, his seventy-five-year-old eyes keen and bright, his guns sleek and oiled and polished. Turner sat in his tiny kitchen using a window ledge for an arm rest.

"I hunted before you had to have a gun licence."

At the age of ten, Turner looked like a veteran hunter of the woods along the river. An old photograph shows a small boy in cap and overalls with the long barrel of a .22-calibre rifle dangling from his arms.

The first animal Turner shot was a cottontail rabbit --- "a cottontail rabbit's the best eating of the whole bunch."

All their lives he and his father, Joe Turner, hunted together. "We used to dig out skunks in the fall for the fur. At that time, if you got a pure black one, you got five dollars. That was a lot of money back then."

After the animal was laid bare in his burrow, a pole with a hood was clamped on its rear quarters. A quick blow to the head killed the creature.

However, the skunks had revenge on Turner. One night he was running for help. His wife lay groaning in bed in child labour. Turner sprinted through the dark and stepped on a skunk. The animal did not think twice. It sprayed him without mercy.

"Oh, man, you remember that Queenie," Turner says with a wild chuckle to his wife.

The doctor refused to let him into the house. "Nobody would." Turner had to bury his clothes for ten days --- the prescribed length of time to absorb the scent, he says --- and dig them up again. He scrubbed his body furiously with carbolic soap.

Turner --- a handsome man with bushy eyebrows and a slight, insistent lisp --- rhymes off an endless catalogue of farms along the river by Poole's Resort Road. He and his father once owned a large stretch of farmland, but the property has been sold. Turner now ranges across the land with his guns and traps.

Turner had other work on the river. He was a steeplejack painter and built cottages and docks for the legendary Eddy Andress. He only fished occasionally.

"In the spring of the year the fish were thick. You wouldn't believe it. There was thousands of them, I would say. There were pike, bass. From our boathouse to Fox Island would be about a thousand yards, from the shore here, and we'd pick up four or five pike in that distance."

Turner and his wife --- she was named Queen Mary by her parents and listed that way on her marriage certificate --- went duck hunting together.
"Remember, you went over with me to Fox Island, didn't you Queenie?"

"They don't call it Fox Island now," she says.

"But we called it Fox Island in our time," Turner replies.

"You could go out there any time, any of them islands, and throw out a few decoys and you killed your ducks in no time. We killed fourteen a day."

Hunting along the river was always his great passion. He remembers the years when wolves and rabbits and beaver moved into the area, and laments the loss of the great numbers of fish.

"I found the first beaver cut and I said to my father, 'There's beaver here.' We checked it out and sure enough, they kept getting thicker and thicker and thicker. Now they're getting to be a nuisance, the beaver. There were no beaver here till about thirty years ago."

His father had permission to set his new beaver traps on other people's land. "And, by gosh, he went to check them out a week later and someone stole them all on him." The Turners were left with nothing.

"We never know wolves around here till about 1937, I'd say. That's when the first wolves came around this part of the country. They came working their way from the west and down, the same as the jackrabbits.

"The first jackrabbits got here, I'd say, about --- how old is Gordie, Queenie, about twenty-five? --- I'd say twenty-five years ago."

The Turners also fell prey to the fickle market for fur. In the 1950s they couldn't give away the fox pelts. During one bountiful year from the first of October to Christmas they caught forty-five foxes. But the pelts would not sell. They kept the batch of skins for six years hoping the demand would change, then finally burned them.

"But later on, they wanted fox." In the 1960s, when the soft red fur had a market, rabies was spreading and the number of the animals fell. "When the price was good, we got maybe ten in a fall."

Then the bounty for wolf kills dropped, though at times in the 1980s Turner could get one hundred dollars for the fur in Brockville. A photo on the kitchen wall shows him hoisting the lifeless body of a wolf. "I got that one on my birthday, I did. I was sixty-five when I shot him. I was over two hundred yards away."

Turner, born in 1914, is still a crack shot. He can put a bullet through the eye of a rabbit at one hundred yards. He rummages through a rack of mugs loaded with odds and ends to make his point. Finally he finds an aluminum disk, about an eighth of an inch thick, sliced in half endways. "There's a hundred yards.

"Billy Hodge and them fellows I hunt with, they know what I can do.

"We were out at Plum Hollow one time. We stopped and got some curd. We went down the road and pulled off."

Turner's son-in-law said, "You see that woodchuck over there. Take a shot at it."

"That's just impossible," Turner replied. "He was five hundred yards if he was a yard. Well, it was across two farms."

Turner lifted his custom-made .243-calibre Browning and squeezed the trigger. Off in the distance, after a brief, tantalizing lapse, the woodchuck dropped. It was as though the ground had collapsed underneath his body. The son-in-law marked the spot with a post and brought his brother and father to see. "They know."

"Now here's another thing, Ben Burley and all those guys, they just go by the book. I told Ben, the generation growin' up today they see a deer, seventy-five or a hundred yards away, they shoot at 'em where they'd only wound the deer. He'd go away and die.

"That's why I don't approve of 'em using shotguns for deer hunting."

After years hunting in the woods Turner has his own ideas how to preserve the stock. The hunting laws need to be changed, he says, otherwise nothing but the smallest of a breed will be left. "I have nothing against the buck law, or the doe, but what I say, they're not lookin' down the road. My opinion would be that, open hunting up every other year for everything, bucks and does. Give the bucks a chance to grew up.

"Because, the first thing you know, in a few years they're going to have all the big bucks killed off and they gonna end up with deer just like jackrabbits."

Poole's Resort Road

To the Bottom of the River and Back

Everett Snider

There were two possible paths of destiny in Everett Snider's life. On one path, fifteen hundred pounds of dynamite sent his corpse to the bottom of the St. Lawrence River. On the other path of destiny, the one that Snider took one day in 1930, he survived and lived a long life...

Everett Snider

Generations of boys from Brockville got their schooling about the Thousand Islands aboard the tour boats run first by Wilfred Snider, then by his two sons Everett and Charlie. The lore of the river was like a storybook passed from adult to child. That is how Everett Snider, who started as captain of a tour boat at twelve years of age, learned about the river and how he taught others like Dr. John Casselman, the professor of pike.

Born in 1911 of United Empire Loyalist stock --- though his mother was a Yankee rebel from Connecticut --- Everett Snider worked all his life on the river, mostly on the family tour boats. In the summer the boats, built from sunny British Columbia yellow cedar either by the Sniders or by Eddy Andress of Rockport, made a one-hundred-and-twelve-kilometre sweep westward to Ivy Lea then back along the United States channel.

The trip was like a mail route and Snider got to know all the guides and fishermen and island residents along the way. From the 1930s Snider remembers characters like Ernie Poole, a tall, slim reed of a man who lived in a two-storey white houseboat anchored at Grenadier Island. And there was Eddy Andress, of course, the boatbuilder who left his "puckish smile" in the memory of almost everyone.

For nine years Snider left the family business to work for the J.P. Porter marine company that dredged and blasted the Canadian channel in the St. Lawrence. A drill boat cut holes in the rock bottom with a row of twelve, steam-powered drills. One of Snider's jobs was to swing a ten-pound sledgehammer all day long to sharpen the point of the drill bits. The bits were dulled by the stubborn granite rock of the shoals. The metal was reheated in a forge on the barge and then, while red hot, hammered into a form to fix the point again. The work gave Snider the massive arm muscles of an ancient galley oarsman.

Once the holes were drilled in the rock, sticks of dynamite were dropped down hollow pipes. The charges were set off by electricity.

Snider remembers the terrible muffled thunder of the underwater blast. It would often leave the surface of the water littered with a harvest of hundreds of luckless fish released from the depths. People from the area would drive their boats into the pools of floating fish and pick out the best ones with a net.

One time after a blast Snider plucked a fifty-pound muskie from the water. Two weeks later he hoisted another muskie the same size.

But the fish were not the only casualties during the channel deepening. One day in 1930 the destinies of men and fish were reversed. Snider was almost left a lifeless heap among the dead bodies floating on the surface.

It was July 19. The blasting crew was working on Hillcrest Shoal off Cockburn Island to make the channel navigable for the big lake freighters. The St. Lawrence Seaway was no more than an idea that needed thirty more years of study and negotiation between Canada and the United States. A storm was rising when Snider, who ran a service tugboat, clambered on board the drill boat. The charges of dynamite had already been laid on the bottom of the river below the *J.B. King* barge.

The barge was anchored by cables to Cockburn Island. When it was time for the blast, the barge would be moved away, then pulled back by the cables.

The foreman, Roddy McNeill, told Snider to take a break until the rain eased up. McNeill invited Snider to the galley for a hot cup of coffee to warm his bones. Nobody warned Snider to get back into his tugboat before it was too late, but then Snider was to be lucky --- if somewhat bewildered --- that day.

"The next thing I knew I was in the water and everything was black around me."

Snider was dazed, confused, desperate. He did not know what had extinguished the light of the sun, why he was plunged into darkness. He did not have long to ruminate, however.

"I was under water so long I passed out."

Snider regained consciousness on the surface. "I looked around. There were some men sitting on the wreckage, so I swam over. The first person I saw was the foreman."

McNeill saw the accident happen from the wheelhouse. He said that a bolt of lightning struck the barge and travelled down the wires that were used to trigger the dynamite. There was no delay in the thunder. The barge, with a load of coal for the drill motors, disintegrated in the explosion.

"When I got on the wreckage I discovered I had no shoes on and my pockets --- shirt pockets and pant pockets and cuffs of my pants --- were full of coal."

"I couldn't see any daylight in the water because the coal was shifting down."

Thirty men died in the blast. Eleven survived. Seventeen of the bodies were never found, Snider says. Also lost in the explosion was the boat's mascot, a Belgian police dog named King. A few days earlier King had been given a gold medal for pulling a crew member from the water.

The survivors, with Snider among them, drifted down the river on the wreckage to Brockville like hapless adventurers on a raft. They were picked up by a United States coast guard boat which was passing by chance.

Snider still remembers the foreman's words to him when he first came to the surface lugging a cargo of coal in his pockets. McNeill said, "You were down there a long time, Ev. I thought nobody else would be coming up."

Brockville

The Dilemmas of Duck Hunting in Bed

David Younge

Once a traveller visited the Pueblo Indians in New Mexico and watched them perform their daily ritual to help the sun rise. An Indian told the traveller, "If we were to cease practicing our religion, in ten years the sun would no longer rise. Then it would be night forever." Everybody has personal rituals, even duck hunters...

David Younge

On a morning early in November an odd warm spell hovers over the water. The wind is strong without making the waves too rough for boats. David Younge looks out the cabin's northern kitchen window and brightens at the scene. In a tiny rock-circled plot of land a few green tomatoes cling rebelliously to the stems among withered leaves.

From March to the end of December Younge spends more nights on the tiny island than at his home in Gananoque. The island is only exposed to one blustery wind, out of the southwest from the direction of Lake Ontario. Across the water from Island 17D --- Younge never felt inspired to change the name of the island from its official number --- is Bostwick Island. Visible on Bostwick is the narrow rock inlet called Half Moon Bay where church services are held in boats in the summer.

Younge, a stout man with curly brown hair and a boyish ease, spends his weekends and some nights after work at the Thomson Rivet plant on Island 17D. Often he is alone, cooking steaks for himself, not the sweet, river-fed meat of the ducks he hunts faithfully through the fall. Around him from September to December are the duck hunters and the hardiest of island dwellers, such as Susan and Eliot Smith wintering on Sagistawika.

Younge, now in his mid-forties, cannot explain why he spends so much time at the island except that it is a need, a demand that must be met, like wanting to get up in the morning to see the sun rise. Yet he does admit that the compulsion, in the form of duck hunting, once went too far.

"When we started huntin' Wolfe Island then we really got into it. Oh, it was terrible up there. Every spare minute we were runnin' to Wolfe Island. We had a black truck with bunks. It got a little out a hand. We'd save all our holidays for the fall. We were runnin' up there two, three times a week."

In a single two-day period at Wolfe the hunting party shot sixty broadbill ducks, also called bluebills.

"When we hunt by Wolfe Island, it's just steady ducks. They like going up and down that American channel. The head of Wolfe Island, Amherst Island, there's always two hundred, three hundred thousand bluebills in there every year. They just come in black clouds."

But the endless trips to Wolfe over a fifteen-year stretch bred a weariness in him, he says. And there was the occasional mishap, like the time he and his longtime friend Doug Gates tipped an aluminum boat into the icy November water.

"The boat sank right down. Luckily you could just touch bottom."

The two retrieved the guns and shells from below the surface, then started bailing out the water with a lunch box. "Of course, the motor won't run. We've got to row back three miles. Oh, we had a great old time."

The Wolfe Island excursions, with the constant driving, the sleeping through the night in the truck, finally took their toll. Younge, growing older, opted for comfort instead. In 1978, he bought Island 17D and within two years had erected a cottage.

From then on Younge was practically married to the island. The bond now seemed too natural to be called a compulsion. And there was a difference between the comfort of the island and the pains of duck hunting. From afar Younge watches the dedication of the muskie fishermen, who ride the river in stormy weather.

"We got up Friday morning, the stars were all out, the moon was out. The wind wasn't blowing.

"If it's teeming rain, we just don't bother. Snowin's not so bad. You don't mind it if it's snowin'. If it's rainin' and we get up, we just go back to bed."

The group takes a boat to Hickory Island or Wolfe about six in the morning, late to be scouting the familiar duck blinds. "If you really want to get the spot, you should be going over there four in the morning." Sometimes the tardy hunters will have to move to two or three different spots to find one empty.

Then they set out seventy-five or a hundred duck decoys in a line over deeper water. The line resembles broadbills feeding. Younge uses plastic decoys from Canadian Tire, after selling the classic wooden Ray Andress decoys that he inherited from his father.

The wooden decoys require too much care and their heads fall off, Younge complains. The live ducks are apparently not as fussy as connoisseurs anyway. The plastic decoys "set higher in the water. They look better."

For a duck blind on Hickory, the hunters merely hide behind cedar branches on the exposed rocky shore. Then the waiting begins. The hunters, armed with shotguns, have to sit until the ducks are drawn to the decoys, within a range of thirty yards.

"You just have to hope they see the decoys and take a run at 'em.

"I have sat in places where the ducks just fly by the end of the decoys and never take a look at 'em. Next time, you can't keep 'em out.

"Last year me and Mr. Gates were huntin' on the foot of Wolfe Island and it was cold. Oh, it was blowin' and cold, fifteen degrees and the first week of September. But we weren't too bad. We were in the lee a little bit.

"Ten o'clock, we had two ducks. Just all kinds of ducks going up the American channel wouldn't look at the decoys. We had seventy-five decoys out. I think the more decoys you put out the better chance you got of gettin' 'em down to take a look at 'em."

The hunters were discouraged and thought about leaving. Then Gates pulled a bottle of peppermint schnapps from his bag. "We got tippin' that a little bit and I said, 'We'll stay till noon hour. That's it.'

"We had twenty-seven at noon hour. At two o'clock we had thirty-five. If we'd a left at ten o'clock, we'd a had two ducks."

Some mornings, when the weather is stormy, Younge is torn over the decision to leave the island for the hunt. He starts debating with himself, fidgeting like a weathercock twisting in the wind.

"Last Saturday, now, I got up at four o'clock. I can't go out there because it's too rough. I said, 'I don't think he'll be comin'. It's blowin' too hard.'"

Still, Younge scurried to the shack to get the bags of broadbill decoys. He started to think of spots on the river where he could avoid the windy stretches.

"I know the wind's blowing too hard. I'm just gonna pound my ass off. So then I come back in here.

"It's about five o'clock and I say, 'Damn, I gotta go somewhere.' So then I go back out ... and say, 'I can't go out there.'

"Then I thought I'll slip down to a little spot in Clarings.

"Then I said, 'There's no sense goin' down there because I know someone's going to be there.' So I ended up I didn't go.

"I was glad I didn't go. At noon hour it was just throwin' water all over the place. It was really blowin'."

Island 17D

Quiet Afternoon of a Faun

Margaret Reid

Not everyone on the river is wild and boisterous, but then not every life is fashioned through the heat of a fiery forge, through the angry clash of a battlefield. Consider the lilies of the field...

Margaret Reid among the pines

Margaret Reid will not even permit herself this one tiny boast -- that she is a river rat. For her, it would be too bold, too presumptuous to compare herself to river folk. Instead, she is happy to stay unobserved in her modest, cedar-shingle cottage on Chinguacousie Island, near Gananoque.

But Reid has been noticed. After returning to the lone cottage every year for fifty years as faithfully as the moon rises at night, she is well-known and deeply loved by the islanders. Her shy manner and quick, happy laugh are as legendary in her section of the river as the skittish great blue heron.

Reid keeps to herself, making grocery trips across the water once a month in her small aluminum boat. She canoes on the still water in the evening, gardens through the day.

By September, after the summer residents leave their islands --- abandoning a season's pyre of magazines for Reid --- the solitude returns to the river. The Chinguacousie resident lingers a month or two longer.

Dressed in a windbreaker, denim dress and white running shoes, the tall, thin woman takes a chair under a straight-backed, eighty-year-old white pine. Behind her, red and orange and white nasturtiums droop in limp, vinelike abandon from a window box. A walking stick cut from a branch leans stiffly against the side of the house under an old ship's bell. Since Reid and her brother, Archibald, now dead, bought the island in 1940, "I've made a lot of paths," she says.

From the cabin her path circles the four-acre island. The path climbs the granite steps that Reid planted herself and follows a layer of nettles she raked and plotted. When Reid comes early in the year, the path takes her past the first of the wildflowers, a pretext of spring, both a calendar and catalogue of creation. The feathery white Dutchman's-breeches mass on a bank as cool as a last, late snowfall. There are white trilliums with a rare red bloom. The Canadian Mayflower is sprouting. On the rocks spread brilliant-green patches of moss made luminous in the shadows by their own inner light. The spaces between the leaves fill with humming birds and nuthatches.

Reid knows the spots to find gingsen with "little white fuzzy flowers" or saucy dogbane. The succession of wildflowers passes through sun and rain to the wild, exuberant black-eyed Susans in the fall, the clusters of mauve asters, the sporadic, deep-blue bottle gentian.

The wildflowers have their spots as particular as their personalities, Reid says. She explains that the island has a frugal soil that has curbed the daring of the wildflowers. "If they get established in one spot, they stay there." The same is true of her. To make the island fertile, Reid and her brother scooped up bucketful after bucketful of dark, wet river muck. They carried it by hand to a plot sheltered by the cabin and a steep hill of rock. There they built stone walls to dam the willful earth and keep it from creeping perversely away. As an experiment, Reid sprinkles wildflower seeds there from far-flung corners of Canada. "It's fun to see what will thrive."

Most of the changes on the island are small, "not very radical," she says. Reid renamed her isle with the Algonquin word for pine because Potato Island sounded too mundane. Lancaster was once called Turnip Island, she says.

According to local lore, although the land was poor on the small islands, it could be even worse on the rocky Canadian shoreline. The early settlers rowed out to an island and planted small plots of potatoes or turnips. Reid also explains that the trees are crooked and spindly because years ago the British navy cut the prime timber for ships and firewood.

In the 1960s, Reid retired as a high school teacher of English and library studies. She and her brother winterized the cottage and stayed year round. The wood stove kept them warm and when the ice froze between Chinguacousie and Lancaster they walked across to a boathouse where they kept a boat. In the winter the pair had to cart their water from the river. "I'm not one of these helpless seniors," she says.

"We didn't feel trapped. It was our nature." The pair would go as long as five weeks without making a trip to Gananoque, where they were born, for groceries. Some people might have found it bleak. The moss and the grasses and the wildflowers were not there for diversion. And as far as the green plants were concerned, the winter was a well-meant but quixotic failure, a night of woeful continence. Still, the pine trees protected brother and sister from winter storms, keeping the piles of snow small and easy to navigate. "It stays so clean. The white snow stays white for ages."

The two made paths around the island in the snow and watched the tracks of raccoons and foxes appear like footnotes at the bottom of a scholarly essay. The animals crossed the river on the ice.

"This is my real headquarters," says Reid of the small cabin where she spends half the headlong year. She has travelled to the hot latitudes of Spain and Guatemala, Malta and Morocco, but she likes the quiet privacy of her island best. Even the storms here do not seem ill-tempered or bullying.

"It's not a very exciting or dramatic life. I can't see that it's newsworthy." Again, the bright smile flashes across her face, widening into an enormous grin. Her voice has been scooped from a rare, fecund soil.

September is a quiet month for an island resident like Reid. The ruckus of boat engines has dissolved like a morning mist, melted and returned to the flux of water and sky like wildflowers once fed by the summer heat.

Reid can tend the autumn blooms. She can pick from a wall lined with books a volume on travel or biography. The great blue heron which likes to perch nearby on the tip of Mulcaster feels at ease too. "Today, I noticed it didn't budge when I started the motor." The jittery nerves of the herons ease in the fall, says the airy spirit of Chinguacousie. "By that time they know no motor boat will shoot at them."

Chinguacousie Island

Enterprise and the Castle Builder

Ferrymen to His Majesty, the King

The Horne family

To the man who makes his living on the river a boat is like the plow and the bag of seed to the farmer. The commercial fisherman and the ferryman rely on their boats as though its skin were their skin, its keel, their spine. The hull of the boat is the seed pod of their lives and sometimes a coffin...

George Horne

For an institution on the river, George Horne does not say much. With one hand on a wooden wheel and his eyes scanning the water he steers the sixty-eight-foot car ferry, the *William Darrell*, with rock music playing from a tape deck. The section of the river between Wolfe Island and Cape Vincent is a bright, brassy stretch of water with waves peaked or chipped at the command of Lake Ontario winds. And the *William Darrell*, says Horne, is the last car ferry crossing the international boundary.

This is the same trip Horne has made ten times a day, seven days a week from mid-May until the end of the October since he won his captain's licence at nineteen. It is also the same trip that his ancestors made, going back to his grandfather Thomas D. Horne.

The most that George Horne will admit --- his characteristic form of expression is a quick smile, masking his shyness --- is that it occasionally gets stormy on the ferry ride between Canada and the United States and that the current along the south side of Wolfe Island can be strong.

Still, rough seas --- "the waves come rolling in off the lake" --- never stop the small, ten-car ferry, Horne says. On stormy days the children from Cape Vincent ride at the front of the ferry to feel the spray of the waves, adds Horne's younger brother Bruce, who shares duties on the *William Darrell*.

The brothers were raised together with their sister Jackie in a handsome stone-block house facing the channel and the ferry dock on Wolfe Island. Here their father Darrell and uncle William once ran the ferry. In 1946, the year after the two brothers, Darrell and William, inherited the ferry operation from their father, they bought a United States army landing ship to carry cars. As more and more visitors came to the

Thousand Islands by highway, the brothers expanded the business with the *William Darrell*, launched in 1953 and named after the pair.

The Horne ferry was an ambitious undertaking. In 1871, Thomas Darrell Horne, George Horne's great-grandfather, built a large structure by the ferry dock with sixteen bedrooms that he intended to use as a summer resort. The large house was useful mainly to house the large Horne clan. In 1936, William and Darrell's father, also William E. Horne, was inspired by another ambitious idea. He bought a large diesel engine ferry --- named after Jacques Cartier, the French explorer who was stopped in his westward venture down the St. Lawrence by the Lachine rapids --- which could transport thirty cars and three hundred and fifty passengers. But the amount of business did not match the dream. Even today the provincially run *Wolfe Island Ferry*, which handles the larger volume of traffic back and forth from Kingston, only has a capacity of fifty cars.

Two years after the *Jacques Cartier* went into service the Thousand Islands bridge was finished, making an easy and less expensive option for crossing the river. If that was not a blow to the ferry, the Great Depression and hard times were.

Over the years, though, the Hornes, descended from Scottish immigrants, have had good luck for mariners. The early ferry service was by steamboat and before that by rowboat, but the Hornes fared well. Earle Cass, a historian married to the great-great granddaughter of the first of the Horne ancestors to run the ferry, Samuel Hinckley, says the only Horne to suffer bad luck was William E. Horne's father, Thomas D. Horne.

Thomas Horne died on November 13, 1884 during a storm when he tried to cross from Cape Vincent in a rowboat. The winds blew in a wild fever and Horne sank, *basso profundo* to the bottom, unnoted. The water rushed over his head until the terror and confusion fell away. The boat was found later, says Cass, in the quiet water at the foot of Carleton Island with a hole in it. The body was never recovered.

Thomas Horne had inherited the ferry operation and the original lease from King George IV after he married Angeline Spinning. Spinning's father had married into the family of Samuel Hinckney, who made the ferry official when he acquired the lease from the king in 1829. According to the terms of the lease, Hinckney was required to transport British soldiers and their Indian allies without charge, though relations between Canada and the United States had quieted after the War of 1812. In exchange for the lease, Hinckney paid a yearly "rent" of twenty pounds to the Crown.

These days the sturdy iron bell-like hull of the *William Darrell*, propelled by its two-hundred-and-fifty-horsepower engines, makes the international crossing without much trouble in ten minutes. The ferry service has come a long way since the Hornes' grandfather, William E. Horne --- remembered for a torso strong from daily exercise --- rowed passengers across from Cape Vincent. When he landed on Wolfe, he donned his cap as Canadian customs agent.

First-time travellers these days do not have to tempt the waves in a rowboat. But, landlubbers at heart, they still look skeptical about the safety of the small ferry. Some travellers stay in their cars during the crossing, peering at the river through their windshields with thin, parched faces. George Horne --- with a puckish inward smile and quick, alert movements in the wheelhouse --- has never lost a car over the side.

Wolfe Island

Hoisting the Duchess from The Mud

Andrew McNally III

From an elegant nook on Wellesley Island the family which literally put much of the world on the map has been observing the feverish changes to the St. Lawrence River through the quiet trees...

Andrew McNally III on *La Duchesse*

The chairman of the board of the McNally corporation saunters onto the deck of his Wellesley Island houseboat with pruning shears in one hand, lamenting that the gardening has fallen behind. It's a July day with the mercury at a surly thirty degrees Celsius and the sunburned summer gardener, Andrew McNally III, wants to get back to his flowers and his two-scarecrow plot of corn, potatoes and beans.

McNally eases his large frame into a white wicker chair on the upper deck of his houseboat. Beside him are big, ragged blooms of white begonia tipped in red, as languorously elegant as the houseboat, *La Duchesse*. In the wake of ships passing along the main channel of the St. Lawrence *La Duchesse* rolls prudently. In slow refrain to the motion of the wakes, the patches of sunlight rise and fall across the floor.

"Before the Seaway all we had were lakers. We liked them. They went slowly," explains McNally.

As a young boy he stood on the shore in the hope that the passenger boats sailing from Toronto to Prescott would salute him, the small heir to the giant Rand McNally map-making corporation. Without the Thousand Islands bridge cutting across Wellesley, the only path to the island was by boat, even for the dairy farmers who struggled for a living among the rocks.

"I was here before electricity and telephones," McNally remarks. When he was three months old his mother, Eleanor, brought him to the Wellesley Island summer home of her father, Royal C. Villas, whose company manufactured headlamps for steam engines. McNally's grandmother promptly made plans to steep the infant in the healthy climate of the river. "She chartered a yacht to take me out every day so my lungs would get full of the great St. Lawrence air." His grandmother wanted to help her infant grandson "survive the terrible Chicago winters."

In 1912, when McNally was three, his mother prodded until his father relented and bought twenty acres on the south side of Wellesley from a farmer named Houghton. The land sat next to the Villas property. Escaping Chicago for summer in the islands was an adventure for McNally. The family travelled by rail through Canada and unloaded at the train station outside Gananoque with "big trunks and dogs and cats and birds and a retinue of servants." Then they boarded the Thousand Islands Railway for the trip --- past the cemetery stop --- to the Gananoque waterfront. The ten-kilometre stretch of track was the sole extent of the tiny railway. The Thousand Islands Railway had an engine and one passenger car, McNally recalls. "It had plush seats with an oil lamp dripping on your head if you weren't careful."

From the Gananoque depot on the river, it was twenty-two kilometres down the river in a boat to summers spent swimming, fishing, watching polo tournaments on Wellesley, or caddying at the island golf course. For the boy who was not yet an executive, the island was the hefty dividend waiting after a long winter. "Chicago was just a big city and school."

In time McNally would take his place in the family corporation, started by his great-grandfather, Andrew McNally, and his partner William H. Rand. The first Andrew McNally sailed from Northern Ireland in the middle of the nineteenth century as an indentured servant. After seven years bound to a printer, he turned his new skill into a job in the print-shop of the *Chicago Tribune*. In 1856, McNally and Rand formed a partnership to print railway timetables and railway maps. Their company grew into the giant Rand McNally corporation which today produces road maps, airline tickets, atlases and also binds books like the Encyclopaedia Britannica.

After Andrew McNally III entered the family business, the islands and the river still claimed his loyalty. It was as binding as a contract signed in his boyhood days. In 1943, McNally reopened a chapter of the fading elegance of the Thousand Islands by buying for one dollar the sunken houseboat of George Boldt, the Waldorf-Astoria Hotel millionaire who built Boldt Castle on Heart Island.

Boldt was building his extravagant, turreted castle of imperishable granite as a sign of his love for his wife Louise when she died suddenly. The castle was left unfinished inside, and the one-hundred-and-ten-foot boathouse, built in 1903 by Boldt as a kind of floating Pullman railway coach, was left to rot. Boldt died in 1916, heart broken, his spirit a bundle of rags. *La Duchesse* subsided in neglect. She eventually sank in twelve feet of water in the Boldt yacht house. However, the upper deck stayed above the waves like a head held high above misfortune.

Divers patched the hull under the water. *La Duchesse*, passive and unquestioning and willing to be led, was towed to Kingston and restored, with a metal hull added later in 1955 like an iron girdle. She was returned to moorage in a girlishly slim channel between Wellesley and a quarter-acre isle named Royal. At the time it seemed as though McNally spent "a fortune" on the houseboat --- he won't say how much --- but he now owned a floating duchy with a bedroom paneled in Philippine mahogany where he could sleep through the summer nights in touch with the river.

On the top deck of *La Duchesse* --- "she's just a big, elegant gal," McNally says to explain the logic of her name --- there is a large screened room with glistening pinewood floors. Next to the sitting room is a living room with carved maple panelling, a stained glass skylight, and a marble fireplace. The lower deck has a dining room with an elaborate brass fireplace and six staterooms outfitted in golden-hued mahogany from Honduras.

The brass doorknobs, darkened by the years, were cast for Boldt. The doorknobs have Boldt's initial with the symbol he adopted as a pun on heart, a hart or deer. The window shades --- turned bright blue by the sun outside --- were built by Boldt, Pullman-style, running in grooves along the edges of the window.

Boldt and the McNallys after him had found a luxurious corner of the world in the Thousand

Islands. It was as remote and secluded as a boardroom. They never foresaw the way the Seaway, highways and bridges, and then powerboats, would change the river. So La Duchesse, without the power to keep pace with time, is edged aside and elbowed by the crude wakes of boats headed down the channel. The jostling comes more often now, and the screened sitting room has no protection against the raw muttering of powerboats, helicopters and aircraft.

"We fuss about it all the time, especially the noise," McNally says. "In the afternoon the boats go by and you can't talk. It's a menace."

"It's just like rock and roll music. It's deafening and very, very objectionable."

McNally is interrupted by an inquiry from a frail, white-haired gardener. Near eighty, the gardener looks, for a moment, as if one of the scarecrows had stirred from the garden and staggered on board La Duchesse. The old man lives on the island and helps with the chores. McNally lifts himself out of the chair for a hushed conference. It's a question about the gladioluses. McNally gives his decision to the gardener.

"He's as old as I am," McNally says when he returns. Yet it is not age he thinks about. His thoughts stray to the begonias waiting to be rooted in boxes in front of La Duchesse and to the vegetables languishing during a dry, sulphureous season. The chairman of the board is delinquent in his chores. He wants to return to the garden that feeds two houses and one houseboat in the summer.

Wellesley Island

La Duchesse

Saxon Ingenuity

Ron Huck

In mythology, blacksmiths are images of creators and inventors. They use their hands and they use their ingenuity to build things. A modern-day blacksmith works without a forge at his creative labours...

Ron Huck

The Ron Huck who returned to Rockport in 1979 was battered and bruised mentally. He loved the riverside hamlet where he was born, but it was remote from the intoxicating power politics of Ottawa where Huck shared the duties during the reign of the ironclad intellectual prime minister, Pierre Trudeau. The election of 1979 which savaged Trudeau and the Liberal party also cut Huck's political veins. In a few hours he fell from the executive assistant of a cabinet minister to an out-of-work father of three children. And it hurt.

Huck had seen the prime minister daily, met with heads of state from foreign countries and oversaw first the department of health and welfare, then multiculturalism. He knew the secrets and inner workings of the government and felt that he made a difference for people who needed help cutting red tape. He was at the centre of national and international affairs, a royal participant in the remaking of Canada. His children could run up to Trudeau and Huck danced with the prime minister's wife.

The "recuperation from the downfall" took six months, Huck says. For a period he had been free to use every ounce of his ability. Now he felt no better than a castoff mariner left behind by his ship. "It's quite a shock, the readjustment. Who have you got here to discuss international affairs?"

It was not the prestige of power in the nation's capital that mattered to Huck, who taught history and English in Ottawa before he was swept into politics in the 1972 Liberal campaign. It was the mental stimulation. And in Ottawa he got that abundantly.

Yet Huck --- in spite of the radical departure from his German immigrant stock on the St. Lawrence River

--- did not return to Rockport like an exile. He came home to Rockport proud of his heritage, moving closer to his family and community as a marina operator. The drive and cleverness that made his grandfather, Fred Huck, a successful engine builder in Rockport, still burned in Ron Huck. The difference was that Huck had transformed his grandfather's Saxon ingenuity into a talent with people, not machines.

Fred Huck might not have come to the Thousand Islands if it had not been for Ellen Slate, a Grindstone Island woman. Huck "left his native land to see how something ticked in the new world," his grandson says. The immigrant met Ellen Slate in New York State. After the couple married they moved to Grindstone on the American side, then crossed the water to Rockport in 1889.

Rockport had earned the reputation as a haven on the river in times of storms. It had a bay sheltered by red granite from the southwesterly winds. The high rock bluff also made it a landmark for boats navigating on the St. Lawrence. Rockport --- once called Stony Village --- was a natural stop for steamers needing first wood, then coal, as fuel.

In the hamlet Fred Huck set up a blacksmith shop and later bought land on the river. The blacksmith made farm implements and parts for boats. Ingenious with his hands, he built one of the first four-cycle boat engines on the river, which launched him into a thriving boat-building business alongside Eddy Andress. At that time it was unusual for a lone craftsman to build one by one a series of engines. Fred Huck had to fashion the crankshaft on his lathe, an impossible feat the scornful engine manufacturers in Brockville told him. Huck built his masterly engine, his *Meisterstuck auf dem Strom*, and dubbed it --- true to his Saxon thinking --- *Invictus*, Latin for "the unconquerable."

Fred Huck was a dauntless man, "very harsh, strong, persevering," his grandson says. He combined that with a knack for innovation that made him resemble another German on the river, the castle-builder George Boldt. "There wasn't anything he couldn't do on a lathe."

Of Fred Huck's six children, five survived. One son left Rockport for vaudeville in New York City. For a while two of the Huck sons, Howard and Ed, helped in the business. Then there was a split and Howard, Ron's father, cut out of the will, drove to work in Gananoque, where he was chief mechanic for the Gananoque Boat Line. Howard Huck, though mellower than his father, was nevertheless resilient. And he could not ignore Rockport. In 1952, when the strong-willed Fred Huck died --- partly from the spiritual loss of his wife two years earlier --- Howard Huck returned. Howard Huck set up his own marina, Howard's Marine, which sits next door to the marina named after his brother Ed.

During Prohibition Howard Huck ran booze across the water in his boat --- "everybody was doing it," his son says. "I don't think it was the money. It was the daring." Huck took the cases of liquor either to a drop spot on Wellesley Island or to Pine Tree Point at Alexandria Bay. The liquor was moved on dark nights "without moonshine." At Pine Tree Point a moving van was waiting. When the sides of the van were removed, there was an eight-inch-deep pocket for the liquor. The same furniture went back and forth from Alexandria Bay to New York City in the counterfeit moving van over and over again.

In 1943, Ron Huck was born. As a child he had a head of hair as black as forged iron and his dark eyes had a devouring look that hungered to learn about the world. Educated in the two-room Rockport school he inherited his grandfather's keen mind and the immigrant's longing to break old ties and cross oceans. Yet now the ties, the oceans to cross, were political and intellectual. Huck's father and grandfather, both Tories, seemed passive politically. Ron Huck wanted to "jump into the fray."

"I felt I'd seen everything locally, but I wanted to see what was beyond," Huck says. "I wanted to see what made things tick and where and how it worked and get involved. To get a clear understanding of something, you have to roll up your sleeves and jump in." He went to Queen's University and started teaching in Ottawa. In 1972, he was picked as campaign manager for Norm Caffik in the federal riding near Pickering, Ontario. That breathtakingly close election changed Huck's life, not to mention history, since Caffik's victory swung the power in Canada.

Caffik lost the election at first by twelve votes and the Liberal party, tied with the Progressive Conservative party for number of seats in the House of Commons, could not form a government. Some sly Liberal strategy during a recount netted Caffik a victory by four votes. That, in turn, broke the tie in the House of Commons, giving the Liberal party one hundred and nine seats to the one hundred and seven for the Progressive Conservatives. Trudeau formed a minority government and Huck was off to Ottawa as an executive assistant.

As a key administrator, an adviser giving direction to one of thirty-two cabinet ministers, he wielded considerable power. "I was one of thirty-two running the country," he says matter-of-factly. But after seven exhilarating years the magic sceptre was smashed. An election put the abortive and short-lived Tory government of Joe Clark in power.

Huck fled to Rockport. The sense of loss was deep --- "There's always the pang to go back. You never lose that once you were in power" --- but life on the river was absorbing. Huck arrived in June, the height of the boat season for Howard's Marine. He became a partner at the marina, trained to be a real estate agent, took computer courses and served two terms as deputy reeve of the Front of Escott Township. Rockport wasn't Ottawa, but then, as the returning adventurer learned, Rockport had rewards of its own. Huck had more time for his family. He was among friendly people with a river-bred sense of grace. Here he could touch the taproot of compassion and feel the spirit that feeds life.

There were characters that mercifully had not changed while Huck was away. Eddy Andress, at eighty years of age, was still perky, still brimful of joy and charm. Huck saw in Andress a man who loved work, children and the sight of a young, good-looking woman. Huck remembers the elderly man nudging and teasing him one day with the words, "See those three blondes down there. I can handle the two. Can you handle the third?"

Politics had never been dry and abstract for Huck. It was the people in politics that Huck liked, he decided, and coming home to Rockport was a sweet reminder of his own needs.

"You never want to leave the river," says Huck, who is a contradictory blend of the wandering immigrant and the man who never leaves his birthplace. Over Huck's shoulder in his office the picture of Trudeau and the 1978 federal cabinet hangs forgotten for a moment. "It's hard to explain. Perhaps it's in your genes."

A sketch of Winston Churchill hangs unobserved, his obliterating stare anchoring a far corner of the room. Huck warms to the topic like a teacher who does not want to bury and hoard what he has learned.

"Never forget where your roots are. That's part of yourself. If you have those roots and an understanding of where you come from, you'll never lose your compassion for people."

There is no faltering in the words. The eyes, too dark to show their depth, are fixed motionless like iron nails from a blacksmith's forge.

"It's part of you and its not going to let you go.

"And the only way it's going to let you go is in death. And I don't think even in death it lets you go.

"You're still remembered. In death, you're gone physically, but mentally and namewise, you're still here."

Rockport

Dynamite in the Hands of a Crown Attorney

Douglas Mackintosh

Some men lead so many lives that you would think they had been reincarnated three or four times. Doug Mackintosh of the Black Macintosh clan is one of these, a man so heroically well rounded that the only thing he needs to complete his character is a patch over one eye...

Douglas Mackintosh

Crown attorney Douglas Mackintosh strides out of the courtroom in the loose black gown of his trade. Behind him could be a murder trial or a nasty sexual assault case. But Mackintosh has other thoughts on his mind as he drives home along the river. After work, he pulls on a pair of battered work boots. It is time to tend his small marina near Ivy Lea.

The same man who read philosophy at Oxford University and swooshed downhill as an Olympic skier is also a river adept. He can handle the controls of a dredging crane mounted on a barge, set dynamite for an underwater blast or build a tugboat in his backyard.

Mackintosh has lived several lives. He founded a marine construction firm which tumbled into insolvency, then paid his debts and created a second company. He fought a corrupt judge hearing a tangled lawsuit which took years to settle. Then, at thirty-eight, entered law school and became a lawyer. He chipped ice off the bow of a boat in a Lake Ontario storm and contended with drunken workers who beached and overturned his boats. After dredging a marsh and destroying the ecology, he helped to found the river watchdog group the Thousand Islands Area Residents Association with his wife Blu, map-maker and cataloguer of islands.

The changes in Mackintosh were part of his versatile, adventurous background. Mackintosh's father Christopher, an entrepreneur based in Glasgow, was an Olympic skier and bobsledder who was "as wild as they come." Once, on a train running through the mountains, Christopher Mackintosh had an argument with the train conductor. In the end he made his point by throwing the man off the train. Christopher Douglas sent his son to Canada for high school during the Second World War. Douglas Mackintosh later graduated from Oxford University with a Master's degree and in 1949 was drafted into the British army. For two years he fought communist guerrillas in Malaysia. "The main difficulty was not getting ambushed," he says.

In 1953, the twenty-two-year-old man returned to Canada for a vacation and stayed. Five years later he incorporated the Black Douglas dredging company with a minority-share partner who supplied equipment and experience. The name Black Douglas was taken from the family line that Mackintosh traces back on his mother's side to a twelfth-century Scottish clan. Feared by the British, the name Black Douglas once meant the bogeyman. Even in Ontario, children were once taught a rhyme that warned them to be good, otherwise the Black Douglas would get them. Mackintosh admits that the choice of the roguish name was partly a blow struck for his independence on the river.

The Black Douglas crew needed a fighting spirit. The company started in the profitable business of dredging sand from a bay on Grenadier Island. The sand was needed to build Highway 401. The hard, well-graded, sharp granite sand was ideal for road construction and the location of Grenadier made it easy to sell the sand in both Canada and the United States. However, Black Douglas quickly ran afoul of a competitor on Grenadier who tried to block access to the Black Douglas Bay. The competitor had created a channel to the bay by dredging sand from property that he owned on the island. Barriers of rocks and piles were erected, and barges were anchored in the way, to block the equipment of Black Douglas.

Some of the Black Douglas crew fought with their rivals. Mackintosh's form of defiance was more civil, if offbeat: he blew his bagpipes across the water to scorn his antagonists with shrill Scottish music.

Black Douglas took the rival company to court for damages to the business. The lawsuit was complicated, Mackintosh says, by behind-the-scenes manipulation of a county court judge who was also a shareholder in the rival sand company. Since the group shared a party line, Mackintosh once overheard the judge tell his rival that Black Douglas was legally in the right, but that they would nevertheless drive the company under.

The judge was "a totally evil man," Mackintosh says. "The judge was directing the whole campaign against Black Douglas." The judge should not have heard the case in his court since he had a financial interest in the operation. However, the judge was dead and buried before he could account for his skullduggery.

Out of court, those were also rough years. Mackintosh struggled for financial stability with a crew that, although loyal during hard times, had its problems. One captain put a tugboat and barge on a rock shoal in a drunken stupor. Another flipped a barge with some help from a bottle. And Mackintosh remembers a December storm in Lake Ontario when the spray of the waves was freezing on the boat, threatening to capsize the craft. Mackintosh tied a rope around his waist and in the pounding of twenty-foot waves chipped the ice away.

The court case over the sand dragged on for fourteen years, with Black Douglas sinking into insolvency. In 1974, the case was finally settled --- though Black Douglas had been dissolved by that time --- with the rival's island land and equipment going to pay the debts of Black Douglas. In the interim, Mackintosh founded in 1961 a marine construction business, Blue Heron Marine, with his pit foreman, Rolly McIntosh, as a one-third partner. A year later Mackintosh bought forty acres of marsh and rocky land west of Ivy Lea as a base, and in 1963 dredged channels in the swamp to create a marina.

Rolly McIntosh, a loyal man in the company, took one acre of land along one of the channels. McIntosh was fiercely independent and kept his thoughts to himself. Suddenly he split with Douglas Mackintosh. "One day he wouldn't come to work. He wouldn't tell me why. He hasn't spoken to me since." Mackintosh says that he still does not know what prompted the split.

Mackintosh also showed his ingenuity with his second business. With no background in boat building, he designed and built, with help from another man, a forty-five-foot tugboat called the *Blue Quail*. He built a crane on a barge that powered itself through the water by a side paddle-wheel.

Mackintosh's method was the same one he always follows: first, ask those who know what to do, then read a book on the subject, and finally plunge in and do it.

Blue Heron Marine became a success, but Mackintosh still was not satisfied. A desire to change, to conquer new seas, urged him onwards. In 1969, the thirty-eight-year-old man entered law school for a long period of study and articling. In 1974, he graduated as a lawyer. He returned to the Thousand Islands as an assistant Crown attorney for the United Counties of Leeds and Grenville in 1980.

Other changes were happening in Mackintosh. The message of the environmentalists in the 1960s had an effect on him. In 1975, when the Thousand Islands Area Residents Association was created to fight the federal government's proposal to expropriate island land for a park, Mackintosh leapt into the fray. He was a founding member of TIARA and the first president. Ironically, the man who destroyed a marsh as a river contractor was now fighting for the environment.

In court, Black Douglas, a man who can handle a tugboat or a stick of dynamite, is a formidable opponent. His knowledge of the river, independence and strength of will would seem to qualify him as a river rat. But Mackintosh disagrees. "I'm only half a river rat." A true river rat --- like Rolly McIntosh --- has a "healthy disdain for government and bureaucracy" and does things his own way, "no matter what." The rebel in Mackintosh still believes that you can find justice in the system.

Blue Heron Marine, near Ivy Lea

Never Say No to the River

Hal McCarney

In the Thousand Islands the spirit of enterprise takes the form of boats and bridges and castles. It comes from an unseen source, roaring like a waterfall through a chasm, bursting, churning without small doubts or hesitation...

Hal McCarney

Talking to Hal McCarney is like talking to the river, all flow and current and no apparent focus. McCarney, the biggest, boldest entrepreneur on the Canadian side of the Thousand Islands, surges all day with boundless energy and ideas. And like the river, he resents being dammed and channeled and ringed by seawalls.

"*Don't* tell me what I can't do," he declares. "*Don't* take duck hunting away from me. *Don't* tell me I can't go muskie fishing. *Don't* tell me I can't go out on the river."

Long before the triple, five-hundred-horsepower engines in his giant tour boats rumble awake in the morning, McCarney hums and throbs as if drawing on a private supply of protein. The energy surges through his six-foot, four-inch-tall, two-hundred-and-sixty-pound frame and propels him around the town of Gananoque, across the river. From a pickup truck where he plays tapes of singing whales McCarney runs the Gananoque Boat Line tours, the Thousand Islands Wild Kingdom, two motels, one restaurant and a constant flux of new projects and schemes.

The St. Lawrence earns him his living and he relies on the river --- just its nearness at times --- to inspire him. The kind of thinking that McCarney likes on the river is the opposite of bureaucracy and the dreaded word *don't*. For him, bureaucracy is bereft of the spirit of enterprise. It is a kind of denial or nihilism that works with rules and regulations, throwing them over living creatures like a deadly net.

In 1969, the forty-three-year-old McCarney, son of a Gananoque hotel owner whose father had immigrated from Scotland, made an enterprising leap. He and Gananoque lawyer Harry Clarke bought half of the Gananoque Boat Line. Under McCarney's industry and ideas the operation swelled from ferrying fifty thousand passengers a summer through the island channels to the 1982 peak of two hundred thousand.

Yet McCarney was never satisfied with a single pursuit, however successful. He coached the Queen's University football team for twenty-five years, patented a football cleat, and collected Indian lore and arrowheads of the Thousand Islands. He sat on the town council. He spearheaded the bitterly contested campaign in 1962 to allow Gananoque's lounges and dining rooms to be licensed for liquor.

In 1970, McCarney started the Algan shipyard near the Gananoque town bay. Gananoque, with boatbuilders like George Andress, was a source of fine skiffs, but it lacked a shipbuilding industry. McCarney's four aluminum triple-deck tour boats were built at Algan, as well as the *Canadian Empress*, a fifty-six-foot catamaran and eight other ships. The world's largest trimaran, built for a Caribbean charter business that McCarney half owns, was outfitted at the shipyard in 1988. The trimaran sailed under the Thousand Islands bridge with twenty feet to spare above its one-hundred-and-five-foot masts.

And yet, in spite of all his accomplishments, McCarney still hears the deadly word *don't* when he hatches a new idea. It seems that nothing can prick and frustrate him so much as the nihilism of bureaucracy. Whether it is zoning regulations in Gananoque that cramp the passionate pace of his expansions, or federal and provincial officials, McCarney thrashes about in the web of rules, regulations and paperwork until he can cut himself free.

One mythic battle demonstrates the kind of beast that hungers after McCarney. He wanted to be a bridge builder in a more or less modest way. A bridge was a creative way to react to the river. It would not be an arrogant attempt to change the current like a dam or a wall. The McCarney bridge was a footbridge, eighty-five feet long, arching from his riverfront home in Gananoque across a narrow, rarely used "gap," to his property on diminutive Island 1. McCarney thought that it would be easy.

"I wasn't interfering with anyone," he insists. The channel was three feet deep, he claims, and nobody used the gap between shore and island "except for one boat a year." But McCarney found himself tangled in regulations from Gananoque, the Front of Leeds and Lansdowne township, the Ministry of Natural Resources and the Ministry of the Environment.

He was forced to take a building permit from Gananoque, which he insists had no jurisdiction since island and water property fall under the township. He took out a building permit from the township. He was forced to rent the land under the bridge as though he were a troll who intended to live there.

Bureaucracy in the hands of nihilistic folk is a scourge on the living, he reflects. "It can make entrepreneurs so fed up, they say the hell with it. Or they do like I did with my bridge and muddle through with it.

"I don't like little guys in Ottawa sitting in an office without a window, trying to make rules about something they don't understand.

"I abhor negativism and negative people."

The river is different. It is alive and it feeds life. In response, McCarney has made a life for himself where he never loses touch with rivers and oceans. When the St. Lawrence freezes in winter, McCarney heads for the Atlantic Ocean to communicate with whales. In 1983, while managing the Caribbean charter business in Tortola, he became enthralled with whale research being conducted by the School of the Atlantic based in Maine. "I got hooked on humpback whales," he says. He sails on the expeditions, sometimes in his own boat, and records the habits and sounds of the sea beasts. "I run whale tapes all day long. Whales have the same relation to me, maybe, as the water."

"I think it's an affiliation that just has to be, like breathing air. As long as you breathe air, you're going to live. As long as I have water, I'm going to live a better life than I would anywhere else."

In the Thousand Islands McCarney dashes about in a pickup truck one size too small for his hulking frame. He has the look of a grandfatherly walrus that cannot be bullied or intimidated or distracted. Over the years he has kept his balance --- if not always his temper --- and his eyes have not lost their sheen.

"I remember as a kid you could see the sparkle on the river. I didn't see as much of that in the sixties and seventies.

"I'm sixty-two and I never stopped drinking water out of the river. That epitomizes my relationship with the river. I would not hesitate to drink water in the river anywhere. The water right now is coming back.

"Am I just dreaming this, or is there more sparkle on the river than there was fifteen years ago?"

Gananoque

Hal McCarney and his bridge

The Escape of Fort Lauderdale's Mayor

Bob Cox

An island can be a catalyst in the lives of people. It can bring a family closer together. It can also be a world apart from the mundane, a place to let thoughts collect and focus in solitude ...

Bob Cox

Rain sprays Bob Cox's face and glasses as he steers his Boston whaler across the water. The rain veils the islands like a cloth of even grey. It hunts impetuously for gaps in his raincoat. Yet it falls sweetly in relief from the humid, sultry July day. "Where are those crazy fishermen?" Cox jokes. His chuckles are drawn out as if he weighed his laughter as thoughtfully as his words. He points the whaler towards Clayton, past Calumet Island where the castle of Charles Emery burned down leaving a lone tower and the servants' quarters. On the water are a cluster of boats with fishing rods absent-mindedly poked over the side.

Cox, engineer, boat dealer and mayor of Fort Lauderdale, feels at home on Grindstone Island. His family has passed the summers on the property --- once believed to be a German spy nest --- since 1918. Cox could be in Bangkok or Tokyo or Kenya if he wanted, but he chooses Grindstone Island in the summer.

Not even the beach resort city of 150,000 can hold him back. Fort Lauderdale and the Thousand Islands have as much in common as "watermelons and raisins," he says. "Fort Lauderdale is a sophisticated, bustling city full of elegant homes and elegant yachts."

But the mayor of Fort Lauderdale does not revel in the sophistication of city politics. He says that he hates hearing the word politician applied to himself. "I'm a businessman who is trying to give back to his community." He has been a member of the city commission, which runs Fort Lauderdale, since 1969 and compares himself to a chairman of the board.

In March of 1988 Cox was elected mayor for a three-year term after his opponent tried to turn his Thousand Island summers into a weapon against him. His rival ran a radio ad which started with the sound of a telephone ringing. A receptionist answered to say, "I'm sorry. The mayor isn't here. He's on vacation." The mud slinging did not work, Cox says. He was elected and does his commission business by phone and mail from Grenadier Island.

On his island, Cox reflects on the destiny that ties him to boats, the water and the islands. He was born in 1917 in Niagara Falls, on the United States side. His father was the president of an American chemical plant built on the Canadian side. The family had a summer home at Fineview, on Wellesley Island, which he says burned in 1918 after children set it on fire. The family bought twelve acres and two bays on the north side of Grindstone the same year and set about raising their son in the unpampered extravagance of the islands.

The family land once belonged to a wealthy man with a German name who was arrested during the First World War, Cox says. A worker on the estate was awakened early in the morning while sleeping in the boathouse. Over him hovered United States federal agents, who arrested the German owner, the butler and the cook. "It was in the height of the German hysteria," Cox says, "and their names were German." The federal agents were suspicious, since German couriers had been discovered among the hordes of summer tourists arriving by train in the Thousand Islands. The spies took a boat to Grindstone, then walked across the island to be picked up by a skiff, which took them to the Canadian side. Once on Canadian land, the German agents made their way home.

After the Second World War Cox, with an engineering degree from Cal Tech and divorce papers from his first wife, decided to live on a boat in New York Harbour "as a change of pace." He stayed on the boat two years, then sailed to Florida to seek his fortune. Approaching from the water like the Norsemen who first landed on the continent, he discovered that Fort Lauderdale lacked good marinas. His knowledge of boats and the water inspired him, and he bought a decommissioned torpedo research laboratory, which he still runs today as a boat sales marina. Cox says that he owns the largest dealership in the world of the unsinkable Boston whaler.

When his parents died, Cox took five of the twelve acres on Grindstone for himself. He started to build a relentless series of small but exquisite cottages of pine and cedar. "I'm a frustrated builder, like a lot of engineers," he says. He builds a litter of small cottages instead of one large building. The advantages are more privacy and less risk of losing everything in a single fire. So far he has built five cabins.

Like others in the Thousand Islands, Cox does not think of land in the area as a commodity to be bought and sold. It is part of the continuity of the family. To keep the island property in the family after he is dead and buried, Cox set up a legal partnership.

The cottage where Cox and his wife Virginia pass the summers is compact in its luxury. He calls it a "saltbox" because of its square design with a jaunty, slanted roof. The interior has the cosiness of a ship's cabin.

The cottage is built on stilts like a design out of *Wind in the Willows*. One end of the main beam rests like a big elbow on the granite outcropping. The porch looking over the water is built around the trunk of a tree as though the cabin were an exotic tree fort. The interior is all pine, with a granite-block fireplace from the Grindstone quarry where paving stones were once cut by Scotsmen.

A home on Grindstone puts you in a transition zone between peacefulness and bustle, Cox says. "It's near and yet so far," he explains. "It's wonderful to live here within visibility of Clayton with the all-necessary amenities --- the grocery store, the post office --- and yet feeling as if you're a million miles away."

Outside the rain picks up its tempo. Stormy, the family's black and white springer spaniel, is getting lonely out of doors. She pushes her humid nose against a low window. "Don't worry," says Cox with a slow, hearty laugh, "that dog's a water dog. She goes swimming." Islands and boats and solitude put you in touch with what's important, Cox reflects. They filter out the unnecessary and help focus your thoughts. "Living on a boat concentrates your mind wonderfully. It concentrates your life."

So does an island.

Yet Cox feels the threat of intrusion in the Thousand Islands. "In this country anything you can reach by automobile is already ruined, or well on its way, and I dearly love living on an island that has no bridges." Then he says with a slow, unrushed, meditative chuckle. "I won't live on a lake. I'd feel trapped."

Later, the Boston whaler skips over the flat, mule-grey water of a windless rainstorm. The fishermen cluster drowsily in their boats in one open spot as though pulled together around an unseen fire. Cox passes them on the way to Clayton to collect the mail of the mayor of Fort Lauderdale. Twice a month he flies to Florida for the day-long commission meetings. After submersing himself in the bureaucracy of the city, he sprints to the airport without dinner. Bob Cox needs to get back to a place without bridges.

Grindstone Island

George Boldt: A Broken Heart in an Unfinished Castle

Clover Boldt Baird

The life of George Boldt the castle builder was a bold tale written by desire and imagination. Then destiny got in the way. The dream was smashed, a heart broken, but Boldt's granddaughter remembers the mighty flame of the man...

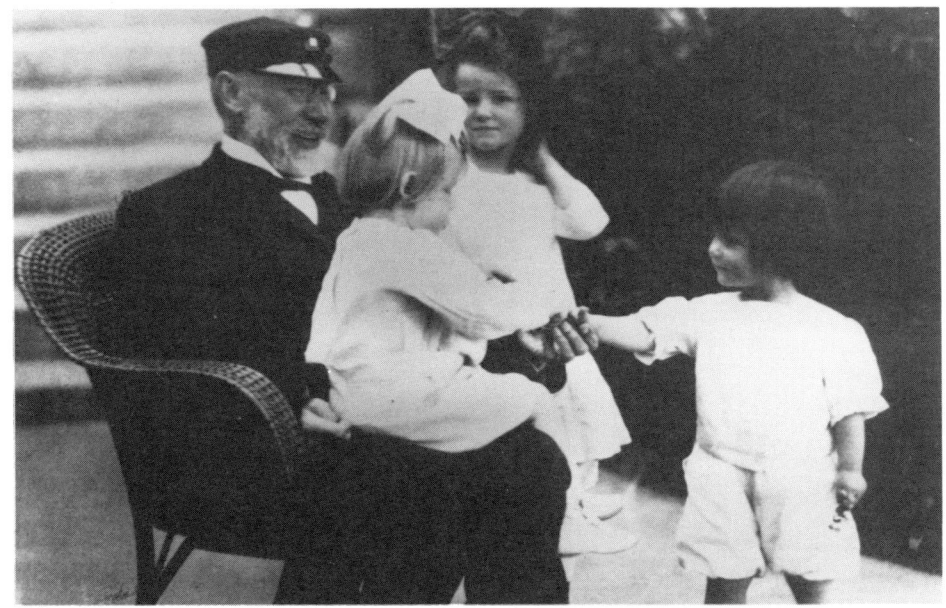

Courtesy of the Thousand Islands Bridge Authority.

Clover in the lap of her grandfather, castle builder George Boldt

The stone-slab walkways of Hopewell Hall sweep past the urns of ragged, red geraniums jostling in the breeze. George Boldt would be pleased. He loved flowers like he loved children, and he wanted to see creation displayed in the sunlight along the river. For his own contribution to creation he built a castle on a nearby island, a reminder not just of his imagination, but the strength of his will.

A picture on a wall in Hopewell Hall is typical of the man. Boldt Castle's builder stands with hands confidently thrust into pockets. The wire-rim glasses frame the dark, indomitable eyes.

Boldt bought the baronial Hopewell Hall on Wellesley Island, then dwarfed it by building a castle on Heart Island. The elaborate five-storey high castle was inspired by Boldt's German heritage. It also reflected his love for romantic visionaries such as the composer of the opera *Der Ring des Nibelungen*, Richard Wagner.

Both Boldt and Wagner had strong wills and large Gothic imaginations. And both were inspired by rivers. Wagner got the idea for the opera *Das Rheingold* one feverish night from a dream of rushing water. Boldt took his dream of a castle on the river and translated it, not into music, but into stone. The castle was an epic project. Hundreds of men were put to work in the Thousand Islands. Ton after ton of granite was quarried from Oak Island. It cost two and a half million dollars just to build the granite outer shell.

Boldt's granddaughter, Clover Boldt Baird, remembers a giant of a man. "He stood about six feet tall," Baird says. She was six years old when her grandfather, then sixty-five years old, died in 1916. "He was a well-built man, erect. He always wore a blue captain's cap with a serge-blue cape. He was a man who was extremely strict, but very, very compassionate, very forgiving. He never held anything against anybody.

"He expected his orders followed. He was good with animals. He loved flowers. He would walk by a pansy bed and see one pansy that bothered him and he would point with his gold-tipped cane to one of the three gardeners that always followed him around and he'd say, 'I'd like to have that pansy taken out.' And the pansy was consequently removed."

Boldt was a German immigrant to the United States born on the island of Rugen in the Baltic Sea. He landed in America without a Deutschmark and built a hotel empire that included the Waldorf-Astoria in New York. Boldt had two qualities which directed his life, a strong will and a sense of vision. "He was a dreamer, a great dreamer," Baird says. "He never would start something but he would finish it. I think the castle was the only thing he didn't finish."

Having established his hotel empire, Boldt shifted his attention at the turn of the century to the Thousand Islands. He intended to outdo all rivals with his masterly *Gesamtkunstwerk*, an island reshaped in the form of a heart with a turreted castle that looked as though it had been plucked from the Rhine River. With rugged outer walls of granite, the castle would have one hundred and twenty rooms. The creation was intended to reflect his love for his wife Louise, born by coincidence on Valentine's Day. "Nothing was beyond his grasp. He would have given her heaven on earth if he could."

But a wayward spirit intruded. Nobody told Boldt that, before the castle could be finished, his wife would die suddenly in 1904 at forty-two years of age. The cause of her death still remains a mystery to the family.

When his wife died, Boldt was shattered. At least the lovers in Wagner's opera *Tristan und Isolde* had a sweet melancholy to console them. Boldt had nothing. Suddenly and without a reason that he could understand he was a spiritual pauper. The death of Louise killed his desire to finish the castle. It was as though he had invested all his Saxon confidence in the giant work of the castle in defiance of the fragility of life. Now he was paying for the unyielding will, for the defiance.

In spite of the compassion and generosity of the man, his tough outer shell made living with him difficult. Part of the Boldt family lore --- perhaps concocted from impressions of Boldt's strength of mind --- was that Louise Boldt ran away. Boldt adored his wife and his family, says Baird, and yet he was a man so driven by his vision that people came second. He loved flowers and yet "his word was law." He was gentle and yet he was unyielding.

Baird partly understands the nature of her grandfather by the effect that he had on her mother. "He adored his family, in particular my mother, who took grandmother's place the minute she died." After Boldt's death, his daughter, Louise Clover, never talked about him, just as she had lapsed into silence about the death of her mother. Boldt's daughter also sold the castle soon after Boldt's death. It eventually passed into the care of the Thousand Islands Bridge Authority. Hopewell Hall passed through the family to the current owner, Baird.

As Baird was growing up, the castle and the Boldt heritage meant "absolutely nothing" to her. The girl fished in the river with the captain of a freighter as her tutor. She flashed across the polo field on horseback. Her father gave her a speedboat called *Alibi Baby*, a joking reminder that the girl needed excuses for her wayward spirit of independence. Yet, if Boldt's influence was ignored at first, his granddaughter was still bound by an unseen spiritual legacy, the power that the man radiated. Baird's rediscovery of Boldt started when she was told that her strong will resembled her grandfather's. That made her curious.

She started thinking about her grandfather. She co-authored a forty-eight-page book, *The Love Story of Boldt Castle*, with the German subtitle, *Liebe Fur Immer*, Love For Ever. The subtitle reflected Boldt's insistence that the family speak in German around him. In turn, the children and grandchildren were always *Liebchen*, sweetheart. The book includes excerpts from Baird's granddaughter Jennifer, who at fourteen years of age daydreamed about islands frozen in time and the romantic desolation of the empty castle.

However, George Boldt was not created in a romance novel. He was a man. He wanted planned and ordered passions and yet he loved his wife too much. He was gentle and yet he was unyielding.

Wellesley Island

Boldt Castle on Heart Island

Footsteps at Jorstadt Castle

Dr. Harold Martin

Buildings and cities, as well as high mountain peaks, have set the mood in the past for inspired thoughts. "Our feet have been standing within your gate, Oh Jerusalem. Jerusalem, built as a city which is bound firmly together..."(Psalms 122:3)

Harold Martin

From the river Jorstadt Castle looks like a small, compact city. The five-storey castle with flaming-red Mediterranean tile roof is the jewel of the Thousand Islands. And a tour does not come without a price. To see the castle from the dungeon to the tower requires assets --- at least ten-million-dollars' worth. That is how much the owners wanted for the place in 1988.

Dr. Harold Martin and his wife Eloise, a gospel singer trained in opera, bought the castle and the ten-acre island in 1963 through their non-profit religious corporation, the Harold Martin Evangelistic Association. The Martins' needy children's camp and religious retreat in Quebec had suffered setbacks. Martin says that the government expropriated land to build a highway and that camp buildings were burned out of religious persecution.

The castle, at least, was unassailable in the middle of the river. The Martins used it as a retreat and centre for visiting missionaries. Their work with orphans and unwed mothers went ahead, as did their sense of a gospel mission. Martin, a Baptist minister, traced his spiritual roots to a lay group called the Plymouth Brethren.

Originally, Jorstadt Island had a more worldly function than Martin intended. The river pilots called the rock Dark Island. At the eastern end of the Thousand Islands where the river widens and the islands lie scattered, the rock was used for navigation. It was the dark spot at night that signaled either the beginning or the end of the thickest stretch of islands, depending on a ship's direction on the river. The sinister implications of the name Dark Island bothered Martin, so in the late 1980s he renamed the rock. The word Jorstadt came from Martin's grandfather, a Norwegian sea *kaptein*

122 Enterprise and the Castle Builder

Jorstadt Castle

named Olaf Martin-Jorstadt, who immigrated to Montreal in the early 1900s.

The castle was built between 1896 and 1904 by the gleeful Frederick Bourne, wealthy president of the Singer sewing machine company. At the time Bourne dubbed the building The Towers. The granite stone for the castle was hauled --- either by ingenuity or piracy --- from nearby Oak Island. The topsoil was begged, borrowed or stolen from the Canadian side to smooth and soften the bare Yankee rock.

Bourne the huntsman liked a challenge, as did his rivals, his fellow castle builders on the river, George Pullman and George Boldt. On Bourne's island the imagination of architect Ernest Flagg had no bounds. He created a false dungeon, a wine cellar, a monstrously large drawing room with a Carrara-marble fireplace and a five-storey clock tower with Westminster chimes.

The castle was given rooms aplenty, like the courses in an endless medieval feast. Among the twenty-eight rooms there were seventeen bedrooms, many with their own fireplaces. The north boathouse --- one of three --- had space for a hundred-foot steam yacht, as well as nine more bedrooms and a staff dining room.

The castle was Bourne's hunting lodge where he retreated to the Thousand Islands in the summer. Bourne wanted to hunt and fish and still be close to the glamour and wealth in the Thousand Islands at the turn of the century. He also wanted privacy.

Bourne had the Westminster chimes installed in the clock tower to remind him of the reverence he owed to his creator. He had a quiet side and needed the sanctuary of a library with rows and rows of books. In the library Bourne could pause and remember the words of the hymn music chimed down the river by the clock tower: "Lord through this hour, Be thou our guide..." In the books in Bourne's library Martin found clues to the nature of the man. Martin traced the passages that Bourne's hand had underlined in religious works years ago.

Other clues to the past, to the purpose and the intention of the castle, are harder to follow. A steep stone path winds up from the boathouse with the

Jorstadt Castle

clifflike face of the castle hanging overhead. At one corner a turret pokes at the sky like a single, straight horn. The first footsteps inside the castle are muffled by the cool stone in the Great Hall. In the grotto of the Great Hall there are huge pillars, Gothic windows and suits of medieval armour. To the left, up two steps, is the library --- as hushed as a monk's cell.

Straight ahead the stone-slab stairway leads to a series of smaller staircases. The steps run helter-skelter like carefree brooks and streams hidden deep in the woods. A sly, secret staircase winds inside a turret.

On the second floor the rooms are dark with walnut panelling. The drawing room is as large as a ballroom and has arched windows along two sides. Set under the arches are carrel booths, private and brightly lit by the sun outside. Presiding over the drawing room is a painting of Charles I. The Stuart king was not a diplomat. He offended Protestant England by marrying a French Roman Catholic princess. Then he outraged the Scottish Roman Catholics by trying to force an episcopacy on them. During his stormy reign the king took refuge in the model for Jorstadt, Woodstock Castle, a hunting retreat.

Further up the main stairway of the castle, the sounds of footsteps are lighter, no longer muffled by stone or lost in large open spaces. The rooms lose their splendour and yet there are compensations.

The windows beckon. The river shines undiminished through the glass panes like an old lantern.

The real worth of the old castle is difficult to calculate. It has an ambivalent place in the islands, noble and yet suspect for its kingly splendour, a sign of enterprise and creativity, yet a contrast to humbler homes and simpler lives. And the ambivalence is not helped by the distance of the Martins, Canadians who live in Florida. Little is known about the couple by the common folk of the islands. These days the Martins, prodded by age and failing health, have put the million-dollar property back on the market.

But Martin does not want to talk about real estate. He waits for the right moment and turns the conversation to salvation and the Lord.

Martin says that some people arrive at his island in storms and need help. Others come for the Sunday chapel services in the sunny west wing --- once a sprightly concert room --- and leave in different moods. Martin makes no demands on visitors. Still, in exchange for help --- a kind of spiritual barter --- the evangelical preacher may ask them for ten minutes to listen to the gospel. There are two prices of admission at Jorstadt: ten million dollars or ten minutes of the Bible. And some pour souls can afford neither.

Jorstadt Island

Gypsy Summer

Steadfast Pride and a Fading Boathouse

Jack Bovey

A boathouse may look like the shack of an old hermit but to a boater it is the door to the kingdom. The boathouse represents freedom on the river. One day the Gananoque town council decided it was time to tear the old shacks down. You might as well tell a river rat that he is a useless and wornout relic...

Jack Bovey

In spring the doors of the staggering line of ramshackle boathouses along the Gananoque town bay are flung open to the river like hungry mouths. As fast as they can, the boats spurt for the river. Behind them they leave the dry husks of the old structures like chaff on a barn floor.

Since the turn of the century, the end of the winter has been measured in Gananoque by two signs: the ice breaking up on the river and the boats slipping their moorings.

However much a boater longs for the river, a boathouse is still a necessity. And that means that only a boater could cherish --- or want to defend through the endless, humbling bureaucracy of the courts --- the line of rusty metal and ailing, smoke-coloured wood. For fifty years Gananoque's landlubbers complained and the town council vainly tried to control the delinquent buildings. But the boathouses flourished.

One episode was a setback for the boathouses, though. A late-night fire consumed half the long row in 1927. The fire was the biggest blow to the pride of Gananoque since the ill-tempered American raid on the tiny settlement during the War of 1812. Gerald Hampton, who would later become the town's clerk, remembers as a boy watching the fire from a bluff overlooking the town bay. It was a stirring sight. The flames from the dry wood leapt twenty feet into the air and set the river ablaze with a red glow. Boats were cut free from their lines and wandered on the river like sheep grazing in a field.

Gananoque boathouses

The fire had more effect in the battle of the boathouses than the resolutions passed by the town councils. And yet it was short lived. The boathouses reappeared with tough vitality like drunken cousins plaguing a wedding reception. Before long they were tilting again at odd angles against the warmth of the sun and leaning against each other for moral support. Some of the town folk saw the boathouses as a sad, if not savage waste of shoreline. The boathouse owners saw them as their link to the quickening pulse and rhythm of the river.

In 1984, the town council underestimated the strength of emotion among the boathouse owners. The council wanted to bulldoze the leaky roofs into oblivion and open the waterfront for everyone. Plans were made for a waterfront park and the boathouse owners were ordered off waterlots technically leased from the town.

An ultimatum from the council to leave by April of 1985 met the defiance of the boathouse owners. Their pride and sense of independence and years of tradition were enflamed by the ultimatum. It was as though two elemental forces, the land and the river, were at odds. Banded together in the Gananoque Association of Boathouse Owners, the forty-five boathouse owners fought back with a law suit that came to trial three years later. In 1988, the town marshalled in court a pile of transcripts from council minutes stretching back to 1902, when the council first became concerned about the proliferation of rogue boathouses. The research was done by Gerald Hampton. The boathouse owners put forward their strongest case based on Jack Bovey and his family's fifty-year-old boathouse.

At 71, Bovey looked frail and nervous on the stand in district court in Kingston. The town lawyers, sharp and hawkish in gowns that covered their arms in loose wings of dark material, nipped at him all morning with their cross-examination. Bovey admitted that the origins of the family boathouse were lost in fading memories.

Bovey learned from the lawyers that the deed for the boathouse he signed twenty years before said that the boathouse sat on "a leased waterlot." Like many others, he had assumed he owned the property because he paid taxes on it.

Bovey is not an assertive man. But no one on the river surrenders a boathouse, no matter how decrepit, without raising a fist. Bovey does not think the boathouses are quaint. He says that he has no sentimental attachment to the structure erected by his father, Reginald John Bovey, a lean, big-boned man who started the Gananoque Boat Line with a partner in the early 1920s.

The son says that his father, after recovering from the poisonous fumes of a mustard gas attack at Vimy Ridge in the First World War, "went to the river for his living." As the boat chauffeur for Howe Island's writer, Henry Bedford-Jones, the eyes of Bovey senior looked into the future. He saw the ripe profits from boat tours of the islands. Bovey senior, with help from his own father, a stone mason and boatbuilder, constructed a glass-enclosed tour boat and dubbed it *Almina*, after his wife. A torn tour brochure from those days has a picture of the *Almina* and proclaims Gananoque as "the Venice of the north."

A tour boat business on the river should have been safer than fighting in the war, but a spark ignited gas fumes and Bovey senior was blown from his boat. The *Almina* burned to the waterline near Wellesley Island with a load of tourists. Bovey was badly burned on the face and hands. Bovey junior, a deck hand, had played hooky to go swimming that day. "If I had been there, I would have been blown through the top," he says.

It took all summer for his father to heal. That winter Bovey senior and John Mallette built a second *Almina*, forty-five feet long. The boat made a fine floating lodge for duck hunting in the cool days of the fall. The rationing of gas during the Second World War made the cost of running a tour boat perilous. The partners in the Gananoque Boat Line sold a business which later blossomed. By the 1980s the boat line would be ferrying two hundred thousand passengers a summer.

The Bovey boathouse rose on the waterfront in 1933 under the hammer of Bovey senior. It was equipped with a telephone for a water taxi business. In that boathouse Jack Bovey was taught to swim. With a rope knotted around his small waist, the boy was dragged back and forth along the inside dock. He learned his strokes in the cool, shaded, still water.

Ironically, the day that Bovey went to court to defend his boathouse, he no longer had a boat. He had sold his sixteen-foot lapstreak cruiser three years before because he could no longer care for it.

But that didn't mean that Jack Bovey could be ousted from his rightful place on the waterfront by the town council. Fighting back against the ultimatum to leave was a matter of principle, he says. "I don't tack sentiment on anything," he insists. "But the fact was that I think we were getting railroaded.

"It's part of the Bovey trait --- we don't like taking orders."

The white-haired judge who presided in a wheelchair agreed with Bovey. The court knocked down the town's claim that after being granted the property by a provincial patent in 1903, it held the shoreline and the waterlots for the good of the whole community. The property was Bovey's through squatters' rights, the judge ruled, a decision the town council would appeal.

When Jack Bovey and the boathouse owners look at the boathouses they do not see a shanty town for boats. They see the invitation of the river beckoning from beyond. It is life on the river that matters to them not the mundane shell that is left behind. The boathouses might as well be a mirage in the heat. The river is movement. It is the voyage that matters for the boater. As Bovey says, "We had no favorite spot. Wherever you ended up, that was it."

Gananoque

The Man Who Gave an Island to the Birds

Bill Browning

The biggest klutz in creation is the great blue heron, a garbage heap of the worst traits of the animal kingdom. The sociable Bill Browning is not taking credit for being the herons' saviour in the islands. He has been cursed on a public dock for his charity...

Bill Browning (right) at Ironsides Island

Across the water the hulk of rock looms in an unbroken mass like the wall of an old abandoned fortress. A sheer rock face runs along the south side etched with a rusty red line of iron pigment like the scar on a gangster's face. This is Ironsides Island, a red granite brute carved by marauding glaciers from the last ice age. The island is so forbidding that the No Trespassing signs are unnecessary. Ironsides has no pleasant welcoming coves, no gentle sandy beaches. There is no place to pull a boat ashore without risk. But Ironsides is not uninhabited. A large, raucous colony of great blue herons thrives here like some Stone Age tribe ruled by a primitive intelligence.

On a steamy July day, Bill Browning steers his boat along the granite cliff looking for herons among the trees. The slender forms are barely visible standing in the highest branches. Browning whistles shrilly, shamelessly shattering the peace of the river. The great wings flap in indignation at the intruder. Browning decides to risk scraping the bottom of his boat and pulls out of the current at the lee of the island. He leaps ashore, clambering over slime-covered rocks and through a crevice.

The air is thick and rank. Over the years the underbrush has grown together into a tangled mass like a single woven fabric. Anything as clumsy and wingless as a human being does not belong here.

The herons nest in tall trees stripped by years of abuse from the birds and the acid of their excrement. The brush under the herons is covered with the thick, ashy white of their droppings. Here and there is the skeleton of a bird that has fallen and died and lain untouched for years. The bones of the skeletons hang loosely together like a wooden puppet, a poor, bird-like Pinocchio thrown aside on a garbage heap.

The heron is a solitary creature, a castaway. On the river the heron is usually seen alone, eyeing people from a distance like the virgin spirit of the river. No one says that if the bird disappeared, the river would dry up, but sentiment about the creature still runs deep. Some love the heron as a sign of the wilderness. Others complain about it as a nuisance. Everyone notices the bird.

A leading authority on the great blue heron, Douglas Mock, says that the birds are "icy customers towards each other." Among its own kind on Ironsides Island the heron is nervous and suspicious. There is little of the co-operation between neighbours that makes life liveable on the river. The male heron has to stay home and brood over an empty nest. Otherwise, the building material would be pilfered by his lawless brethren. This is no model for a Utopia in the wilds.

By the 1960s the number of great blue herons in the Thousand Islands had fallen dangerously low. The creature could not cope with the advance of people and the disruption of its privacy. If disturbed during the breeding season, the whole colony departs in a fluster. The infants are left behind as bewildered orphans. And then some people just like to shoot the heron for target practice. "As large birds they are easy targets for idiots with rifles," Mock says. "I'd be jittery too if I were shot at as often as they are."

The decline of the bird might have continued if not for the exuberant Bill Browning. A man who acts according to his own impulses, Browning decided to give a fellow creature on the river a chance. He bought the thirty acres of Ironsides Island for $9,500 --- a golden piece of real estate that he estimates is worth half a million dollars today --- and gave the rock as a heron sanctuary to the wildlife conservation group the Nature Conservancy. The number of herons breeding on the island has risen from a low of two hundred in the early sixties, to over 1,500.

Browning is not looking for gratitude, though. A boisterous man with a toothy grin and a booming voice, he sets an impulsive pace for himself, doing things with an air of festivity and accident. Giving Ironsides back to the river was a typically off-handed gesture of the man, a bachelor in his sixties who is happiest among the colony on the river.

When he was thirty-two years old --- then a successful businessman destined to rise to the top in the *Reader's Digest* corporation --- Browning was one of the great partiers on the river. He and some friends bought a thirty-foot cabin cruiser which they named *Hangover 1* and plied the river looking for fun. They roamed through the riverside taverns or past the mansions and castles of "millionaires row" in the Wellesley Island area. Then Browning decided that it was time to pay his dues. "I'd been raising hell down the river in *Hangover 1*. I thought, you ought to turn around and do something good."

Most of the time Browning's benevolence takes the form of the good host. He has a special knack for gathering a flock around him. His hospitality extended to the herons by giving them a home of their own.

Browning has since retired as a vice-president of *Reader's Digest*. He has a summer home on Lyndoch Island, mistakenly called Ash Island on the charts. Browning owns most of Ash-Lyndoch, just west of the Thousand Islands bridge, as well as most of Wallace Island across the channel. He started buying and selling land in the Thousand Islands for reasons that boaters understand best. He needed a place to dock his forty-two-foot cruiser. "Till 1965, the river was empty. Then you had to buy a piece of property to tie your boat up."

The need to have a base --- a human rookery --- in the islands was important. It meant survival of the spirit, a call from within that Browning had to answer. Being a successful executive had a lonely side. And the islands were the antidote. They were a vessel or container for friends, drawing a group together like the wood stove in an old country store.

If success were all that mattered, Browning might have taken wing in the business world and never looked back. Raised in Kingston, he started to work in the advertising department of the *Kingston Whig-Standard*. He later returned to Kingston to start a radio station with three boy scout buddies. A

Courtesy of the Canadian Parks Service.

The great blue heron.

hearty, well-liked man, Browning was working for *Reader's Digest* in the United States within a decade. He was flying to Europe, Africa, Australia and Hong Kong to manage international advertising for *Reader's Digest*, but he always commuted to the islands from the corporation's base in New York City. Browning ritually kept all the airline stubs from his commuter flights, which fill eight large plastic garbage bags.

In the 1970s, the Canadian government proposed to buy and expropriate the islands and turn the scattered property into one large park. It was only one alternative in a draft plan, but the mere suggestion outraged Browning and other local residents. One group of rebels banded together to form the Thousand Islands Area Residents Association or TIARA. Browning --- who had given one island to herons --- refused to sell his island property to the government. "I fought the battle of the islands," he says in words that suggest a civil war. The massive expropriation never took place. "The best government is no government," he declares in the spirit of people on the river.

Browning never wanted to be hampered by rules and regulations. He liked working for *Reader's Digest* because the corporation gave him room for initiative, just as the river gives him scope to do whatever he wants. He once owned an imperial cottage on Ina Island with thirty bedrooms and a massive ballroom in a boathouse. Now he has settled for a collection of century-old cottages on Ash-Lyndoch under a sign which reads Camp Browning. Here Browning entertains a constant stream of guests, the booming voice presiding like a medieval lord of the feast.

Browning is proud to be a river rat. It means that he has a home, that he is not an outsider. There was one encounter in particular which made him feel that he had been accepted into the fraternity of the river. One day while his boat was docked in Alexandria Bay a thief crept aboard and stole Browning's laundry. It was the ultimate indignity, not just to lose the laundry, but to be victimized by the people that he loved. Browning fumed in an Alexandria Bay tavern. His words were heard. Somehow the right river rat learned that the boat of a comrade had been violated. The laundry was returned. That was an omen for Browning. "It means you're accepted as a good river person by the local people," he says.

Browning has a home on the river. He comes back faithfully every summer. For some people, that would disqualify him as a true Thousand Islander, since he is gone in the winter. But then so are the great blue herons. The herons know that they have a sanctuary in the Thousand Islands and so does Bill Browning.

"Somewhere you need a place where you belong," Browning says. "I feel like I belong here more than any other place."

Ash (Lyndoch) Island

A Full and Authentic Wind

Albert Bangma

When Noah built the ark he struck upon an ingenious idea --- though not without some outside help and inspiration. The ark was not just a vessel for crossing the water. A boat was a way of creating a small and manageable universe...

Albert Bangma

All Albert Bangma needs is a good, strong wind. His eyes lift up from the deck of his thirty-five-foot wooden sailing ship, the *Magellan*, which he built with his own hands, to watch the sails stretch round and full and ripe with St. Lawrence wind. He felt the same exhilaration years ago when he went to sea as a child in a Dutch fishing *kot*. Later he raced homemade iceboats across a lake in Holland. The times have changed, there may be some grey in his silvery-blond hair and beard, but the wind still stirs him like a living creature.

In the summer Bangma lives on the *Magellan* in an intricate labyrinth of pine-panelled cabins below deck. If he has carpentry work in Gananoque, he sails on the first east wind from Brockville, where he lives, through the islands. He moors at the Gananoque municipal marina. "I've seen so much of the world," Bangma says, who as a Dutch army recruit sailed to the Philippines, the Suez and the Indian Ocean, "and this is it. When God created the world he did the Thousand Islands last, and he really knew what he was doing."

Bangma was born in 1925 beside Lake Tjeukemeer in Holland. His father was a carpenter who supported a family of eleven. Bangma, left to himself, was given his own set of tools when he was five. "I grew up in the carpentry shop," he says. The woodworker's axe had to be taken away from the child after he cut himself on the leg. The scar is still visible. For Bangma, carpentry, the wind and sailing are the threads that bind his life together.

His first boat, he jokes, was a wooden shoe with a tiny sail in it. When he was eight years old he made his first trip out to sea in a fishing vessel belonging to friends. He remembers the bobbers and the eel nets being set. Then came the excitement of eels and herring shimmering and writhing as the nets were hauled on board. The trip was such a revelation that the boy, who had longed to be a carpenter, asked his father why the man was not a fisherman too.

The fascination with the power of the wind was growing stronger, amplified by Bangma's Dutch sailing heritage. The songs that he heard as a child advised, "If you want to become someone, you go to sea. The lazy man stays home." He and his friends built sailing boats and an eighteen-foot iceboat for the lake, using the same mast and sails in both summer and winter. "We sailed in anything...pig troughs...anything that could float."

There was a thrill in "the speed and going by the wind." In Holland, the wind is so steady, he insists, "I could leave the kites up in the morning and they'd still be up when I came back from school." So, accepting the challenge of the wind, Bangma built a windmill that lifted water in buckets. The iceboat that he built with a friend had a twenty-six-foot mast to trap the wind, could seat six, and reached speeds of fifty kilometres an hour. Sometimes the iceboat hit open water. "The momentum kept you going," Bangma says with a throaty laugh. "You didn't know the hole was there."

Bangma was training as a carpenter when the Second World War broke out. Since building material became scarce, Bangma told his father that he would train as a sailor. After the Nazi occupation of Holland, the seventeen-year-old was forced to join a crew taking a freight barge up the canals to Berlin. In the German capital, Bangma arrived in time for an Allied bombing raid. He watched three ships in front of him catch fire and sink. Bangma decided to become a fugitive. Returning home, he was hidden from the Nazis, along with seventeen others, including a Jewish girl. Bangma remembers hiding in a hole in the ground with a wooden lid and straw over top. His father fed an extra household on top of his own hefty family and never complained.

After the war, Bangma was conscripted into the Dutch army and saw the Middle East and the south Pacific. But he wasn't impressed by the windless

Bangma's *Magellan*

corners of the world that could not fill a sail. "There was no wind, and it bothered me. Sometimes I wished a strong wind would blow."

He returned to Holland as a partner in his father's business, married and started a family that would grow to eight. Yet he felt something was still missing. "I wanted to go sailing again. It was just too dull."

Africa and Australia were possibilities, but in 1951, the twenty-six-year-old man and his wife chose Canada, and moved to Belleville. "We came here for adventure and we were going to stay ten years." Then a moonlit drive along the highway next to the Thousand Islands changed his mind. "I'll never forget that night. I said, 'This is my country.'" Bangma moved to Brockville to be closer to the river and the islands.

He also started building sailing boats in his spare time, first a sixteen-foot boat, then a thirty-two-foot vessel. But his real feat was the *Magellan*, started in 1980 in a shed he built for the project. By the time he had the *Magellan* in the water in 1985, its hull length was thirty-five feet, six inches, and it had two masts for five sails. Bangma adopted a Rossborough design from Halifax called Pilgrim, which gave the ship the look of an old-fashioned, sea-going fishing ship. On deck, the ship has a rudder stick instead of a wheel. It also has a sunken wheel house which doubles as a tiny galley. The half-decks at the prow and stern are raised to give the boat a flat half-moon look. The planking is cedar, with golden-coloured elm on the main deck.

The ship is so steady, Bangma says, "I can walk away from the rudder and sit by the mast."

Much of the time Bangma sails the *Magellan* by himself. He likes the simplicity. The wind picks up the sails of the *Magellan* from across the water and fills them like a melon swelling and ripening. The planks stretch for the load. It is a thrill to sail a vessel made with your own hands. The ship has a timeless look. Bangma has found his way home through the passing fever of the twentieth century.

Brockville

A Community of Boaters

Peter Small

Rats are social animals. Crowded together in a laboratory experiment they become nasty little brutes. No wonder the river rat behaves differently from his cousin caught in the rat race of the city...

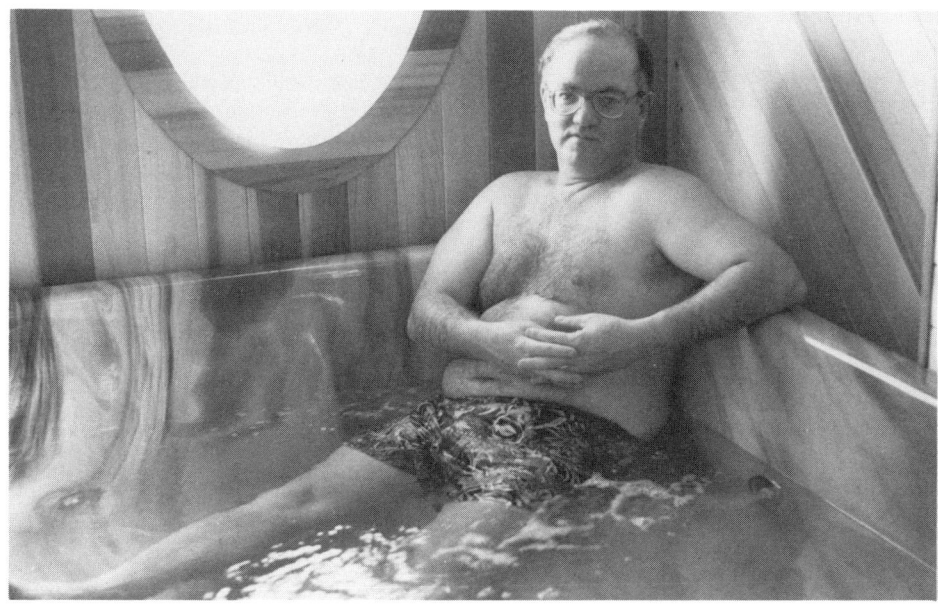

Peter Small in his living room hot tub

In the Thousand Islands there is a group of people known as crashers. The crashers have dry mouths and sweaty palms and eyes wide with fear. They come to the islands full of the confidence of people on holidays. That mood is shattered in an instant. What seemed simple and certain vanishes. They are handling the wheel of a boat for the first time.

Peter Small remembers meeting a group of teenage crashers from New York City on McDonald Island. "We knew that they had rented boats because they smashed into the docks."

"One of them --- I guess he'd be about twelve or thirteen --- he tore up to the outhouse and came back down and said, 'I can't believe this. There's only a one-holer up there.' "

Small jabbed back, "That's the bad news."

"What's the good news?" the boy asked.

"You didn't get mugged on the way there," Small said.

Small divides the boaters into three groups: the sailboaters, aloof and absorbed in the academics of mast and lines; the powerboaters, drawn together in herds grazing in the shelter of island moorings; and the crashers, manoeuvring a houseboat through current and winds as though it were an iceberg with a will of its own.

"When they show up at a dock there's a mad rush to help them. They get more help on the river than anybody, because people want to save their boats and the docks."

Small is a jovial man. He thrives on the social world of the town of Gananoque and the Thousand Islands like a muskrat feeding on clams on the river bottom. Small was born in Gananoque. He thought he could leave the area, but discovered after five years in Toronto that life in the city was unliveable.

In Toronto, he learned "how the other half lives --- survival." "It's a totally different pace in the city. It's two hours of your life every day just driving in traffic."

Small and his wife Linda returned to the three-stoplight town of Gananoque after their spell in an urban purgatory, but traces of frantic city life remained. Small's nervous system took time to adjust. "It took me six months to unwind. I'm sitting at the stoplight at the TD Bank racing my engine. My wife says, 'Where are we going? We're only going two blocks.'"

Small comes from a versatile small-town breed. He started his own sports shop in Gananoque, was town welfare administrator for a year, and then switched to the job that suits the sociable --- and sometimes controversial --- sportsman best, town recreation director.

Small is on the water for the opening of the season for each fish. During the summer he and his wife spend the weekends on their boat camping at one of the park islands. Camelot and Aubrey, which are protected in the spring and the fall from the wind, are the favourites, though there is also a series of islands where the Smalls dock and renew old friendships.

"It depends on which way the wind is blowing where you go. That's the key, really."

At the island camps the boaters separate themselves into two clusters, the dockers, who have cruisers and are hungry for company, and the sailboaters, who moor by themselves out in the water and are looking for peaceful coves and inlets.

Dockers behave like one large family, Small says. They share their food and watch over each others' children. And for a small town boy, the summers on the water are an important part of the social life.

"You get to meet people from all over the place. It's like the United Nations out there. You don't know who's going to show up from where.

"It expands your boundaries beyond Gananoque. And there's a great deal of sharing out on the river. You have one cook shack and in foul weather you're all in the one cook shack."

At least once a summer Small organizes a "seafood extravaganza." The group meets on an island for a dinner of perch or bass or pike, shrimps, scallops and maybe even a turtle, which if boiled for two hours tastes "like leather."

After the meal, with the flames from a campfire glinting on his round, wire-frame glasses, Small pulls out his guitar and picks at a folk tune. Small puts into words what others in Gananoque grasp instinctively, that the rhythms of life are dictated by the call of the river.

Small says that he knows the longing of the town factory workers before the opening of fishing season. The workers start looking at their watches at nine on a Friday morning impatient for the end of the work day.

Every angler has a story about a big fish that slipped the hook or a mishap on the river. Small has a tale about the boat that he lost in his own backyard. It happened in April as he was preparing his boat for the new season on the water.

Small was treating the fibreglass with linseed oil and stopped to have a beer inside the house with a friend. Suddenly a child ran into the house yelling. The boat was on fire, the child screamed. Small lunged for the door. Outside he saw flames "twenty feet in the air" and black smoke spiralling over his house like a town on fire. There was nothing he could do. "It all burnt up right in front of my eyes."

Small thinks that the rays of the setting sun glanced through the window of the boat and ignited the pail of rags and linseed oil. The boat was a total loss. Small bought a replacement as fast as he could. He could not afford to miss a summer on the river. "You take a ribbing when you buy a new boat. People say, 'Geeze, I'm going to burn my boat up too.'" And Small has not heard the last of the boat-in-the-bonfire. "That's a tough act to follow," he admits.

Gananoque

Hallelujah Heights

Rick Wiley

Someone with a fear of falling should stay out of the sky, but when did a daring man ever obey the voice of timidity ...

Rick Wiley

At ten thousand feet Rick Wiley turns a valve to shut off the hiss of the small propane burner. The wicker basket creaks lazily from time to time like a miniature wooden sailing ship. The basket hangs suspended in a solitude as absolute as the night sky. Yet it is day, the sky is a psychic blue, and beneath Wiley's hot-air balloon the whole intricate maze of the Thousand Islands is spread out in a single view.

Inspect me, says the scene below. Have a closer look over the side. What is so far away seems near. The boats are pygmy chips of wood stuck, as if with a dab of glue, to a speckled pigment of motionless grey and blue and green. The cottages are flat specks among the bristle of transistorized trees. The shorelines of the islands are as clear and legible as the rings in the stump of a tree.

Wiley will not say it is a spiritual, out-of-body experience, but few people in a balloon want to do more than float quietly and meditate. "You float like a dandelion seed," Wiley says.

The balloonist remembers one day when he climbed the wind as though it were a ladder, high into the sky over Cape Vincent. The river and the islands were laid out for his inspection. "It was incredible, a cold day in late August. I could see Galloo Island in Lake Ontario. I could see Oswego, the Ogdensburg bridge, the Adirondack Mountains, Canadian lakes. I could literally watch the river narrow into the Seaway."

From that height, the world looks better organized, he says, comprehensible with a single sweep of the eye. "It's amazing to see a tree from the top down, to

Ballooning over the St. Lawrence

look down into the forest and see the whole forest upside down." It is as though barriers had crumbled and unknown shackles fallen. "You are wide open to the elements," he says. "You feel no wind because you are going with the wind." And the balloonist, in a rare moment of power, controls destiny with a hand at the propane valve.

Wiley's desire to see the river from the air is an old dream in the Thousand Islands. Balloonists were crossing the river before there were motor boats and airplanes. When the war historian Benson Lossing visited the area in the 1860s he mentioned the flight of a balloon passing over Clayton. "Toward sunset the quiet of the little village was disturbed, and the faces of all the inhabitants were turned skyward to observe the passage over them of a man in a balloon, a thousand feet in the air, who had ascended from Kingston." The balloon, Lossing wrote, "descended far toward Sorel, the outlet of Lake Champlain."

Wiley, however, belongs to the twentieth century. A native of Cape Vincent who teaches computer technology to grade eight students in Baldswinville, he has made four hundred and fifty balloon flights since he first flew solo in 1980. Almost one hundred of the flights have been along the American side of the river, with a dozen trickier flights across the river to Canada.

It is more difficult to make the trip northeast across the river from the United States to Canada, Wiley says. Normally the prevailing winds of the St. Lawrence are southwesterly, which naturally carries a balloon down the path of the St. Lawrence Valley. To cross the river from Cape Vincent, Wiley has to hitch a ride on an early morning breeze blowing from the shore out onto the water. He must stay about one hundred feet off the ground. If he climbs to four hundred feet the off-shore breeze would collapse and he would be caught in the tug of the westerly wind. River crossings are also complicated because the Canadian side is rocky and heavily forested, and the bureaucracy has grown more insistent in the past few years.

The times that Wiley has crossed the river in his balloon have been full of discoveries. He flies over the water low enough to see the perch and bass and muskie in the clear depths, and skims the tops of trees on islands. Balloonists, he says, test their skill as pilots by brushing the grass on a field. If Wiley crosses the bow of a freighter, he is greeted with a rock-blasting, bird-flustering burst of the whistle.

He can fly so low in the slow-paced balloon that he can talk to people on the ground. During one flight a woman heard the mystifying hiss of his balloon and ran outside. Alas, she had dashed absent-mindedly out of the shower without a towel. "She was so excited she was waving," says Wiley. "She came running out naked. I said, 'I won't tell if you won't.'"

As a child in Cape Vincent, Wiley says that he dreamed of seeing the islands from the air. As an adult he gained a fear of heights that he would have to break. But in those boyhood days he was a daredevil. He jumped from the roofs of boathouses into the river and swam under the docks to avoid the wrath of adults. In the winter he and his sister rode the ice floes from dock to dock.

One day he and a friend decided to cross the river from Cape Vincent to Horne's Point on Wolfe Island in rubber inner tubes. They made the two-kilometre trip both ways. There was one heart-rending moment when they found themselves in the path of a mighty freighter. The boys paddled frantically to get out of the way. When the freighter passed, they rode the rolling wake in celebration. When the boys returned to Cape Vincent a worried group of adults had gathered with the priest, Father Riley. "There was a lot of commotion I didn't understand when I got back." The boys also swam across to Wolfe Island, riding back with the ferry. They swam three to five kilometres because they went diagonally to take advantage of the current where Lake Ontario empties into the river.

Wiley left Cape Vincent to go to college and later to work, but he keeps a place in the village and returns to visit his family and to test the sky with his balloon. Over the years Wiley --- a descendent of a revolutionary warrior who fought with Washington at Valley Forge --- also learned to overcome his newly acquired fear of heights.

The secret, he discovered, is whether you are tethered to the ground. The bond makes you queasy. It is the attachment that defeats you. "When you're not attached to the ground, there's no fear," he claims.

Cape Vincent

'Ramming It' on the River

Bruce Jasper

The ticket to independence and freedom in the Thousand Islands is the price of either an island or a boat. And then even independence comes with its temptations and dangers ...

Bruce Jasper

It was a Friday night late in September. The sun was burning weaker. The stag party started at the fire hall in Gananoque. Three epic days later Bruce Jasper --- nearing thirty and no longer the wild reveller of the rugged waves he once was --- would wind his way home through the Thousand Islands.

A friend was celebrating the eve of his wedding. It was an invitation to party, with the usual adversities to overcome. That night a broken engine bolt marooned the five in Clayton after the bars closed. The groom passed out and the group slept in the boat. On Saturday --- though by then Jasper longed desperately to return home --- the boaters passed from island to island, from party to party.

Saturday evening was spent in the International Tavern in Gananoque, where Jasper, only a few kilometres from his apartment on the river, slept the night in his black Trans Am with the large gold eagle painted on the hood.

Jasper admits that the years have made a difference. He is more reflective now. His eyes glitter darkly, mixing pain and compassion and reserve with a strong streak of independence.

When Jasper came to Gananoque in 1980 at the age of twenty he was an outsider. To change that he needed entry to the social world set on the rim of the river. Then he would have another family, a river family. Jasper had broken with his parents at fourteen. He went to work to support himself in his native Sherbrooke, a mixed English-Canadian and French-Canadian city in Quebec.

His first job was pressman's helper --- once called a printer's devil ---- at the daily newspaper in Sherbrooke where his grandmother worked. He drifted from city to town as a pressman until he found work in Gananoque with the publisher of the town's weekly newspaper. Then Jasper might as well have been reborn. He had a purpose. He lived for the weekends.

He quickly made friends with the young Gananoque people whose boats took the place of sports cars in the city. They sped across the water and anchored at their favourite spot, the long, sandy crescent of Brown's Bay at the United States island of Grindstone.

"There's quite a few of us that still river together," Jasper says a decade later. Some married, a few drifted away, but the main link was that they met "through the river." Jasper explains, "Like most people say around here, they had a boat before they had a car."

On his modest pressman's wages Jasper bought a sleek sixteen-foot Baja speedboat with a shallow draft and sexy stiletto prow. The red metallic paint of the boat burned fiercely in the sun. Jasper boosted the craft's credentials with a one-hundred-and-fifteen-horsepower Mercury engine. The boat was Jasper's certificate of independence, his graduation diploma. He joined the Gananoque circle as an equal.

Still, even Jasper was worried by the recklessness he saw. For some, the power of a boat on the river was absolutely intoxicating. Jasper was not timid, but he refused to lend his craft --- which makes sharp, wing-tip turns with the water rushing against one side --- indiscriminately. Some "don't realize how quick you can lose it." The first time Jasper let his girlfriend drive he was sitting on the back of a seat balancing two drinks. She cut the motor sharply. He was catapulted helplessly forward over the windshield fracturing two ribs.

Jasper's Baja will do a respectable eighty-eight kilometres an hour open throttle without the nagging interference of wind and currents. Speed is a thrill of its own, he says, "just ramming around on the river, putting it down and letting it go." Others fed on the intoxication like dope. Jasper recalls a doomed and restless boater who often shows off with a seventy-foot feather of spray behind his motor. "You can't keep him in one place," Jasper says. "He comes shooting into the beach with a rooster tail."

When Jasper first bought his speedboat, he loaded it with clothes on Thursday nights in the summer and fled to Alexandria Bay after work. He slept with only a tarpaulin between himself and the pure, untarnished stars of the river. The next day he crawled out and was ready for work cleansed and refreshed. He spent the entire weekend on the water.

The group would anchor in a bay and inflate their air mattresses. They paddled with their arms waving distractedly like flippers. Out came the cans of beer. The bright voices gabbled and brayed over the water. The sun gave his blessing, fattening his followers with the rewards of a healthy life. They laughed and joked and made friends with boaters on both sides of the border. By the end of the day, thin, drowsy and baked, they looked as though they had been slain by an excess of sun.

Besides the drinking, some of the boaters smoke marijuana, Jasper says, "just like you'd see in a bar." Untempted himself, he marvels at the recklessness of a cocaine user from Kingston with a fleet hydrostream boat. "He just scares the hell out of everybody," Jasper says. "He's just ramming around not looking where he's going." The man's fingers are taped from burns, which Jasper reads as a sign of freebasing coke. The cocaine is burned for use with a small flame.

Jasper --- who has never hit one of the green-brown shoals that lie under the water --- remembers the friend who thought the river forgives any kind of carelessness. In a drunken stupor the friend slammed into a stone breakwater. He was headed home the wrong way at the time.

The river is not kind, Jasper acknowledges. "If you don't respect it, you're going to end up getting hurt."

Jasper thinks he is mellowing as he nears thirty. The epic weekends can be brutal. "It takes a lot out of you when you sit in the sun all day. Last weekend I felt like forty."

Married at nineteen and then divorced, with no children, Jasper wants to settle down. His back aches at the bucking it takes from a speedboat on choppy waves. He is in the mood to trade the speedboat of the rebel for the slower galley of advancing years. "It must be old age. I guess you just can't be nineteen the rest of your life."

Gray's Beach, east of Gananoque

Bruce Jasper "ramming it"

Lifting the Sails of a Fertility Goddess

Roland Jones

For some people boats have an overpowering appeal, like buried treasure or a relentless force of destiny. An exceptional boat can make life lively or shackle it in chains of subservience...

Roland Jones on the *Freyja*

Early in the morning the burly, bearded figure of Roland Jones rises from the hatch. He scrambles across the deck of his racing yacht with one thought in mind. With cloth in hand Jones conscientiously wipes each drop of dew off the rich Oregon pine. The labours are not finished yet. Once a day the four hundred brass fittings are polished. The hull and the deck are washed two or three times a week and then buffed with "a real chamois," not a mere rag. A worker hired for the summer revarnishes one patch of the mahogany hull each day to keep the deep-brown complexion near perfection.

Jones treats the *Freyja III* like a fertility goddess, which she is in a way. The sleek, mahogany yacht was built in 1949 for the sea for King Gustof VI of Sweden. The lively eighty-nine-year-old king named the vessel after a goddess from Norse mythology who was a favourite of the opposite sex.

For five years the king sailed the forty-one-foot sloop through the salt waves, her Honduras mahogany hull obscured by a protective coat of ice-blue paint, the brass fixtures sealed under chrome. Then the monarch died. The *Freyja* was sold to a friend of the family, a banker in Buffalo, and shipped as deck cargo across the ocean. The new owner died before she arrived.

The *Freyja* lost her lustre --- or at least lost her admirers. She gathered dust for five years, then was sold and resold without compassion until a blustery stock market analyst named Roland Jones bought her for $10,500 in 1973. Since then, every summer the *Freyja* has cut the salt-free waves of the St. Lawrence River and anchored off Camelot Island.

Jones is passionate about the yacht. She stands as a symbol of daring and distinction and elegance for him, the image of the perfect life. Thus the *Freyja* was not cheapened with a cute name or a catchy slogan across her bow when he bought her. The yacht bears a name from Norse mythology, Jones explains. Freyja is "the goddess of love and beauty. She is a goddess." A golden-haired, blue-eyed deity, Freyja was the daughter of Njord, a god of fishing and seafaring. She represented fertility --- or what is known in less inspired times as hormones. The amber found in the seas was once said to be the tears of Freyja's sorrow when her husband, whose hormones ran amuck, starting roving after other female deities. The gods and giants and mortals cherished the goddess Freyja, who swooped down from the skies to select fallen warriors.

All this, Jones thought, made the name Freyja an apt choice for the celestial racing yacht. Under the entrancing sheen of mahogany and brass there is almost a living creature, Jones insists. "A wooden boat has a personality, its own character --- a warmth, a kindness, a spirit, a vitality."

"The boat owns us, as opposed to we owning it. We're its custodians while it's in our care."

The attention he lavishes on the boat is part of Jones's philosophy of life. From his father, a country doctor who loved boats, he inherited a dictum that he has never forgotten. "Dare to be different," the elder Jones said. His son has tried to live that way, rising from a telephone clerk on the stock market floor to the vice-president of a large stock brokerage firm. He also made a career as a lecturer and author. Now he runs his own investment fund company in Toronto.

Jones is recognized in the volatile stock market circuit as a fount of cautious wisdom. The *Calgary Sun* once described him as a "larger-than-life" figure among Canada's "premier stock analysts and seers." He has entertained the billionaire Bronfman brothers on the *Freyja* and Peter C. Newman wrote in his column in *Maclean's* magazine that Jones, pictured beside the rigging of his boat, had "a remarkable record" for investments.

Jones is so attuned to sailing that he uses it as a metaphor for aspiration in his book on stock market investment, *The Common Sense ¢ of Investing ($ Millions)*. In the introduction to the book Jones compares an investor who knows the risks to a sailor who prepares for a storm. "In today's uncertain investment markets, we have to think like the sailor." Then quoting fellow sailor, Garfield Weston, the founder of the Weston empire, he adds, "It's the set of our sails and not the gales that determines the way we go." The secretary who typed the draft of the introduction was not a sailor. By mistake --- and with a landlubber's lack of imagination --- she typed the words "the set of our sales."

Jones is accustomed to the attention that his daring brings. On his yacht he has clippings from newspapers and magazines that describe him as a stock market guru. That celebrity status vanishes in the Thousand Islands, where the *Freyja* overshadows the stockbroker --- a twist that delights Jones.

He lavished care on the sloop and had her refitted with improvements that outdid the King of Sweden. Thus the *Freyja* looks like it was fashioned in a mint not built in a shipyard. It is luxurious --- insured for a meagre $48,500 in 1988, Jones has been offered $250,000 --- however this is a luxury that transcends money. It gives a reflected shine to the owner like the glory of owning a painting by a master.

After Jones bought the *Freyja* in 1973 he entered her in a race in Lake Ontario. The crew, familiar with the Thousand Islands, persuaded him to take an excursion eastward after the race. The anchorage that Jones found for the *Freyja* in the islands, among people with a history of sailing and a love of antique wooden boats, was the start of a pilgrimage each summer to the area. Jones and his wife Kit anchor off Camelot Island, where the water is deep enough for the full keel hull and nineteen-foot draft of the *Freyja*. In the sheltered spot, the Joneses entertain friends or float in an inner tube reading a book.

One of Jones's favourite anchorages in the islands is "a hurricane hole in the back side of Georgina

Island." The hole is a rocky, sheltered bay, one hundred feet in diameter and twenty feet deep. The bay is ideal protection in a squall, but it also comes with its own slow whirlpool, Jones says. The whirlpool keeps the boat suspended in the middle. "You just sit in it and spin around all night."

Out on the water, the *Freyja* handles like a sea-born creature. When the sails tip the boat to the side, the water surface of the long, pointed hull expands, increasing the speed of the boat to its eight-and-one-quarter-knots hull speed. The yacht has been made to cut the water with regal poise, not bounce like fibreglass boats, Jones says. In a run before the wind the Freyja cuts smoothly and evenly, finding "the groove" like a path of acceleration. Then the sloop, like the soaring Norse goddess she is named after, doesn't labour with the vulgar propulsion of a powerboat. She "plays" with the strength of wind and the flux of water.

The *Freyja*, Jones would say, has the strength of her own convictions, like the man who cares for her. "We look after this boat in our own way," he says. "It's really in essence being true to yourself."

On Board *The Freyja*

Deer Island's Skull and Bones Society

Coit Liles

People come to the Thousand Islands for tours and lessons in history. The tales get retold, distorted by memory, embellished by pride. And sometimes there is deliberate irony in the tales...

Coit Liles and burnt library

The tour boats have bizarre tales to hoot and bray from metal amplifiers as they swing past Deer Island. One tour boat says that the island near Alexandria Bay has a nudist colony. Tourists who are prudish are warned to look away. Another says that the fire in the island's great stone library destroyed a Gutenberg Bible, a rare and priceless copy of the fifteenth-century printing of the holy book.

The blame for some of the extravagance of the stories belongs to the secrecy of the Skull and Bones Society, a Yale University association whose members have sole use of Deer Island.

The Skull and Bones Society is mocked for readers of newspapers across the continent by the artist who draws the Doonesbury cartoon strip, Gary Trudeau. In the cartoon strip the Skull and Bones members act like a strange academic cult. They consult the dead in seances and wrestle in the nude. The cartoons are pinned to a bulletin board in the boathouse dining room on Deer Island.

The society has attracted attention across the United States, particularly during the inventive mud wrestling of the 1988 United States presidential campaign. George Bush and his father were both members of the Skull and Bones. The leader of an Apache tribe claimed during the election campaign that George Bush's father once stole the skull of Geronimo for the society to use.

Other rumours say that the society also has the skull of the Mexican revolutionary Pancho Villa and that the mud wrestling is done by initiates in the nude. And then there is the riddle, native to Deer Island, of the roasted corpse.

The tales make Coit Liles laugh. A small, bony alumnus of the Skull and Bones Society, Liles has been coming to Deer Island since 1972, more recently reincarnated in the form of its bustling honorary caretaker. He has seen nothing more supernatural on the island than the spectacular ruins of two buildings and some spirited conversation around the supper table with Yale alumni.

Still, the members of the Skull and Bones Society enjoy their notoriety. The tale of the nudist colony, Liles says, was probably spawned by skinny-dipping in the river on a hot day. "I think everybody up here on the river that has a house out on an island does that. The river just invites you. On a hot day sometimes it's easier to strip it off and jump in.

"Unfortunately, we happen to be right on the channel where the tour boats go by. And I would not say that the presence of the tour boats doesn't provoke it some times. You get some of the younger guys up here and once they hear the nudist colony story they're liable to want to perpetuate it.

"No, we're not a nudist colony. Anybody who went into the business of having a nudist colony up here would soon lose his shirt with the mosquitoes at night, the cold weather in the early part of the summer, the fifty-five degree water."

As for the story of the great library fire and the destruction of a Gutenberg Bible, Liles is skeptical. George Douglas Miller, a Yale graduate from the class of 1870 who inherited the island from his father, built an exotic three-storey stone structure out of the native pink granite. Miller was a collector of Yale memorabilia and year books as well as a member of the Skull and Bones Society.

In 1949, the library and wooden interior of the building were gutted by fire in the middle of the night. The stone shell was left intact like a skull with empty round windows for eyes. "Had the wind not shifted during the course of the blaze the island probably would have burned," Liles says. "We never had a copy of the Gutenberg Bible and if we did, we wouldn't have had it out here.

"I don't know how these stories get started."

Liles remembers a story told to him by an eighty-year-old man. Another of the elaborate granite structures erected by Miller, this time on a point of rock, burned, leaving people from the area shocked when a skull and ribs were found among the ashes.

"On a day in the summer of 1927 the house called the Outlook caught on fire. Apparently guests were expected later in the day and a maid was cleaning one of the upstairs rooms. She had lit a small fire in the fireplace with some trash or newspapers to take the chill off the room.

"A gust of wind blew the burning paper back into the room and started a small fire. The maid panicked and ran away. By the time help arrived the upper floors were consumed. Meanwhile, down in the kitchen they had been preparing a big rib roast.

"Because of the affiliation of the Deer Island Club with the Skull and Bones Society there were items, reportedly a human skull or human femur, in the building as a curio. After the fire they found a skull or two and a number of charred ribs. And the belief for a while was that two people had been killed in the fire."

One of the tour boats also claims that Skull and Bones members must pledge one-third of their estates to Deer Island if they want to use the property in the summer. That is not true, Liles says. Miller, the owner of Deer Island, bequeathed the forty-five-acre island in the 1930s to the Deer Island Club, a loose association of Yale members who once belonged to a senior class society known as the Skull and Bones.

For a fee, members of the society, the Deer Island club and their families can stay on the island in the three large cottages. Miller, who made his money in the industrial boom after the American Civil War, developed Deer Island as "his little fantasy world." That was the style on the river in those days as people like hotel millionaire George Boldt, on neighbouring Heart Island, let their whimsy run wild in stone.

"I think he tried to create an earthly paradise here on the island. Perhaps there was a little rivalry among the rich men to see who could build the most elaborate spread on the river."

About one hundred and fifty people a year spend summer on the island. Television is forbidden and there is no telephone. There is a meadow in the centre of the island where children and adults play baseball and a crude tennis court of rolled earth. The highlight is often the discussion at the dinner table, which suits the original intention of the Skull and Bones Society.

Liles will not say much about the Skull and Bones Society because part of its charm is its secrecy. However, he explains that it admits fifteen senior class-men from Yale for one year only. It is not a university fraternity or a social club and actually bans liquor during its meetings. The Skull and Bones Society is a male-only group formed for *bone* fide discussions. The talk is sometimes intellectual, sometimes frank and personal.

Liles will not reveal how the society got a name with an eerie, occult sound. "That, of course, is one of its secrets. We don't talk about its internal features outside the society.

"There's nothing grim or mysterious about it. The name actually is a bit of a put-on. Looking back I think we might have found something a little less forbidding."

Deer Island

Muskie Lords and Muskrat Men

Photo by Shawn Thompson/Courtesy of the Gananoque Reporter

Muskellunge: The Great-grandfather of All Fish

Martin Copp

Among the most quixotic of quests in the Thousand Islands is the tale of one man, bitten by the romance of muskie fishing and pursuing an ancestor's hot ghost, that old pioneer and father of muskie fishing on the St. Lawrence...

Martin Copp

In 1887, an oil millionaire from Pennsylvania named C.A. Duke came to the Thousand Islands to fish. He was a strong, physical man with a bushy mustache and a line to his jaw that was firm, determined. The initials C.A. in his name stood for Charles Alva, but the millionaire was always called by the more impersonal form, C.A. Duke, which he obsessively branded in wood and stamped in metal on everything he owned.

When Duke came to the area he stayed at first on Grenadier Island at the Angler's Inn, run by Joseph Senecal. Before long Duke was a compulsive muskie fisherman, trolling for the fish every day with his guide Henry Senecal from August to October through the years 1903 to 1907. Just as he kept every letter and rubber band that touched his fingers, he meticulously recorded every catch.

In 1906, Duke bought property at the west end of Grenadier. He filled the space between Grenadier and a small island to create a peninsula, which he named Muskellunge Point, after his passion for the fish. His children did not have the same intensity for muskie trolling and the family fortune slipped through their fingers as it was divided and taxed and lost over the years. But Duke left a golden riddle for the great-grandchild who felt the closest to him, Martin Copp.

Some parts of his great-grandfather's life are a puzzle to Copp. He has been drawn back to the Thousand Islands year after year, gathering, for more than a decade, material for a book about muskie fishing on the river. Copp resembles his great-grandfather both physically and mentally, and both men share a fascination for the elusive predator king of the St. Lawrence, the muskellunge. Yet their destinies in the end separated into different paths, as though Copp had been robbed or disinherited of the true direction his life should take.

Copp's great-grandfather was an intelligent man whose energy was directed not to books, but to the physical labour of running an oil field. Copp --- whose remarkable memory stores scientific facts like an encyclopedia and forgets everything else --- has never settled down to a steady job or family life. He dropped out of college while studying to be a biologist. Now he is a bartender living in Florida in the winter. And yet Copp is drawn --- even though he feels like an outsider --- to the physical life on the river, particularly bass and muskie fishing.

Part of the riddle and the legacy that Duke left his great-grandson was the compulsion to pursue the muskie. Duke was a pioneer of muskie fishing on the St. Lawrence. He had what Copp sees as the essential ingredients, the time and the money to persist day after day trolling for the fish.

A technological breakthrough also helped. The single-cylinder engine was adapted as a boat motor for the St. Lawrence skiff at the turn of the century. Trolling for muskie can be a long and arduous task in a skiff moved only by the power of an oar. But with the one-cylinder engine, Duke could troll as long as his patience lasted.

After Duke died, when he was sixteen years old, Copp discovered a box of his fishing photos stashed in the boathouse lodge on Grenadier. The cache of photos was like the slag heap of the riches of the family. Copp did not know what his destiny would be and he would not see any of the family wealth, but the urge to fish bass was awakening in him. At night the boy went to the Grenadier home of Ed Senecal to be fascinated by the tales of fishing and the river.

Senecal was Copp's river guru, as he was for others, such as Dr. John Casselman. Senecal had the knowledge and understanding of an expert. Senecal had peered into the mysteries of the muskie like an astronomer gazing at the stars in the night sky. "He had an awareness of wildlife, fish, that no one else seemed to have. He would talk about muskellunge like they were almost human beings.

"He'd catch one. It would get off. He'd claim they understood what was going on. He figured that they were a very intelligent fish and that you had to use intelligence to outsmart them."

From memories as a child and the records left behind, Copp began to wonder what kind of man his muskie-fishing great-grandfather was.

"He was a perfectionist in everything he did. Everything had to be perfect. Everything had to be in place. He kept track of every penny that was ever spent for anything.

"That's getting really strange.

"He had a very cold personality. People were frightened of him. He was an authoritative figure.

"He was only interested in hunting and fishing. He had come from a wealthy background. He had no education because he dropped out of college and chose a different life, almost an uneducated, red-neck life --- out of choice. It's very bizarre because his father was very well educated."

Muskie fishing appealed to Duke as a challenge that required an unswerving, steadfast nature. He was, his great-grandson says, a muskie fanatic.

Duke's perseverance paid off. The photos show him posing with racks of muskie. His supreme moment came in August of 1906 when he caught one hundred pike and four muskies in a single day.

But Duke also had a compulsion to keep and catalogue whatever came into his possession. That included the day's catch, which he scrupulously recorded, making it almost more fetish than fish.

Ironically, the muskie has eluded Copp just like the full reality of his cold, imposing great-grandfather distanced on the other side of a barrier of time. Copp has tried to recreate the past. He has accumulated fragments of information and old photos from other fishermen, sometimes to find startling images.

One series of photos shows a muskie treated with cruelty. The anglers have spiked a muskie illegally through a hole in the ice. A man holds the fish roughly by its gills, a lack of reverence which revolts Copp. In another photo --- a desecration by death and by indifference --- the man holds the trophy in the air by hooking his fingers through the eyes of the fish.

Copp, by contrast, had a compassion that did not bring him luck on the river. By the time of his mid-forties, he had only caught one muskie, and that fish was so trifling, no more than two pounds, that Copp had to throw it back. Still, he speaks of the experience like a revelation.

Copp was fishing near Beulah Island when the small muskie grabbed the minnow bait --- almost as a challenge --- and leapt fighting out of the water. Copp netted the fish and was amazed at the fiery colours. "I could not believe the beauty. It was a beautiful little fish."

The fish had brilliant blue spots "the size of nickels."

Copp believes in the intelligence of the muskie, even to the point where the creature will taunt a human being.

One day Copp and a friend hooked a muskie off Hill Island. The fish, however, broke the line. Copp was staying on board the *Amaryllis*, a floating hunting lodge from the 1920s anchored off one of the Alimar Islands. He had gone to bed. In the middle of the night he was disturbed from his sleep and went to the windows. He recalls hearing the muskie stir in the water outside.

"At three o'clock in the morning a huge fish came up trying to throw the hook."

Copp has never been able to shake the image of the fish on the moonlit river. It was like an illuminating piece to the puzzle of destiny, like a moment of feverish insight, gone before it could be fully grasped. The fish was no better at answering questions than Copp's great-grandfather lost in the depths of his grave.

Courtesy of Martin Copp

Wellesley Island

C.A. Duke (left) and muskies

No Cure for the Dedicated Angler

Clayton Ferguson

The nature of the muskie is explained in these words by Harold Herrick: "It is an unpredictable fish. At times it takes its bait in open, deep water, on the change of wind, in shallow weed beds. At other times it will prefer a dark day, rough water, with white caps." To understand an unpredictable fish takes an unpredictable man ...

Clayton Ferguson

Even two or three beers on a Sunday evening do not diminish the passion of a fishing guide like Clayton Ferguson. In a corner of a tavern in Clayton, Ferguson's dark eyes flash hotly. That fire is invoked naturally on the subject of fishing, since a single-minded force drives the man. He calls it dedication. From his lips the term almost sounds like a form of torment.

"There are no secret spots," he insists. "There's muskies all over the river. I have no secret spots. It's the same as anything. There's no secret. It's persistence. It's in your heart. It's dedication.

"You lay in bed at night thinking of the plugs that weren't working right."

The words flow with a fierce, unchecked, headlong momentum. Ferguson dominates the conversation.

Scornfully, he repeats the charge from a fellow guide that he is "burned out." In a scrap book kept in the rank, untidy fertility of his bedroom he has page after page of photographs and newspaper clippings of champion muskellunge. In the pictures Ferguson's face evolves from a scrawny youngster to a bearded, middle-aged guide. Now, above one eyebrow, there is a small crescent-shaped scar, like the slip of a chisel on a wooden face, a moment of lost innocence perhaps.

In the tavern, Ferguson recites the figures, computes the proof. In the last twelve and one-half days he has landed eleven muskies. In twenty-three years as a guide he has caught twelve trophy muskie between forty and fifty inches in length.

If he remembers the beer on the table he takes a long draught, admitting he drinks too much --- but nothing interferes with his work as a guide.

"There's no best guide. There's some awful dedicated fishermen out there. The best guide is dedicated."

He was nineteen years old when he made his first solo trip as a guide. That day started a chain of miraculous catches. Ferguson had found his destiny. A guide, respected for his catches, had overbooked and Ferguson was handed two temperamental fishermen from Kentucky. From the beginning the two complained that the elder guide had produced no muskie the day before, a serious charge and one that Ferguson bitterly resented in silence. It rained that day and the three men, who had been fishing for bass, decided, as a parting gesture, to make an attempt at muskie, though the water was turning as dark as the bottom of a wine cask.

The miraculous happened. They landed a fifty-two-inch muskie off Potter's Beach at Grindstone Island.

"I was new then. It was all an accident. That's just nature's luck."

The wind came up. Ferguson shifted to the lee of Wolfe Island, trolling distractedly in a straight line. The miraculous happened again. A thirty-eight-pound muskie was landed in the dark.

Ferguson was burning with pride. He wanted to hoist the traditional white flag, one for each trophy muskie. "I wished it was daylight so people could see what I did on my first day."

Since that day in 1955 --- aside from winter voyages that took him as far as the Black Sea on a commercial fishing boat --- Ferguson has been pursuing the muskie like a man possessed. He learned the craft from his father, a farmer who switched to guiding after he returned from the Second World War. The war left the farmer physically wasted and unable to manage a farm. His reward for service was a metal plate in his head and the bits of shrapnel dug out of his body like worthless nuggets.

Fishing for bass is like hunting rabbits, Ferguson says. Success is almost assured and the angler can return with large numbers of small game. But where's the achievement? Muskie fishing has more dignity.

"It's the muskie that make one do it. Bass fishing is so easy. They're either biting or they're not.

"Anyone can catch a bass. Not many can catch a muskie."

In his boat --- a 1951 mahogany day cruiser that mocks the "plastic" of other boats -- Ferguson is a hard and sober guide. He fixes on his task with a determined, short-tempered severity, dropping the distracting chatter. "In my mind I know what I want to do to catch fish. Watch me, but don't ask me seven thousand f*****g questions. Keep your eyes open."

If there are no secret spots, Ferguson is nevertheless feverish about the precise details of technique, how the plug behaves in the water. In his apartment overlooking the river he grabs a handful of plugs and exhibits the teeth marks of countless muskie to make his point.

Towed on the line behind the boat, the plug vibrates in different ways, depending on the size of propeller and the revolutions per minute of the motor, Ferguson explains.

He fine tunes the revolutions per minute for the exact vibration he wants in the plug, then weaves the trolling line in the pattern that instinct tells him attracts the fish.

"It's hard for me to explain to customers."

Ferguson will not divulge the strategy of the plug. He has no idea why a particular vibration attracts the fish. "I know how to produce them. I don't know what the muskie's thinking."

After the brief muskie season in the fall, Ferguson turns to other pursuits. He works as a stone and brick mason, and when the mood strikes him, he grabs his guitar and picks at a bluegrass tune.

"It'll build up in me. It's singing out of your heart, singing the blues. I'll get sad."

Sometimes the urge strikes late at night. There is no resisting. He composes a ragged, patched tune as he goes along. Where it comes from does not matter. "It'll be the prettiest god-damn music."

The conversation moves forward like a refrain, mixing music, the memory of today's catch, the longing for the big fish tomorrow. "Fishing is the dedication. Your heart is dedicated to it."

"It's not how much you catch. It's how much you put into it."

Clayton

A Few, Finite Words

Bruce Woodman

Hunter Grimes' shrewd definition of a river rat is "a subdued extrovert." The definition may be apt, but there is always a blunt extrovert waiting to give it a kick...

Bruce Woodman

Bruce Woodman talks the way he smokes a cigar, in brief, assured, wolfish puffs. A large man at six feet, two hundred and thirty pounds, he flicks the metal lighter open, relights a smoldering cigar. "We spent the whole bloody day rockin' and rollin' in the rain," he says gruffly. That, from an armchair in a home on Wolfe Island, summarizes a day's work. The peaked cap stays fixed on his head as though it still shaded him from the sun. Two eyes focus with the intensity of one. A detective show flickers on the TV set.

Woodman knows where the shoals are, where the bass and pike and muskie feed on smaller fish. The rest is chance, for which he is not responsible. Fishing guides, he says, fall into two classes, those who know the river and those who claim they know the river. The latter category are not guides, he says. They are boat operators.

The lighter snaps open again and the cigar is lit like a burning spit of wood. Woodman speaks as a man sure of his facts. He is no fool caught with an empty boast. He has good reason for confidence.

Woodman's family settled on Wolfe Island in the mouth of the St. Lawrence in the last century. The island was still a wild outpost exposed to storms rolling off the lake. From his father Woodman inherited something that cannot be bought, a knowledge of fishing. In an average year he lands thirty of the big, handsome brutes known as muskellunge. Compared to the muskie, anything else looks like a puny, good-for-nothing, little runt of a fish.

Woodman now insists that, unless it is going to be mounted, the muskie be released in the water. He does not want the fish to be thinned from the river. "We're going to leave a little legacy here for the kids," he explains. That's the end of the discussion. Don't ask for more.

In the mid-1800s Woodman's great-grandfather, a United Empire Loyalist, left Wisconsin for Wolfe Island. He cleared land at the wind-scoured western tip of the island that faces Lake Ontario and started farming. The farm passed to Woodman's grandfather, William George, who had two sons, Stanley Livingston Woodman, named after the two African explorers, and George Washington Woodman, an oddly patriotic name for United Empire Loyalist stock.

Bruce Woodman's father, Stanley Livingston Woodman, and his grandfather tried to start a coal and grain shipping business on the island, but it failed. Stanley Woodman made a break with the family tradition of farming to become a river guide.

"I guess you'd say he was a God-fearing man," Bruce Woodman says. Stanley Woodman was tall, skinny and rugged. He didn't drink. He took the labours of a fishing guide seriously, learning the shoals the hard way, by sounding the depths painstakingly with a lead line.

Bruce Woodman was born in 1928 in the white wooden house across the road from the water. Woodman and his wife Margaret still open the building in the summer as a tourist home but live across the street on the side of the river. Woodman started fishing at five years of age at the end of a dock and says, "I'm still learning. You find new spots to fish, new ways to treat people. Everybody's different. You've got to be a father confessor to some of them."

Woodman began as a guide when he was fifteen --- "I haven't got a nickel more than when I started," he insists --- and fishes one hundred to one hundred and fifteen days a year. In the winter he drives a snowplow for the Ontario Ministry of Transportation on Wolfe Island. A fishing guide cannot survive without a second job in the winter, Woodman says.

He fishes a twenty-kilometre stretch of the river, concentrating on the mouth, and is one of the top half dozen muskie guides in the Thousand Islands. American muskie biologist Steve LaPan calls Woodman his mentor, a guru of the river, though the guide has to be approached with the same respect as a man-eating giant.

Muskie are not easy to catch. In the fall, when the summer residents and visitors depart, the muskie return to shallower water to feed. "You go three days and don't get any," says Woodman. "You go the next morning and get three. I guess you never can tell." Yet Woodman says fishing is only one-quarter chance. He knows ten muskie spots on the river. "Some guides know approximately where to go, but they don't know exactly." His biggest muskie was a fifty-four-inch monster he landed in the 1960s.

Some of the guides are switching to down-riggers for muskie, which shorten the length of the trolling line by a large weight that pulls the line down. Woodman scoffs at the success of the down-rigger --- "that's open to a lot of debate," he says --- and insists that the legitimate way to catch muskie is with a flat line and jointed plugs as lures. "Let the records speak for themselves." End of debate.

Woodman has lived all his life on Wolfe island, except for a brief stint in Gananoque, where he trained as a police constable. In the 1950s, he was Wolfe Island's sole municipal police constable. He worked part time to settle car accidents, break up fights and intervene in family squabbles.

After seven years he quit, preferring to guide. "The money was no damn good" and Woodman liked the freedom of the river. Yet thirty years later a copy of the Criminal Code still sits threateningly on top of a stack of books in his living room. Woodman was the island's last municipal police officer. The Ontario Provincial Police took over after him, using the ferry from Kingston as transportation like other outsiders.

Woodman roots for a new cigar. The metal lighter flicks again, putting fire in the grotto of his eyes for a moment. The metal snaps shut like an axe hitting a chunk of wood. Woodman has no patience for indecisiveness. Six months later on a winter afternoon he will decide to quit smoking cigars forever. Being fickle at anything is a waste of time. You either know where the fish are or you do not. The rest is endurance.

"If I'd wanted to be doing something else," says Woodman, "I'd be doing it."

Wolfe Island

Blessed Are They Who Wait for the Fish

Clarence Huntley

Muskie guide James Brabant of Clayton has this to say about the muskellunge: "A lot of muskies are known to be in the same spot year after year ... I think these fish are like dogs --- some stay home and don't want any others in their territory; and others are roamers." As for muskie guides, well, some are roamers and can't wait to be gone, while others settle down as though the river were home ...

Muskie Jake

"I've been an outdoor man all my life. I couldn't work in a factory. I'd feel as if the walls were pressing on me."

The words lengthen in a sunny drawl, simple and straightforward like a fishing line unravelled slowly into the water. What Muskie Jake says, he means. Boasting and bad temper and deceit would be a waste of energy.

Muskie Jake is so even tempered it's easy to forget that he has inner needs, unlike a rock or a tree.

The face is long. The features are large with two white sideburns sweeping across the cheeks. The eyes have a spare blue innocence as open to inspection as a chart of the river depths.

Gone is the stormy manner and rough look that the romantic demands from the river rat. The wolf and the cougar and the muskellunge fit the definition of a wild creature. But what about the deer and the rabbit? Do they belong in a cage or running free? Are they as full of creation?

Muskie Jake has no definite answers. Speaking what is on his mind would be pushy, disrespectful.

"I guess we're all river rats," he says. He treats the term as a distinction dreamed up one night in town, of no more consequence than deciding the number of islands in the Thousand Islands. It is still the Thousand Islands. Can anyone throw a net over a river rat and define one?

"They see us out there all the time, huntin', just like a rat huntin' round the yard lookin' for somethin' to eat. You're rattin' around lookin' for the fish.

"I think it's just a name. That's all it is.

"I can't explain it myself."

Clarence Huntley is a private man. He can endure the long wait for muskie --- and what destiny dispenses --- with patience. His boat is scrupulously tidy, thoughtful, like his manner with people. If a river rat has to dress like a scruffy beggar, "Well, then I'm not a river rat," Huntley declares.

On the wall of his small home workshop hangs a rack with duck hunting guns --- Huntley won't hunt inland game like deer and moose --- a large stuffed muskie and an old photograph of one of his mentors, a handsome fishing guide named Frank Lalonde. The old guide is hoisting a thirty-five-pound muskie.

Lalonde belonged to times that were both rougher and gentler. He wears a tie. He has suspenders and, on his head, a respectful working man's cap. A stubby cigarette dangles from one corner of his mouth.

Huntley has been Muskie Jake for so long it takes a moment to remember his real name. The Muskie Jake tag evolved gradually, he says. It was natural. "They started to hang it on me," the guide explains without elaborating. "I like it. It kind a rhymes, doesn't it?"

Clarence Huntley was born in Gananoque on December 10, 1916. He was raised by his maternal grandparents, Jacob and Louise Huntley, whose last name he adopted as his own. His first memories are full of wonder at the large fish seen through the eyes of a child. When he was six he remembers watching from the shore as his grandmother trolled alone for muskie. It was like a puppet drama on a distant stage. Something magical happened. A fish pulled on the line from below the surface. The elderly woman pulled back in mimicry, alone against the giant unseen muskie. Then, too weak to heave the beast into the boat, she towed it behind to the land. There, for the finale, it was lifted out of the water.

The child looked down at the muskie. The fish, pulled from hidden depths, was real, yet gone now, dead. There must be more fish out there invisible below the surface.

Jacob Huntley, the first Jake, was an inspiring sight too. He had a kingly handlebar mustache, a balding scalp and a tiny island --- jokingly called Huntley shoals --- with three bent trees and a cottage. Grandfather and grandson spent hours on the water, fishing and sailing in a St. Lawrence skiff. Under the guidance of his grandfather and his grandfather's son, Ken, a fishing guide also called Jake, the boy was inducted with steady, unrushed ceremony into the life of a river man.

Aside from five years of service during the Second World War as a Royal Canadian Air Force transport driver, Huntley has been a local fixture around Gananoque. After he returned from the war in Europe in 1946 he started as a guide with a St. Lawrence skiff and a four-cylinder engine.

Huntley earned his reputation as a guide fishing for the most challenging and elusive of predators in the river, the muskellunge. Muskie is fished by trolling or dragging a line as long as one hundred and sixty feet behind the boat. As a long-lived beast, the muskie is crafty. It has been the prize fish of the St. Lawrence for over a hundred years among generations of Muskie Jakes.

In the 1860s Benson Lossing came to visit the ruins of the British fort on Carleton Island and recorded his ambition --- that day denied --- to land a muskie. Lossing wrote of the attempt near Clayton: "We trolled faithfully, but only a solitary pickerel of moderate size rewarded our watchfulness of the lines. Our dreams of mighty masquelonges, forty pounds in weight, which some young ladies, they say, sometimes 'hook', were dispelled."

To sooth Lossing's pride, the oarsman commented that the wind had stirred the water so much that "nobody couldn't do nothin' at fishin' when the creeturs couldn't see the spoon."

To add to the difficulties of guides like Huntley these days, there is a relatively small number of muskie. Nevertheless Huntley keeps guiding for the fish, making sure his equipment is modern.

Huntley --- unlike some Canadian guides --- has adopted a down-rigger, in addition to a depth finder. The down-rigger is a nine-pound weight in the shape

Photo by Shawn Thompson/Courtesy of the Gananoque Reporter

Muskie Jake, Angler Donald Anderson and fifty-two-inch muskie

of a fish which drops down in the water. The fishing line clips to a release on the down-rigger. Because of the weight, a shorter, time-saving line can be used.

As for the depth sounder, Huntley says that he knows the shoals and fishing grounds in his twenty-kilometre territory on the river from Landon's Bay to Howe Island and the Forty Acres, the expanse of water bounded by Wolfe, Howe and Grindstone Islands. The depth finder saves the time of "sighting" the fishing spots on the water by co-ordinating the landmarks. The device also makes it easy to distinguish the fish below.

In spite of a lifetime spent on the river, Huntley will not venture for muskie east of Landon's Bay. He says that he knows the whole river for navigation, but not for fish. For muskie in his own territory, he knows twenty-five fishing spots in the Forty Acres and another ten in the channel between Kingston and Gananoque.

"It takes an awful lot of time. You've got to hammer at it, never give up," he says.

"I've seen people troll in places for muskie they haven't had a muskie there in a hundred years.

"I troll the Forty Acres from the foot of Wolfe and Huckleberry Flats and Sugar Island. This is my native waters right up here."

Duck hunting requires the same patience as trolling for muskie. Huntley carves his own decoys, spreading sixty-five on the water in the pattern he thinks works best, then waits by an island.

"The main thing is sitting still and don't move --- and keep your face from looking up in the air." The pale-grey fleshy saucer of a face is a signal that warns the ducks, he says.

"You either fool the ducks or they fool you."

The days on the river do not get better or worse, Huntley says. He does not intend to stop working as a guide --- "If I feel like I am now, I'll go right to the end" --- though the years have not spared him pain. He was hurt by the loss of his fifteen-year-old son in 1970, followed by the death of his dear wife Margaret in 1987. The son drowned inland in a pond a few hundred yards from the Huntley home.

Huntley was teaching the boy to shoot and fish. "He was a great lad," Huntley says simply, recording a fact, not asking for sympathy. "He would have been a guide. John could have carried on."

The boy's hunting cap hangs beside his gun in Huntley's workshop.

"I have a feeling that over the years there aren't going to be any guides."

But these days there is still Muskie Jake. In the unpredictable, dirty weather of October when the muskie feed and fatten for the winter, the guide is not sitting idle on the shore. His mahogany boat plows across the swells of the river with a relaxed, good-natured roll. Huntley's blue eyes scan the water. He does not need to curse and rail against the foul weather. The rebel in him refuses to be gruff. He has inner strength, like fruit that needs no rind to protect itself.

In a boat as neat as the kitchen of a chef, the drawl of his conversation is deep and unhurried and straightforward. In one corner of the boat is a symbol of the closest thing that Muskie Jake has to a philosophy. It is a waste paper basket. Muskie Jake is a man who is tidy with time and the river and people.

Gananoque

A River-Bred Gent Retires to His Nets

Allen Cook

Some people have lives punctuated by grand --- and fleeting --- accomplishments. Then others lead lives of common joys in a single unending flow like the movement of a river...

Allen Cook (right) and his son, Aurthur

Allen Cook talks like he fishes, in one long, sweet, unending line. All his life he has been fishing commercially, accepting the licence of his grandfather, handing it to his sons as part of their heritage. Along the way he marvelled with simple delight at a river rich with fish, a river as sleek and powerful and seductive as the apparition of a cougar he saw one morning by the spot where he tends his nets. For nineteen years Cook also worked as a school caretaker. But, when he retired in 1977 at sixty-five years of age, he was eager to fish commercially once more for perch, sunfish, bullheads and eels with his two sons, Arthur and Herbie.

"Now I was born down by the waterfront here in Gananoque, 1910, so you see I'm no chicken. My dad died when I was very little, four, five years, and I don't remember much about that --- but what I'm coming at is this fishing business. It originated a way back, way back. Now I can't go into those years because I've gone to 1910 for you. Now granddad he --- those licences that I have now and the boys have, was handed down to me at that time. That's a long time ago. I don't remember dates too well and I don't remember names ... I guess I'd be about eight when I started fishing with the grandfather there, Rastus Cook --- and he had a fishing licence --- and uncle Harry Cook. They were very good fishermen. Now we're speaking about nets, nets and commercial lines, so therefore you have got to have a certain amount of cleverness about it or you're not going to carry on with it...He seemed to have a knack to know where to go and put a net and catch some fish. I'll show you a picture here."

Cook rummages through his wallet with dark, suntanned fingers. He lays out a pile of family pictures till he comes to a sturgeon taller than the man beside it. Proof. No disputing it. The Cooks are fishermen.

"They fished every type, you might say, off the river. Them days you could catch pike, which you can't now, and those days you could catch in general everything was on the river, but no bass understand.

"There's two types of fishing, evening fishing and daytime fishing, you know. In other words, if you're going to fish eels and catfish, you do that after supper. You use three-hundred hook line, you see...

"I guess I'd be about sixteen when grandfather had me handle a couple a nets to see how I could make out with it --- I maintain that I fish. And I'll be putting nets in the river --- seven, that's my limit --- and I'll be putting seven in the river the day after Labour Day this year, the boys and I, the two boys. I never seemed, really and truly, to find the commercial fishing."

He pauses for the word he can't find. His face is bright and friendly. Then he resumes: "All I did find was good, hard work. It's like farming or anything... You got up, you had your breakfast, naturally, and the procedure you used was to take your lunch always, just in case a wind gets you out and you couldn't get back so you have something to eat.

"All right, well then, you go --- if it's netting season --- you go look at nets, clean them off, take care of your fish, or put them in live fish boxes ... Then, why maybe one net wasn't fishing as good as another, so you're going to shift that net around. This going to sound crazy. I can set fifty nets and out of fifty nets you'll have thirty fishing good. It wouldn't be any use asking why. We don't know. You've got to be on the spots where they're travelling ... There's some days you do exceptionally well and there's other days not so good. Fish has a habit of moving very quickly from shallow water to deep water and they'll follow where they're good feed.

"Say it's a shipping day. Now you want to be out, oh, try to be out six o'clock, eh, in the morning. All right. So you're going out there and you're going to look at the nets. Then you're going to sort your fish. Pack them and ice them and ship them. And them days it used to be that we run the fish to Clayton. Now we do it all local here in Canada. Now we're dealing strictly with Picton.

"Well, when we put the nets in the river they don't come out of the river unless there's bad damage by muskrat or somebody cutting them. The point is you have to keep moving them around.

"It's interesting. Something gets in your blood and, by golly, it's just like these fellows with moose hunting and deer hunting. Now we're looking, like little kids we're looking very much forward to September. Because we put the nets in the river. In other words we'll be going to work.

"It's a pretty nice sight, supposing you see half a dozen good, big, golden walleyes swimming. You know what you've got to do with them, release them. But you can always take time to look at these things, if you understand me. Don't take them out of the water, but leave them in the net and look at them. Then release them.

"This river never --- I'm going to state this, I know Arthur will back me up on this --- there's never been the conditions on the river below Gananoque since they started these devilish cesspools --- am I using the right name, cesspools? Sewer lagoons! That's the thing I'm looking for. And that is supposed to be purifying going into the river. It's running out into this creek here, the Gananoque River, and from there into the river. And it's not very dang healthy this."

Allen Cook and his son say that they can tell the difference by the weeds, and by the green slime and moss that collect in their nets, which they have to burn out with the sun.

"I spent nineteen years with the school board as a caretaker. And all the time I'd work I'd still have the river on my mind. So when I became close to sixty-five I was getting pretty excited about going back on the river, getting myself some equipment, going on the river and going to work. So that's the way it can affect me. It was in my blood --- because fishing is interesting, Arthur will back me up. You can get up in the morning and you can have the thoughts on your mind, 'I wonder where today I can put a net.' It's always something new cropping up.

"We had that black cat, you remember two years ago, the cougar. About half past six in the morning at Landon's Bay. He came up, stood in the middle of the highway. And then he seen me, ran like a deer, jumping up on that big hill and was gone. Jet black. Long, long tail. Big heavy fella. But I did see him, true as I'm sitting here, 'cause I told the boys the same morning.

"You know what was odd about that? First off, a fox came out on the highway and then went across so easy. And I stayed quiet. I was just getting ready to go out, but I sit quiet in the car. And Mr. Fox came down off the same rock. Then lo and behold comes the big cat. But the big cat, he sit down out on the highway and looked up and down. And then spied me and away he went. Never have we seen heard tell of him since, that fella ..."

Gananoque

The Muskrat School of Love and Cunning

Richard Senecal

The muskrat is an ingenious creature, schooled in the ways of the river. Like the muskie, it is a sly adversary for someone who needs the challenge of a strange intelligence ...

Richard Senecal

On an October afternoon the wood smoke drifts from the chimney of the Senecal home at Buell's Point. The trees shelter the smoke --- a warm, welcome, familiar smell --- from the clutch of the wind blowing off the St. Lawrence. The scent of the smoke carries the spare, unfevered musk of the forest.

Richard Senecal, island child, retired trapper, opens the door before there is time to knock.

Before long, he is scrambling into the mole-burrow basement of his cottage-home to retrieve a wire cage trap. The small fingers grope through the trap door at one end, showing how the muskrat, his ingenuity put to shame, enters. Senecal also lifts a foot trap, sets it deftly with his fingers, touches the trip from below. The trap snaps shut angrily on metal and empty air.

Senecal has the same simple delight that a mechanic takes in an engine humming smoothly.

Life as a trapper was a natural choice for Senecal. He was born in 1923 on a Grenadier Island farm to a trapper with a family of eleven children. The family ate muskrat meat at the dinner table and quite often bullfrogs' legs too. "I've tried beaver. There's a lot of meat in beaver." As a teenager in the late 1930s it was easy for Senecal to earn the princely sum of a dollar a pelt with a handful of traps. The money looked good and he could work outdoors.

Yet the times were changing. The rich, rewarding farms of Grenadier Island were falling behind economically. The Senecal clan was brought to the island to farm in the 1880s by Richard Senecal's great-grandparents, Joseph and Catherine Senecal. Joseph and Catherine Senecal ran a dairy farm and built the three-storey Angler's Inn on the north shore. Later their stout, hard-working son Anthony "Tone" Senecal ran the hotel.

By Richard Senecal's time the families were leaving the island. The days of providing everything from the land were disappearing --- actually a brief flash in a history of fishing thousands of years old in the Thousand Islands. On Grenadier a family could no longer grow and stitch and build whatever it needed. And trapping was seasonal work.

Senecal tried other jobs temporarily: factory work in Brockville, driving a tour boat, carpentry. For fourteen years he was caretaker on an island owned by a corporation and he also laboured in the Rockport boat works of Eddy Andress. But nothing satisfied like pitting his wits against a wily, web-footed rodent like the muskrat.

On a good year, when prices were high, Senecal might catch as many as three hundred muskrats in a month and sell the lot for a thousand dollars. Those were the golden years of the 1960s. The fur pelts had a rich, erotic splendour which sold easily and the supply seemed inexhaustible. "At that time the 'rats were really thick," he says.

Senecal was licensed to trap along the shore of Grenadier and on the mainland opposite the island. At the beginning of the season he would place one hundred traps. Early every morning, he would return to the traps, collect the muskrats and reset the traps. By the time he finished skinning the beasts it was probably after dark. Senecal learned about trapping from his father and from observation.

Two kinds of traps were laid. There was a long cage trap laid in the burrow that led through the mud from the muskrat's weed home. And there was a leg trap hidden in the marsh where the muskrats fed, frolicked and made love.

"The weeds have to be just above the water and your trap is set in the centre," Senecal says, explaining in arcane detail how to set a leg trap in a marsh. Don't put the trap too close to the weeds, he warns. The muskrat, with its leg caught, keeps circling until the chain of the trap takes hold in the weeds. Then the creature breaks the bone in his leg, followed by the skin. It is a simple choice. The leg stays a prisoner in the trap and the muskrat escapes.

In the spring the muskrats are bitten by love and mate, which in their temporary folly makes them easier to catch. The female leaves her musk in the weedy marshes and the male gets careless looking for a companion, Senecal explains. "After that, you don't catch them."

The fur pelts were better in the spring because the hide was tougher, thicker after the winter. But the mating muskrats also bit each other recklessly in their love-making. That left holes in the pelts and made them a less valuable catch.

Poachers were a problem in the 1940s around the islands. The trappers were licensed, but not to specific zones as they are today, and not everyone abided by the honour system. The marauders came in the night before the season started and slipped into Senecal's territory like human weasels. They hid their traps well below the water and Senecal never caught the thieves.

Time added other corruptions. Even the flavour of meat seemed to change. In the 1970s Senecal and his wife noticed the difference in the meat of ducks shot on the river. "They tasted terrible, muddy," Senecal says, a feeling echoed by others, such as Muskie Jake, a fishing guide from Gananoque. "They smelled just like muck," Senecal observes. He thinks pollution affected the meat.

"Black ducks were the best --- and wood ducks, mallards."

Senecal and his wife Evelyn, after raising a family of six on Grenadier, left the island in 1983 as a grudging concession to their age. It was difficult travelling across the river in the winter. "I'd still like to be back there because it was my home. It's nature, I guess you'd call it." His sister, June Senecal Hodge, is one of the few remaining residents of the island.

Richard Senecal nevertheless gets out on the river, especially in winter with the sixteen-foot-long plywood iceboat he built himself. The iceboat is blown across waves and ice by a sixty-five horsepower aircraft engine mounted at the back. It travels forty kilometres on hour on the river and flies at ninety-six kilometres an hour across the ice.

The only time Senecal left the river was during the Second World War when he served in the Royal Canadian Air Force instructing the men what to expect in poison gas warfare. Cut off from the river and the people he knew, he was trapped. He has not forgotten that period of exile. The weekly letters from home eased the pain. Still, "It was pretty damn lonesome," he says. "You're lost and sad.

"You'd sit by the shore and look out on the ocean and wonder where Canada was and if you were going to get home again."

In time, the trapper came home to the river.

Buell's Point

Bait Shop Talk: A Public Forum for What Ails You

Ed Shaw

On the river, fishing is a common folk art. It distinguishes one individual from another. And so is the conversation and debate held beside full tubs of bait...

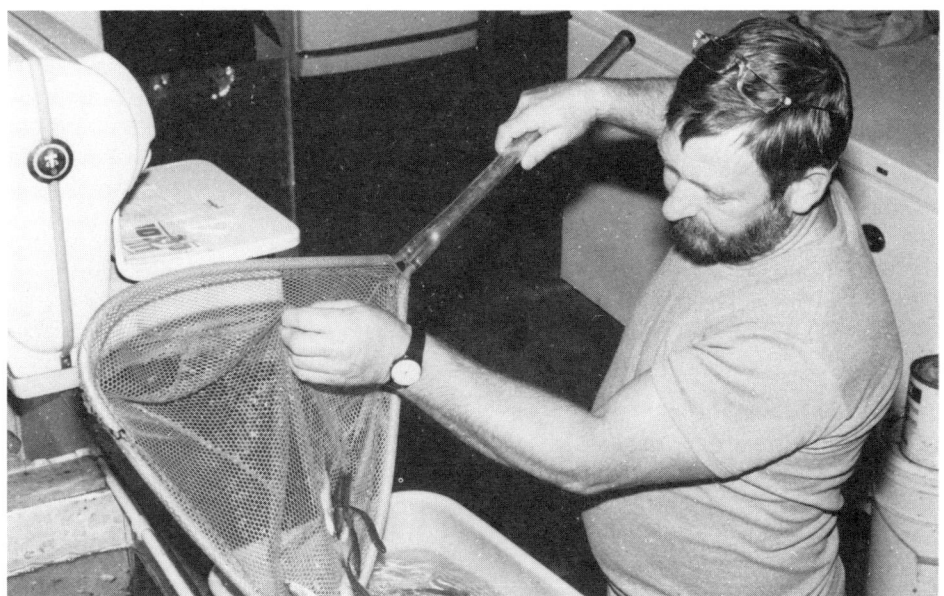

Ed Shaw in his bait shop

Ed Shaw lounges shrewdly in a corner, listening. A short American with a dog's head carved on the tip of his cane rants about blacks and foreigners and Japanese cars. Even the outspoken Ed Shaw will not leap into the conversation this time. He keeps quiet at the racist monologue. Then two tourists with thick German accents ask where to find lures. That makes Shaw, also a river guide, chuckle to himself. Lures are stupid. Sheer folly. They won't let you fish at the depth of river fish in the summer, Shaw explains later. A real angler would know that.

For some, the sizzling topic of the day may be the nearly criminal exchange rate on the Canadian dollar, the insult of the latest fishing regulation, or Shaw's favourite outrage, the scandalous loss of the winter lake trout season in 1987.

With plastic bait buckets in hand the fishermen troop through Ed's Live Bait Shop. The converted gas station garage in Gananoque is cluttered with metal bait tanks, refrigerators to cool the worms and stuffed fish hanging on the walls. The fishermen want to gab as much as they want to buy live bait. Aside from the Muskie Lounge in the tavern across the street, Shaw's place is the best unofficial public forum in Gananoque. Here the bearded radical of the river, the uninhibited master of no ceremony, Ed Shaw, holds court on the troubles of the day.

Starting a debate with Shaw is no more difficult than getting a bull to charge. "I like an argument now and then," he confesses. "It keeps you going. It keeps your blood flowing." A passionate man in his fifties, he has an old-fashioned set of values about river life.

And Shaw loves an impromptu wrangle. "If I'm wrong, prove me wrong. If I'm wrong I'll be the first to apologize, but prove me wrong."

He hisses like a hot coal dropped in water at the thought of anyone fishing beyond the limit. That is a devilish problem in the Thousand Islands. In addition to some renegade anglers, the issue is confused by the division of the river between two nations and two sets of regulations. Cross the line and the fishing rules change by magic. But that does not excuse lawlessness.

Shaw recalls two American fishermen who wanted bait before the opening of bass season. They bragged about what they would catch. Why should a bait shop owner care? "You talk about getting hot under the collar," Shaw says. He lapses into silence and fumes at the memory. The renegades got a surprise. Shaw refused to sell the two any minnows. He told them to get lost.

And yet Shaw --- no stranger to contradiction --- found himself embroiled with the Ministry of Natural Resources over a program to protect lake trout. Shaw fought back with a public petition. He phoned the minister at home when the ministry decided to close the two-week lake trout season in 1987. Shaw was so incensed that at one public meeting he had to force himself to sit down and cool off. The river battler said that the ministry's own figures proved the winter season didn't harm the trout as much as the summer season, which was left unchanged. The ministry disagreed.

As far as the bait-shop rebellion wages, it's a simple allegorical clash between bureaucracy and free choice. Shaw is convinced that the big money of tourism, the power of tourism operators and the summer cottage owners, influenced the ministry's decision. "Your tourism --- and this is a fact --- controls any season, especially in the fishing." Fishing in the winter, he says, was a ritual cherished by local people almost as much as Christmas and Easter. "Our lake trout fishing was like the opening day of duck hunting. Everybody looked forward to it. It was a tradition."

As a guide, Shaw leads the kind of life that summer fishermen envy. He can make a living from the river.

Yet it's not the fantasy life it seems, he insists. It was a break for freedom but it came with a new set of shackles.

For fifteen years Shaw, who was born in Gananoque, worked in the Stelco steel-forging plant in town. In his spare time he raised budgies. He broke with the plant job when he started a taxidermy business --- "officially" licensed --- in 1973 and then added a bait shop four years later. But at least the plant work had regular hours that gave him free time for the river, Shaw says. "It's nice to be working for someone else. If I was able to work back in the plant again, I'd probably enjoy it. You got an eight-to-five job. You're done at five o'clock. If you're running your own business, there's a lot of stress."

Shaw can only go fishing for fun himself one or two times a summer. To keep a stock of minnows, he rises at four in the morning in the summer. "This shop keeps me going all the time trying to keep enough minnows for everybody."

"Some of the bait men, they'll lay down in the morning and have a snooze or lay down in the afternoon and have a snooze. Not me. I'm on the go all day long. I don't kill myself, but I'm still on the go. It's long hours."

As well, a guide is under pressure to produce fish out of thin air. On the water everyone is an authority and everyone is a critic. "You take a day where it's windy and you can't get very many fish. You got to produce. And there's some people that don't understand. They think they can go out there and drop a line in and bang. Some people aren't satisfied unless they're steadily pulling them in. The guide's supposed to do miracles. It doesn't always work that way."

The temperaments of the fishermen vary too. The American anglers, "They're all pretty good Joes," he says, though Shaw --- a mite high strung and explosive himself --- admits some are domineering and volatile and "a little harder to please."

And fishing is not as quiet as it once was. The boat traffic has mushroomed on the river during the weekends. "You're buzzed all the time." Boaters and fishermen don't mix, Shaw pronounces. They are different breeds --- as separate as the sun and the moon, lure fishermen and bait fishermen. And never the twain will meet.

The conversation is interrupted by a man swinging a plastic bucket. Shaw pauses to scoop minnows out of a tank of cold running water. Then he plucks a styrofoam cup of worms out of a refrigerator. There is some good-natured banter. The ritual calls for old friendships to be renewed.

Whatever the issue, Shaw thinks that how people behave makes the difference --- and that's how he rates a fishing guide, by attitude, not by the size of the catch. "We're all good guides," he says, refusing to name the best. "Anybody that produces fish out there half decently for a party and treats his customer with respect, I think is a pretty good guide.

"There is days if the wind's blowing hard and it's raining, it's tough. You go get some, but it's still tough. We all have our good days and we all have our bad days."

Gananoque

A Hole Behind the Rocks That's Always Good for Bass

Ernie Manse

The image that sticks of Ernie Manse is a man with a fishing rod in one hand and a frying pan in the other. The frying pan is his emblem of hospitality and lifelong passion for making friends...

Ernie Manse

"I get up at daylight in the morning in the summer and run up below the Canadian bridge --- a favourite spot of mine --- and I'm back to the island to eat breakfast with a limit of bass by eight o'clock."

The bass do not sit cooling in a refrigerator. They are fried right away "in a little bacon grease and a little butter" on an outdoor brick grill.

That's how the sweet-hearted, nearly toothless Ernie Manse inspires himself for another day on the river. His island, called Away From It All, is a small fry in a big river. No larger than one-quarter of an acre, other islands circle it like a litter of small animals sleeping together. To the west is Arcadia Island, recalling the name of the rustic paradise of ancient Greece.

Manse feels safe here. "No matter how the wind blows I'm protected."

For thirty-five years Manse ran his own marina in Alexandria Bay. He was a fishing guide as well. And if the property is sold now, the river has not been bartered away. Manse spends his summers on the St. Lawrence, with an island cottage to fix his bearings like a polar star.

Manse has done everything on the St. Lawrence and met everyone. "I fished ever since I was big enough to hang onta a fishin' pole." When he was barely as tall as a table he marched to the creek down the road carrying "a little stick with string and a hook on it to catch little perch." Then spurting upwards as a teenager --- he has the massive, tanned hands of a giant --- he started hunting illegally at fourteen years of age.

In his twenties Manse shovelled coal for the boilers of the ferry that steamed between Alexandria Bay and Rockport nine times a day. After work, he swam the five kilometres from the Bay to Rockport to train for swimming races. By swimming from the United States to Canada for exercise Manse says that he started his own international development program. Another name for it was friendship.

During the Second World War Manse did not abandon the water. He saw the South Pacific as a first class carpenter's mate in the ship repair unit. His job was to fit the plywood landing boats on the USS Minos. For a river man accustomed to the craftsmanship of fine old boats it was a revelation. The landing boats were an introduction to the throw-away philosophy then gaining hold. "They were made for one trip. Anything they did after that was free gratis."

Back in the Thousand Islands Manse fished commercially for sturgeon and built boats for the Hutchinson Boat Works in Alexandria Bay. In 1955, he bought waterfront property and built his own marina. But the real Manse was the man who hunted, fished and trapped --- and acted as a kingly host in an island hut.

A relationship to the river was no throw-away philosophy. Like a good marriage, it was enduring, never satiated. In the spring of 1988 Manse and his grandson trapped seventy-nine muskrats in six days. He is proud of photos that show the muskrats piled like small sacks of fur on a dock. The feelings they stir in him make him marvel, "No matter how old you get, you're still a little boy."

That excitement was as keen as ever on a recent hunting trip along the river. It was October but the hunters were caught in a fierce early snowfall. "That was a son of a gun," he says with a long, delighted cackle. "Don't think it wasn't rough out there in the storm.

"There wasn't over an inch of snow on the ground, but it was an awful storm. I never seen snowflakes quite so big and quite so thick. They come down and hit ya just like they was a half-inch thick and ninety-nine per cent rain and just like a blotter. Boy, it didn't take long for ya to be wet through."

The deer escaped back into the woods without falling to a bullet.

As for fishing, it is partly a social activity. After guiding for years --- fishing for "mostly bass and northerns" --- Manse knows fishing grounds along the river on both the Canadian and American side.

"I'm a live bait man," Manse declares as though it were a badge of honour. "I go out there in August. Why, you can catch bass all over the river."

The river opens to Manse like an old, intimate companion. He knows dozens of inlets and shallow water spots where the fish like to linger. With barely a pause he thinks of "one nice little hole in behind the rocks. It's always good for one or two bass.

"After four or five casts, if I don't get one of those big bass, I get right out of there, because tomorrow there'll be one in there."

Manse catches fish and puts them in a pool that he built in the water beside his island. "I catch them so the bass boat guys don't get them." The pool, the size of a large room, was made out of a cement and rock wall fixed on a rock ledge. Manse lets his family catch fish for supper from the pool. They also swim there. Some of the catch he releases late in the fall. On a typical year Manse, more a preserver than a destroyer, returned to the river --- with an unspoken amen --- this litany of fish: seventeen bass, one northern pike, two catfish and two dogfish.

"I like to catch 'em. I get a kick out of catching 'em. You take one of those big largemouth bass. He jumps about three feet in the air. His mouth is as large as this," Manse says, opening his hands as wide as a frying pan.

"I took him over to Peck's. Peck said, 'What did you catch him with?'

" 'Oh,' I said, 'I caught him on a sucker.'

"He says, 'They ain't supposed to bite on suckers.'

"I said, 'Well, you go down to my island and there's seventeen in my pond and you tell 'em they wasn't supposed ta bite.' "

The crackling laughter rolls out at his own tale, sweet, long, honeycombed.

On weekends, friends and family come for the meals Manse cooks outdoors on his fireplace. "I'm cooking dinner for fifteen or more every Sunday," he says unfurling another long, lively laugh. In an outdoor cooking hut he keeps a sink, fridge and an arsenal of large iron frying pans.

It is true that he is older now. Age has stiffened and slowed the body. But the smile has not been worn away. Manse is content. On the river he never felt empty, never fretted about what he did not have. "You could do what you wanted to do. There wasn't anyone that wanted to be a millionaire."

And Manse knows that success means little, that people defeat themselves. "You don't have to do much to enjoy life."

Alexandria Bay

Squatter's Rites

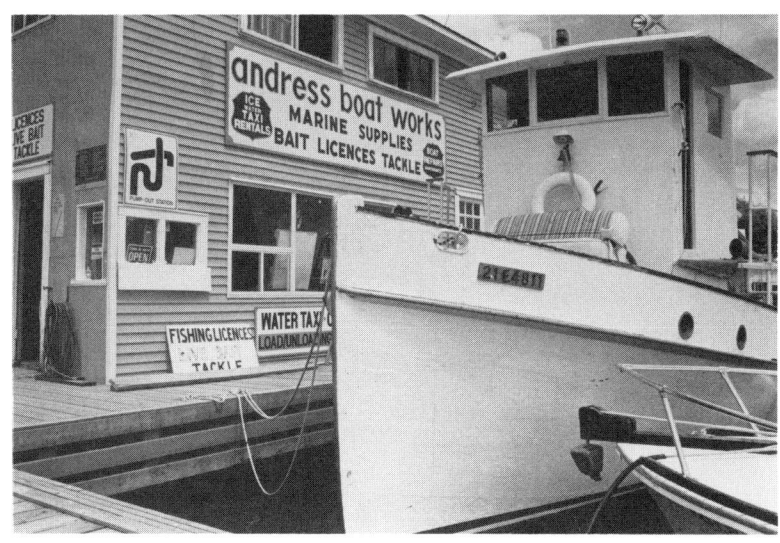

A Puff of Tobacco from a Briar Pipe

Leon and Marjorie Rusho

Islands are a good setting for either a paradise or a prison. They can be a school for life or a purgatory. The choice depends on the type of person who lives there...

Leon and Marjorie Rusho

In the nineteenth century an island like Grindstone was a small kingdom. It was one of the giants in the St. Lawrence, along with Wolfe, Howe, Wellesley and Grenadier, so it could support a colony of farmers. The border between Canada and the United States was not the great divider that it would eventually become. A more important distinction was life on an island itself, which tested the spirit and initiative of a family.

Leon Rusho and his wife, Marjorie Dano, are American beef and dairy farmers on Grindstone descended from Canadians. Rusho's ancestors drowned, gave up in disgust and moved to the more convenient mainland, or stayed on Grindstone's south shore where the island was all the universe they needed.

Leon Rusho was born on December 2, 1908 in a Grindstone farmhouse on Rusho Bay, named after a distant ancestor, probably his great-grandfather Christopher Rusho. The first Grindstone Rusho came from Canada in the mid-1800s. He left behind, for his great-grandson to read, his signature, chiseled into the timbers of the barn he built. Christopher Rusho and his wife Julia, with a few cows, a team of horses and strong backs, found life good on the island.

The farm of Christopher and Julia passed to their son, Freeman, whose fame in the family annals is the unadorned record of his death, a river funeral. All that is known of Freeman Rusho comes from the obituary that calls him "a respected farmer." The fifty-five-year-old man disappeared on the evening of May 7, 1904 crossing from Clayton. His body was never found. A capsized skiff was discovered a short distance from Freeman's home beside his sail and his hat.

The farm passed to Freeman's son, Manley, who transported the family from the Rusho Bay homestead a few hundred feet west to where Leon Rusho lives today. "I thought he was the greatest," Leon says of his father, a black-haired, clean-shaven man who had the soft-spoken, gentle manner of the Rushos. Manley would pause in his work, light his briar pipe and draw a few thoughtful puffs to put life in perspective. Manley Rusho married Alice Atherton, a woman born in Manchester, England and brought to Grindstone by her mother to be among her maternal kin, Welsh stonecutters who worked at the island quarry.

Marjorie Dano Rusho's family also came to the island from Canada. Her parents, Ambrose and Delia Dano moved from a farm near the village of Lansdowne to a two-hundred-acre dairy farm they share-cropped on Grindstone. The family was large, with eleven brothers and one sister besides Marjorie, and there seemed to be nothing that the island could not provide. Grindstone had two schools, two general stores and one Methodist church. Since the roads were poorly developed on the mainland, the transportation problems of living in the middle of the river did not seem bad in comparison. Marjorie was happy to make an imaginary dollhouse on the rocks with a few pieces of broken plates and a doll. The owner of the general store gave her stick candy.

As a girl Marjorie remembers her grandmother, Sarah Vodray, who wore seven petticoats that puffed out her dress and smoked a clay pipe. "I thought grandmothers did that," she says. Marjorie's older brother brought tobacco for the woman's pipe. "She'd grin when she'd see that." Then Sarah would light the pipe and tap her foot as she smoked in a straight-backed chair. She hid the grey in her hair by dying the strands with coffee.

The children from about thirty farming families went to the school where the main entertainment was getting closer to the wood stove in the winter. The children often arrived wet after tramping through the snow, Marjorie remembers. Drying out was one of the morning rites. The school, like the homes on the island, was not designed for comfort, says Leon Rusho, who went to the same small school as his wife. "They were not built to live in. The wind blew in one side and out the other."

"We loved it here," says Marjorie Rusho. "I never had any desire to go anywhere else." A week-long trip to Rochester one time was not the adventure she thought it would be. The visit stretched into an eternity. Marjorie learned her lesson. "It was a terrible ordeal to be in that city --- hot and dusty and noisy." Her husband adds, "The island was home. The family was there. We were close. We had good neighbours. We were never lonely in the wintertime."

One disadvantage was the lack of a marine weather forecast on the radio. Without a forecast, the storms rose with little warning, the suddenness adding to the force. Rusho remembers that when a river storm buffeted the house as it rushed down the river his mother would lament, "I pity those lake sailors tonight." The Rushos, with sailors among their kin, knew the brutality of storms. Rusho's great-uncle Truman Rusho drowned when the wooden sailing ship *Bell Mitchell* sank in Lake Superior with a load of lumber. "The only thing they ever found was a hatch off the companion way," he says.

Another great-uncle, Alexander Rusho, had his own schooner sink under him in Lake Michigan after a collision with a barge. "He never sailed again. He had enough. He told us he thought he was going clear to the bottom of Lake Michigan." The combination of losing a ship and gaining a wife helped persuade him to give up the risky life of a sailor and settle inland. "They all sailed," Rusho says of his ancestors. "Some of them stuck to it. Others didn't."

Even the farming Rushos led a double life as sailors. In 1949, Leon Rusho bought a fifty-foot marine landing craft from the United States navy for $2,500. Used first as a way to transport farm goods and machinery, before long Rusho was hauling cargo for others in the craft. The boat was licensed for the Great Lakes and Rusho took loads as far as Oswego. He moved lumber and bulldozers across the river and helped lay underwater cables from Cape Vincent to Chippewa Bay. In 1975, Rusho replaced the navy craft with a fifty-six-foot cargo launch called --- in a radical snubbing of every nautical tradition --- *Oak Grove* after his farm. His son Leon Jr. operates the *Oak Grove* now.

Of the four Rusho male children born on the farm, all have kept ties with the water. Manley, a retired telephone lineman, was busy in the Mediterranean Sea in 1988 teaching American history to marines on the helicopter support ship the *USS Guam*. Robert lives in Louisiana and works as a captain aboard an oil company supply tug in the Gulf of Mexico. Milton is a United States Customs agent on the narcotics water patrol in Florida.

Although farming has declined on Grindstone and the Rusho children, aside from Leon Jr., have departed, Marjorie Rusho says, "This is a great place to bring up a family. After dinner they were always in the house. And I didn't have to worry about the kids getting run over."

Rusho has watched the changes to Grindstone, the gradual replacement of farmers by summer residents, the growing isolation of the large, fertile island with no bridge like Wellesley, no ferries like Wolfe and Howe. But, with a typically sweet smile, he makes no lament. "You can't go back," he says. "You have to go forward. That's the way it is."

Grindstone Island

Leon Rusho and the *Oak Grove*, his cargo launch

The Corn King and the Cows

Ralph and Mary Ann Hodge

An island, with the right inhabitant, can be a small, fertile kingdom. As a character in the play The Slick of '76 *says: "Everything on our island is very small. Even our national island flower is small --- the seed."*

Ralph and Mary Ann Hodge on Tar Island

One day in 1945 a handsome man with a square chin, soft blue eyes and a teenage wife did an amazing thing. He bought the most quixotic of all properties. It was farm land isolated on an island. And since there was no bridge or ferry to the island, the farm land might as well have been a bog or a rock ledge. The couple did not see it that way. For the royal sum of $3,000, they took the deed for sixty acres of sandy loam on the sloping south side of Tar Island. They also got a ramshackle farmhouse that looked over a channel called The Narrows in the St. Lawrence near Rockport.

But Ralph Hodge knew what he was doing. He was buying back a piece of his past, redeeming it. He now owned the farm that his father George had only rented. Hodge could take off his shoes and sit in the parlour where his mother gave birth to him on an August day in 1916. The purchase could have been a disaster. But by working seven days a week and increasing their income through market gardening, the Hodges made the farm a success. Better yet, the two were such unique creations, they became part of the local folklore.

It was as though the two had a natural ability to make the river and the land yield its wealth. Ralph Hodge was a king of corn and muskrats on the St. Lawrence. His crop was fabled to be the sweetest in the Thousand Islands and his traps filled with muskrats like seeds in a pod. His wife Mary Ann left her mark as the small, indomitable woman who rowed a skiff through the islands, sometimes in rough seas, to sell vegetables door to door.

The river was no summer vacation for the Hodges. Many times they found themselves battling stormy waves in their small boat. And in February of 1986 the river showed that it felt no loyalty to the devotion of its people. The Hodge's thirty-four-year-old son Roger froze to death off the point of Tar Island. His snowmobile had run off the ice into dark, open water. "It was really cold that night," his mother says. "The wind was blowing. He turned the wrong way." Roger Hodge left a wife and three children on the island.

Still, Ralph and Mary Ann Hodge do not cling bitterly to memories of the bad times. A warm and friendly couple, under their care acres of corn, potatoes, beans, beets and lettuce thrived in the sun in the same spot where the Iroquois camped to fish eels.

Ralph's father George, as a renter of land, didn't understand the concept of owning property. George Hodge was a hard-working man with fourteen children --- four more children died while young --- and nine dairy cows. After milking the cows, Hodge senior rowed the milk to the cheese factory in Rockport, then set off for Club Island, where he worked for a dollar a day as the caretaker. His son would follow the same routine when he bought the farm.

Ralph Hodge remembers the time his father bought a monstrous black bull for fifteen dollars, an amount that took him two weeks to earn. The bull was too wild to be herded into the barn. The family decided it was better to let the rough, hunchbacked beast roam the island, since the water was as good as a fence. One winter day Hodge and a brother "saw this big thing in the ice. It was the bull. It drowned." The family had a practical solution to the catastrophe. "The bull was still warm. We hitched a team of horses up and pulled him out and slaughtered him and ate him."

Ralph Hodge left the island in his twenties. He was working at the Kingston shipyard as a driller building the wartime corvettes for the navy, when he met a fifteen-year-old girl in a restaurant. Hodge was not a man with doubt or hesitation. He decided that he wanted the girl as a wife. Mary Ann Lamure, an Indian from the Golden Lake Reservation, was a tiny but independent woman who looked even younger than she was.

After a brief courtship, Hodge said, "I looked her right in the eye and said, 'Would you like to get engaged?' " The girl's response was simple and full of the wisdom of an adult. "I'm too young."

Hodge wouldn't listen. He prodded her. "Make up your mind." He bought her an engagement ring and a wedding ring of bright gold. She resisted the temptation and threw the gold defiantly into the fire of a stove. The girl was convinced that marriages did not work. Hodge did not give up, however. After a two-week acquaintance, the two were married in 1943 with the young bride muttering under her breath, "I'll get married and maybe it will be a lifetime." Someone should have told her not to worry. Forty-five years later, after raising seven children, she says, "I guess we made it."

Yet, in the beginning, when the future was still unknown, the Hodges needed a place to start. They returned to the old family farm that was languishing on the island. They picked an apple from a tree that never noticed the land had been abandoned. They peered through the slits in the boarded windows and decided that independence was another word for an island farm. Hodge had one shock, however, when he became landowner. His family had always rented farm land and never held a deed. "I thought I owned the farm," Hodge says, "and then I started paying taxes. I never thought I had to pay taxes on my own property."

The farm was purchased from Edna Andress, one of the Root clan from Grenadier Island and wife of the famous Rockport boatbuilder Eddy Andress. One day at the end of October the new landowners carted their possessions to the Rockport dock to make their move. The scow scheduled to take them across the water never came. Undeterred, the two spread their mattress on the dock and bedded down under the river stars. When Hodge woke up in the morning, he turned to his wife and found her transformed. Her raven hair was silvered with frost as though she had aged thirty years overnight. The dock was dusted with a light, snowlike covering. "We didn't mind the cold," Hodge says, "till we got out of

The islands in winter

the blankets." The pair knocked on Eddy Andress' door to claim their ride to the island, but the boat builder, like a medieval host of a castle, insisted on observing proper courtesy. "I ain't moving you till you have your breakfast," he told the Hodges and ushered them inside for a meal.

After settling at the island farm, Hodge found that his neighbours were as generous as the earth and the sun. He only had enough money for a second cow to add to the fourteen-year-old relic that his father gave him. But, with the carefree words "I don't mind helping a young man out," Albert Hunt insisted that Hodge take two cows and pay him later. When the two men ferried the cows to the island, Hunt had another inspiration. He said to Hodge without ceremony, "You just as well might have two more." However, Hunt was crafty. He wanted to help Hodge and himself at the same time. Hunt made a secret deal with Hodge that the farmer would make payments now and then directly to him. That way Hunt could spend the money that he never saw again if it fell into the hands of his cautious wife.

Hodge's cattle, raised on the island, soon became amphibious creatures. They learned to swim the slim channel when they came and went from pastures on the mainland. One time Hodge was leading his small herd of eleven cattle from the mainland to the channel. He asked a neighbour to help to steer them into the water. However, the cattle were thinking faster than Hodge. "You should see them go into the river. They knew they were coming home," he says. Other times the beef cattle would "blat" to the dairy cattle on the island. The dairy cattle "blatted" back. With those comforting signals, the beef cattle flew into the water like ducks. "You never had to say anything to them. You'd think they were educated."

On one occasion Hodge came home from the tavern and decided to inspect his herd. The number had increased miraculously and Hodge stared in bewilderment. The herd was twice as large as it should have been. The answer lay in the magic of hormones --- which also dictate behaviour in the social world. A purebred herd of a dozen cattle had swum the six hundred meters downstream from Caiger's Point, heroically inspired by Hodge's big, lusty bull. "There was one cow in heat," Hodge says, "and they all took off. We had a heck of a time getting them all back." Hodge's bull was worth a fortune in hormones, but the farmer never encouraged it to lure any more young cows to the island.

Another time the Hodges sold a short-winded horse and forced the animal to swim across to the mainland where its new home was. Poncho the pony --- who also had hormones to worry about --- couldn't bear the heartbreak of being left behind. "The son of a gun took off and swam after the horse."

Then the Hodges bought a black-and-white team of horses, called Star and Buck, for plowing. The team belonged to two brothers, who each owned one. One brother had been killed after he was struck by a train. "I've got the nicest team you'd ever want," the surviving brother told Hodge. For one hundred and sixty dollars, plus another fifteen dollars for a wagon, the farmer had a team. But Star and Buck had other ideas. They were not particularly keen to get in the traces and plow, which was hot and heavy work. That meant that Hodge often spent till noon hour chasing Star and Buck around the field. Later, when Hodge bought a tractor to plow, Star and Buck were dumbfounded. Gone were the sweet mornings wiled away running through the field with Hodge. "They'd stand at the fence and watch me plow. They'd say to each other, 'What's he doing?' " Hodge says. "They'd hate to see us leave the farm. They would stand at the fence at the river till we came back. I suppose they were lonesome and felt they shouldn't be left alone." Both horses lived over twenty-five years.

As soon as the Hodges learned that they could make money selling vegetables, they set to work. For the first two years, before they bought a five-horsepower boat engine, Mary Ann Hodge rowed the vegetables three times a week to Rockport and around the islands. The smallest child sat in the boat beside her. One day she landed on an island and a customer asked her if she knew where she was. "See that flag," he said, "You're in the United States." That meant that her vegetables were contraband and she was a corn and tomato smuggler. But the islander bought the vegetables because they were the best corn and potatoes that he had ever seen.

Mary Ann made her rounds in the river and, in spite of her fear of water, never wore a life jacket. "I figured, if the river was going to take me, it would take me," she says. Sometimes the swells were so big that they rose higher than her head. One time a storm came that was so fierce, she couldn't get around the windward side of Tar Island. She didn't go home. Her solution was navigate the leeward side. Neighbours said to her later, "Did you know you were in a hurricane?"

If Hodge did not appreciate his wife's determination yet, he learned the day that she hitched the team by herself and drove the horses to Rockport and back across the ice. Mary Ann Hodge had never hitched or driven the team before. Her only mistake was putting the horses in reverse position, with their heads turned together. The result was that they ran at a frantic clip like mice on a treadmill.

Mary Ann Hodge also hunted deer with the boys on Grenadier Island and excelled as a trapper. Her muskrat pelts attracted attention because they were expertly skinned and stretched. Hodge swells with pride and admiration for his wife. "I wish you could see her skin a 'rat. She can skin a 'rat faster than I can."

Hodge will not forget the first time he laid a trap for a muskrat. It was his boyhood initiation into river life. He was thirteen years old and knew a spot where a small muskrat had the habit of climbing out of the water onto a tree. His father let him set the trap himself without instructions. The boy made a mistake. He set the trap so that the animal could break its leg and get free. "I said, Dad, I got a leg." Hodge senior replied to the lad with wry backwoods humour, "That's no good. You've got to get the whole 'rat."

Tar Island

River of Sensation, River of Desire

June Senecal Hodge

Down the road of the river is a house in a pocket of rock on an island where the people are captives of wind and current and ice. But far from feeling shackled and confined, these two think that other folk live behind the dull walls of a prison...

June Hodge

Grenadier Island wouldn't be the same without June Hodge. The families that farmed the island in the nineteenth century departed one by one. But she and her sweet, one-eyed husband Fred stayed behind in the oldest house on Grenadier. In that house, heated in the winter by a stove fed with island wood, the Hodges raised five hot-blooded children. From the porch championed by three birdhouses, within earshot of chimes that ring in the wind from three trees, the Hodges have kept watch on the river for more than half a century.

Now in her seventies, the bright-eyed woman with the thatch of white hair was born a Senecal. The Senecals farmed on Grenadier in the nineteenth century along with key island families like the Roots, Burtches, Fishes, Pooles, Buells, Elliotts, Mallorys and Masseys. Many people remember them and the wise old man of the river, Ed Senecal. But now only Hodge, her husband and her brother Beverly keep the winter stoves burning on the island.

"I'm a river rat," says June Hodge with tough pride and confidence. The river is more of a country to her, particularly since she was born a water babe with tangled citizenship. "I was born on a houseboat on the American side. It gives me a bit of trouble, but I've got it straightened out now."

Hodge was born in 1918 in a houseboat tied at the dock in Alexandria Bay. Her father, Paul Senecal, a Canadian trapper and fisherman, married an American woman. It was only by accident that June was born a citizen of United States waters. The family returned to Grenadier Island after her birth to live beside her grandparents, Anthony and Agnes Senecal, who farmed and also ran the Angler's Inn on the north shore. One of twelve children --- including Richard Senecal, the trapper interviewed earlier in *River Rats* --- Hodge was educated in a one-room schoolhouse now boarded against the sun's rays. Inside the schoolhouse the children of the island, including her own, were taught.

In 1934, after the sixteen-year-old girl married Fred, ground-keeper at the island's nine-hole golf course, Hodge moved into the two-hundred-year-old frame house. She settled down to the chores of a housewife, raising five children and earning extra money by washing and ironing sheets for the summer residents.

At first the sheets were washed in a hand-cranked machine. Only later did Hodge graduate to the technology of a washing machine powered by a gas engine. The price for washing and ironing a sheet rose over the years from ten cents each to thirty-five cents. Some of the men had fourteen or fifteen white dress shirts which had to be ironed as smooth as ice. "I washed all day and ironed all night," Hodge recalls.

Life on an island was all the world that Hodge wanted. She couldn't imagine what kind of barbaric pleasure people could get from the strange wilderness of a town or city. On Grenadier, life was orderly and sensible. The shopping was done from a catalogue and the purchases carried across the river by her father, who operated the island's post office from the family's kitchen. When Hodge was a child, the doctor still hurried to the island by boat to deliver the children. These days Hodge's children and grandchildren bring the groceries to the island and chop the firewood for the winter. Without a motorboat of her own --- she has a skiff she rows to Tar Island and back --- the next generation is her contact with the mainland, her safety line. "We've dwindled down to three people who stay on the island all winter," Hodge says. "Sometimes it gets a little scary when you think about it in bad weather."

The chill of winter can dig into the bones of an old, un-insulated house on the river. The wind outside, gusting, changing direction, rising and falling, makes the heat of the kitchen stove seem temperamental. "It's hard to keep it at a happy medium. We're either too hot or too cold." The fuel for the stove is still cut on the island, though the Hodges also burn discarded wood, such as old dock lumber, soft and dry after being reprieved from years in the river. "In the winter you want good, hard oak," says the expert.

The Hodges have to be careful what kind of wood they burn. A fire set loose on an island has a life of its own and cannot be stopped. "I won't burn pine. It soots the chimney up and I'm scared to death of a fire. If the house caught on fire, the only thing you can do is get out." And Hodge knows. When she was eight years old she watched a fire burn the schoolhouse to the ground like a malicious spirit. The men had to raise another school building in its place.

Hodge thinks the winters are warmer these days, the ice on the river no longer as thick. When Fred Hodge was twenty he drove a car across the ice from Grenadier to Mallorytown Landing. That foolhardiness makes him chuckle in times of thinner ice. "Isn't that wild to think of ice that good?" June Hodge marvels. "It must be the pollution ... or the currents are different." Still, in the winter, with the wind lifting puffs of snow off the ice like smoke, the ice is welcome. June Hodge skiis across a bridge of frozen water. She takes a path from Grenadier to Tar Island, where Fred's brother Ralph lives, and from Tar to the mainland. "We love it when the ice is good so you can come and go when you want."

"We're the lucky ones," Hodge says. "Not that we're rich. We bought this old house years ago. We're sitting on a gold mine." The impractical island land that put farmers like the Senecals and the Roots and the Buells out of business is now valuable real estate. Yet Hodge and her husband have no desire to sell and move to the mainland. The thought is monstrous, barbaric, worse than losing her citizenship again. The river is her real treasure, the pure, unextracted Rhinegold of her heart.

"There'd be nothing to look at," she insists. "The river flows by. You watch the ice go out little by little." Hodge watches the changes of the fall and the winter and the spring written in the freezing and thawing of the river. In the spring she climbs a hill on the deserted golf course looking southward and watches the icebreaker clear the main channel. One year a crowd of skeptics collected on the hill for the battle of the giants between the icebreaker and a

June and Fred Hodge on Grenadier Island

powerful sheet of ice. "The minute there's an open hole in the ice you watch for the ducks," she explains. "Then the geese start flying."

"It would kill me to live in the back country and not be near the river."

Even spring is radically different on an island.

The wind changes direction. It no longer sweeps out of the north or the west with the old cynicism of winter. The wind blows from the northeast down the channel toward Grenadier, warming the earth for the tiger lilies and purple swamp flowers in front of the Hodge's home.

From an island, spring comes with the violence of a calamity or great upheaval. The shell of ice on the river rends, breaks, cracks with an exuberance that makes the land seem weak in its pale and sober thawing.

Sometimes, Hodge says, the spring wind blows for too long from the same direction. She gets tired of the monotony. But then she can lie in her bed waiting confidently for the river to change. She can hear the broken ice rattle and jostle impatiently. The cakes of ice thrash and burst with sound in a pantomime of harvest. She has heard the cool, unfevered clamour since she was a girl. As a woman in her seventies she can hear the ice from her bedroom at night and again in the morning.

The sound of the river thawing quickens the blood with excitement, like the first flock of geese, the first wildflower, the first day of school. "When the ice is going out you lay there and hear it tinkling," she says. Her voice is thick with admiration.

Grenadier Island

Shaped by the Andress Skiff Mold

Ethel Andress Johnston

There is a mercy in time that comes to gentle folk, the settlers by the side of the river, the craftsmen. They are the people that adversity could not twist or cripple...

Ethel Andress Johnston in her St. Lawrence skiff

In the spring of 1920 a three-year-old girl stood on the farm where she was born at Kerry Point, east of Rockport. She watched the back of her eight-year-old brother Elmer striding down the lane. It was a moment of upheaval fixed in a child's frightened mind. The family was moving. The girl saw her brother hugging the cat in his arms as he trudged behind a wagon loaded with possessions. The little girl ran after her brother and the wagon. She was called back by her mother standing in the doorway.

That was the decisive year that William Edward Andress, a generous, light-hearted man who loved children and had the giddy, impish humour of the Andress clan, transplanted his family to Rockport. There Eddy Andress began a boatbuilding business that is as much a part of the islands as Noah's ark is of the Bible. Coming to the river liberated the craftsman in Andress. He would no longer build St. Lawrence skiffs in the barn during the dark of winter. Andress raised a boat works and started a tradition that his descendants still follow in Rockport. But Andress left more behind than the skiffs, the fossil remains of his life. The image of the gleeful old shipwright stuck in the minds of people up and down the river.

After leaving the farm, Andress went to work in the Rockport marine shop belonging to German immigrant Fred Huck. In the fall of 1920 he bought from Captain John Carnegie, a tour boat operator in Rockport since 1888, the big white house on the highest hill in the riverside hamlet. Eddy Andress wanted to build boats like his father William F. Andress. The elder Andress built sleighs and buggies in the hamlet of Caintown, north of Brockville, before

Rockport, with St. Brendan's Roman Catholic church

he moved to La Rue Mills by the river in 1902 and started to build boats.

That same year William's brother George, who had the dark-brown eyes and bushy eyebrows of the Andresses, moved to Gananoque to build skiffs. With George in Gananoque, the Andress boat works were spreading along the shoreline. If building skiffs were a military campaign, the Andresses could not have planned it better. George bought a house at the mouth of the Gananoque River, where his granddaughter, Olive Stevenson, still lives. The boatbuilding strain was unshakeable in the Gananoque Andresses, and George's son Ray also made a name for himself as an expert carver of duck decoys. As a boatbuilder, Ray Andress was "a perfectionist," his daughter says. "He didn't make any money because it just had to be perfect."

In Rockport during the 1920s Eddy Andress was building skiffs and mahogany cruisers with workmen like Clifford Hunt, who would soon start his own business with help from Andress. The craftsman inherited from his father skiff forms used as a mould to build the frame of the boat. Carefully, through the mist of a steamer that helped to bend the cedar strips, the boat evolved from a skeleton of white oak beams. Then, after working all day in the boat works, the men retired upstairs to play cards. There the curls of men were clipped. Hunt, who also played music on the violin to pass the evenings, wielded the barber's scissors.

Andress' daughter Ethel remembers the smell of fresh lumber, the soft, pliant sound of wood being shaved and hammered in the boat works. Andress clamped a cedar board in the vice and let his daughter plane it as a game. The shavings fell to the floor in long, flowing curls. She tucked them under her cap as though she had blond ringlets. "The shavings always smelled so nice, especially when it was cedar."

Ethel and her brother were given pieces of wood which they sharpened with a spoke shaver to a pointed prow. They hammered a nail into the front end and tied on a piece of string. Then they towed their great, worldly boats back and forth along the dock.

Ethel was a restless child. She swam and climbed the big tree by the house and then clambered over the roof of the porch. She played on a large, layered outcropping of pink granite by the house. She and her brother made a game of cleaning the skiffs their father rented to summer guests. The boats had to be scrubbed and rinsed after the guests had been fishing. The children soaped the inside, then pulled the plug in the bottom of the craft. The unsinkable skiff filled with water like a pitcher dipped in a well. The brother and sister dove off the side of the skiff and prolonged the chore half the day.

Meanwhile Andress was building his reputation on the river. He made cottages and boathouses and docks among the islands and built tour boats. He ferried people back and forth across the river from Brockville, Alexandria Bay and Gananoque in boats that he built. The boats were named *Elva*, his daughter's middle name, and ranked I, II and III.

Andress's only son Elmer --- an image cut from the father's gleeful mould --- was being groomed to continue the tradition. He helped in the shop, he says, "as soon as I could hold a clinching iron." When the son was sixteen, the father built an eighteen-foot cedar skiff. The skiff had a cantankerous one-cylinder engine that took "hours" of cranking to start. When the son was eighteen he was tour boat captain on the Andress-built *Elva II*. In 1946 --- a bustling year when the Andresses built twenty boats --- the name of the boat works was changed to W.E. Andress and Son.

Eddy Andress was a sunny if sometimes quick-tempered man whose anger passed quickly. And he was also a fast wit who liked to tease the visitors with strange explanations. As he drove the tour boat past the sheer rock face near Club Island called the Palisades, he had his own way of describing the unusual depth of the channel. "No one ever drowns here. They starve before they reach bottom."

The visitors would ask like school children about the water that frothed over fast-moving eddies. Andress was happy to explain. "The water froths because the fish are taking a bath," he would say.

He also had an explanation for the bright-green colour of the water at Benson's Rift. The man whose house was there had an Irish cook, Andress said. And the water was green where the woman washed her feet.

As Andress grew older his strength was as enduring as a tree rooted in rock. He loved his family, his community. He had lost two fingers to a buzz saw and nicked a third. Age could not bend his frame and Andress --- nicknamed Hurry-up Eddy --- never lost his childlike enthusiasm. Still, the years were catching up. His daughter remembers that his head would nod sleepily at the wheel of his boat. He hit the same shoal at the foot of Grenadier Island three times.

Andress died on December 30, 1981 at the age of ninety-five.

His daughter Ethel lives in Rockport, where her son Dick works at the Andress Boatworks owned by her daughter Wendy and her son-in-law Art Merkley. And two or three times a week Eddy Andress' daughter escapes from the current of mundane cares. She pushes her St. Lawrence skiff away from the dock and picks up the oars.

"It's such a relaxing feeling. The skiff is so buoyant and it has spoon oars. You don't have to lift them out of the water. You just skip them over the top.

"People think of rowing as work, strenuous exercise. It isn't. It's relaxing.

"The ripple of the water under the skiff --- if you're coming into the wind --- it's almost like music on the side of the boat."

The skiff was built by her great-uncle George ninety years ago.

Rockport

Boy in a Boat with Chorus Girls

Robert Gareth Service

There is a joke in the Thousand Islands that if you look over the side of the boat you can see the border painted on the bottom of the river. Some people look. But then others believe that the line makes the difference between Canadians and Americans...

Robert Gareth Service

On a day in October Gareth Service is hunched over a canvas in his garage. The retired newspaper editor is working on his new passion, painting pictures of the ducks that he once hunted in the fall. It was his son-in-law, the irrepressible Hunter Grimes --- the river rat who entranced and then married his quiet daughter Martha --- who prodded Service into picking up a paint brush. He tried a duck scene on the river. He was amazed when his first painting sold in an auction. Nothing was holding him back now, he realized.

Actually, there had never been anything holding him back. Change and openness were a way of life on the river for Service and others. Before the St. Lawrence Seaway and the Thousand Islands bridge existed the boundary between Canada and the United States was only a polite formality. The typical greeting was a good-day-and-how-are-you exchange between people who shared the same river. The river families were not affected by abstract political distinctions that now divide the St. Lawrence into two halves. Their choices were made practically and by inclination, not by nationality.

And Robert Gareth Service had the river state of mind. Born in Alexandria Bay in 1910 to a Canadian father and an American mother --- "I just happened to be born here in Alexandria Bay" --- one day he would teach himself to be both a newspaper writer and a wildlife painter. From those early days of informal borders he remembers crossing the river with his father, who ran the family-owned grocery store in Rockport.

The ancient United States customs guard was often posted in his dock-side chair in Alexandria Bay when Newell Tilden Service arrived in a boat with his son. There were no cold, clinical questions to answer, no litany of sins from the man-made morality of trade and commerce. The official might ask the elder Service to sign a book in the back room. He might wave him through with a hearty "good day." After all, Service was a citizen who belonged as much in Alexandria Bay on the American side as across the water in Rockport.

What made the Services such cheerful, adaptable hybrids? It may have started with Robert Henry Service, a roving Scotsman who passed through Ireland in the 1800s. He immigrated with his family to a farm on the St. Lawrence just west of Rockport. From then on the Services could not decide which side of the border suited them best. The Service family moved to Alexandria Bay and then worked in a mammoth tourist home, the Thousand Islands House, which has now been replaced by a riverfront hospital. Service and his wife Zelpha Jeroy, a superb cook, prospered and bought the St. James Hotel in Alexandria Bay. The Services sold the hotel --- for reasons his grandson does not know --- to buy a grocery store and three-storey hotel in Rockport at the turn of the century.

When Gareth Service was two or three years old his father, Newell Tilden Service, moved his family to the Union-Jack country of Rockport --- though his wife, Edith May White, insisted that she was a Stars-and-Stripes American. For a while, the family also lived in Kingston, but the twin river hamlets of Rockport and Alexandria Bay became the magnetic poles of Gareth Service's youth.

As soon as school ended in the spring, Gareth and his sister were packed onto the side-wheel steamer the *Britannic* in Kingston and dropped off in Rockport. There the French-Canadian steamer picked up a cargo load of cheddar cheese from the Rockport Cheese Factory, bound for Montreal. "Everybody on it spoke French, which enthralled my sister and I, and the purser only had one hand."

The seventy-five-year-old cheese factory was destroyed by fire on June 3, 1932. A ferry from Alexandria Bay steamed towards the factory that day without the usual screen in the smokestack to catch the sparks. A spark set the cedar shingles on the factory roof ablaze. A fire boat that rushed from the Bay was unable to quench the flames, though it had an inexhaustible supply of water from the river.

Ethel Johnston remembers the factory and the fire. As a teenager she rowed from her house in Rockport to the waterside door of the factory to get curds as a treat. She took off her straw hat and the workers at the factory filled it for her with free curds. She recalls the farmers from the islands bringing their huge milk cans across the water every day. Among them was Ralph Hodge's father coming from nearby Tar Island at eight in the morning. George Hodge stands out in Johnston's mind because the other island farmers had motor boats and he alone rowed his milk to Rockport. Once the factory burned, it was not replaced.

While Gareth Service was growing up the Rockport Cheese Factory had not yet caught the fatal wind-blown cinder on its roof. It was still producing its rich, yellow crop, as fertile as the boyhood summers on the St. Lawrence. And the Thousand Islands bridge --- which joined the land and sundered the river into political halves --- had not been built.

In his grandfather's gaslit hotel in Rockport --- started by Charles Cornwall in 1848 --- the boy moved among a flock of chorus girls, dancers, and husband and wife comedy teams from the New York City vaudeville.

The entertainers would sing at the piano in the well-stocked hotel library. They amused the boy with tales from the classics of the theatre. The books that they left lying on tables intrigued him with the lure of knowledge. He had no idea that the spark of inspiration would catch, that he would become a self-taught newspaper reporter and, in his later years, a wildlife artist.

A fight promoter from New York taught the boy how to box. The women entertainers taught him love and desire and the meaning of the word hormones. One of Service's tasks as a teenager was to row a load of chorus girls across the water in a St. Lawrence skiff while they trolled for northern pike with a hand-held line. Service laughs at the memory of the exotic and worldly wise entertainers teasing the young boy. His reward, if the fishing was good, was a peck on the cheek. "I remember I'd fall in love every summer with a different one."

Service remembers his grandfather as a "sporty" man with a long, drooping mustache and a passion for fast horses --- the type of bold and lively man who knew what entertainers needed in a summer retreat.

With a horse named Bob, after himself, the elder Service swept recklessly down the icy country roads in the winter. He loved the speed. "On those back roads you used to tip over," recalls the grandson. "We tipped over several times. Fortunately, the horse wasn't hurt."

Service had other close escapes as a boy. He remembers the time that he almost drowned in the St. Lawrence. Through the clear water someone spotted the boy lying on the bottom of the river near the dock in Rockport. The man dove in to save him. Service was given the typical cartoon-like revival treatment. "They rolled me on a barrel. I can still remember coming to and the water spurting out of me. But it didn't affect me. I survived."

In 1924, Robert Service had a stroke and could not manage the hotel. Newell Service took over, but Prohibition in the United States, which made river taverns on the Canadian side profitable, affected the character of the place. Boatloads of parched Americans arrived in Rockport on tour boats. The beds were taken out of the hotel rooms and replaced with tables and chairs.

To meet Canadian law, a sandwich had to be supplied with the beer. Edith May was determined not to be a drudge in the kitchen making endless throw-away sandwiches. She wrapped the sandwiches tightly so that they could be used as props over and over again. The sandwiches had a long life. "When the sandwiches got too dilapidated, she'd have to make new ones," Service says.

Service, though his family lived in Rockport, went to the closest high school, in Alexandria Bay, staying with his fully Americanized set of grandparents. He worked in a pharmacy and became a correspondent for the *Watertown Daily Times*.

Service was in Alexandria Bay when two Canadian aviators crashed in a snowbank in 1939, creating an international incident. The Stars and Stripes, unlike the Union Jack, had not entered the war yet. Service was at the centre of a great story. His stories and photos went onto the wire system to the nation's newspapers. The bridge had been built across the river the previous year and bridge mastermind Grant Mitchell took the aviators to his home, using the event, Service says, to help publicize the Thousand Islands.

Service had a wife and family, but the romantic --- and he later realized one-sided --- tales of the war he wrote from interviews with American soldiers had an effect. They stirred those wandering, hybrid genes of the Services. A gleeful draftee in 1942, Service fought until he injured himself escaping the enemy from a building. He jumped twenty feet to the cobblestones with ammunition belts adding weight to his body.

Service eventually returned to newspapers, as a reporter and editor for the *Watertown Daily Times*. He also stayed a child of the whole, undivided St. Lawrence. His mind was as open as it once was to the chorus girls and the vaudeville entertainers and the fast rides down an icy road.

Thus a day in October finds Service with a paint brush in hand, his river rat of a son-in-law at his elbow. The two are absorbed in the task. Service relies on help from others to find the right shade of colour for his palette, since he is colour blind.

"You can't be afraid to paint," Service advises. "If you're afraid to work paint, you'll never be a painter."

Service and his son-in-law fret over the way the waves look on the canvas. Something is wrong. The waves are too stiff, too formal. They do not have the capriciousness of the river.

"You don't want it to look like a plowed field," Grimes says with concern. Grimes himself plays his role on the river with whimsy. He is dressed like a scarecrow with patches of flesh showing through the wild rips in his jeans.

Service does not argue. He labours with the tip of a brush. The smooth, civilized line of the wave disappears. There are no conventions to hold him down. He can change as easily as he once crossed the river from Alexandria Bay to Rockport. He alters the white spume on the crest of the wave. Now the wave inspires. Now it is ragged and torn. It is a boundary that has been broken, as free in the wind as a flag without a country.

Alexandria Bay

The *Britannic*

Courtesy of the Museum of the Great Lakes, Kingston

'They Don't Know My Right Name'

Bud Hunt

Some people earn respect for their force and vitality. Others earn respect for the gentle flow of their lives, like a current of creation that makes itself felt without the need of glaciers and volcanoes...

Bud Hunt

A woman climbs the steep lawn towards Bud Hunt with worry in her eyes. The *Flox* is long overdue on the river. The woman wonders if the *Flox*, a 1912 motor launch said to be the oldest of its kind in the Thousand Islands, has broken down. Bud Hunt, calmly sitting under two fraternal willow trees in Ivy Lea, a stubble of white on his chin, reassures the woman. He has been on the river since he was born and takes life with a confident grace.

The *Flox*, with Paul Webb at the helm, will come eventually to the small marina. There are a dozen slips which Hunt rents by his home to keep his ties with the river and tradition.

"They don't know my right name," he says. His first name has long been forgotten on the river. "Call me Bud Hunt."

Hunt traces his ancestry back to his great-grandfather, Henry Hunt, who built a home on one hundred and fifty acres stretching in a long strip from the river at Ivy Lea to where Highway 401 cuts through the countryside. Henry Hunt also ran a boarding house in the summer named The Willows after the towering willow copse that surrounds the property. Now only two enormous willows stand side by side at the edge of the water. Time has not been idle.

"All the willow trees used to be whole until that truck tipped over on the parkway and the acid came down and killed them all. It killed all the trees down through here. It cleaned them out."

The Ivy Lea farm passed to Bud Hunt's father, Philip, who ran a dairy farm with twenty-two cows on the tipsy, rocky land that cannot be farmed profitably in such small patches today. Out behind the barn were two good springs that ran year round. Sometimes in the morning and the evening his son and daughter transported bottles of milk across the water to customers in cottages.

"Milk was ten cents a quart and cream was a dollar a quart. Milk-fed chickens ready to put in the pan were a dollar apiece." But then regulations were established for pasteurization and it was not practical for the small Hunt farm to buy pasteurization equipment.

World War Two came along and claimed men from the river, including Bud Hunt. He joined the Canadian Navy in 1939 when he was twenty to work in the boiler rooms of ships. Hunt kept the engines running during escort duty in the Atlantic, and was shipped to the Pacific in an armed cruiser.

"Hot in the Pacific?" he responds. "I've seen it one hundred and twenty degrees in the boiler room." The Navy took him around the world's oceans, and Hunt returned to the Thousand Islands, to the family farm in Ivy Lea, where he has lived ever since.

"In those days people stayed in the islands a lot longer than they do now. People stayed the whole summer," he says. Hunt and his wife Jean operated a river grocery store with gas pumps in Ivy Lea. At first the customers were as plentiful as the fish. The Hunts would have to stock a hundred loaves of bread on the weekend. But times changed. The islanders came for two weeks and shopped at grocery stores in larger centres. The people on sail boats, Hunt reflects, brought enough provisions to keep their solitude unbroken. And it was cheaper to buy gas on the American side. Eventually the Hunts closed their store and gas pumps.

But in spite of the changes, the river stays the same, Hunt says, sitting on his breakneck front lawn under the willows to let the cool summer breeze blow over him. Susie, the small white poodle, takes a friendly lunge at Donald, a Muscovy duck, who was sleeping with his red face swivelled and tucked into white feathers. The duck was rescued on the front lawn, Hunt explains. "He came in here one day last winter. I looked out and he was sitting under a tree." At first no one could get close to the refugee fowl. "He used to sit in a timber under the dock. He got frozen one night and I had to come down and cut him out." The operation cost Donald a few feathers and most of his dignity. "He got disgusted over that and left for a day. He came back later." Hunt has been feeding the duck corn twice a day and the duck has learned to tolerate people.

Hunt breaks off to look east down the river for Webb and the *Flox*. The woman comes near again, concerned. Hunt offers more reassurance. Many times he has pulled sailboats off shoals, including the popular shoal at Goose Island --- "They're on it pretty near every day," Jean Hunt adds --- but the *Flox* is in capable hands, if slow. Hunt recalls the winter that he and two relatives had to go out on the ice to rescue an islander who stayed too long and was trapped between the ice floes.

He waits patiently. His faith is unruffled.

The river has delivered many things. Hunt hoists a prize paddle. It had to be scraped of the garish yellow paint laid over the wood. The paddle rode in on a wave by itself. That reminds Hunt of a river man who uses the river as an alibi for his pilfering. The man had a grindstone that a neighbour thought looked familiar. "Well," said the man with a characteristic long drawl, "it just floated in on the river one day." Hunt recalls one island farmer with a row of toasters which he also claims came floating in the river. Hunt left the paddle in the barn for years until moved to restore it and put it to use.

"That's my pride and joy," Hunt says, leading the way to his antique mahogany skiff-putt which once belonged to a mayor of Ottawa. In 1949, the sixteen-foot boat, discovered sunken in an old boathouse with its planks and ribs soft with rot, was given to Hunt. "I rescued it and brought it home. It hung in the barn for thirty-five years."

Then Hunt decided to mend the motorized skiff. He replaced the planks and stripped the red paint off the hull, the grey paint from the inside. Underneath was healthy mahogany and cedar. Hunt discovered that the space between the planks inside was sealed with elegant strips of brass. The original brass and metal one-cycle engine, built by the St. Lawrence Engine Company in Brockville, worked the first time. "Oh, she'll go. I don't worry about the engine. She'll kick over. The engine runs like a clock." The rudder turns by a small spoke wheel on the starboard side. So now, thanks to Hunt, the wood glistens and the brass shines under the sun.

Hunt turns and scans the eastern horizon. In the distance is a small boat attracting the attention of other boats. It draws a small flotilla in its wake as though there were royalty aboard. The boat is flying the Union Jack. "Well, there she is. Here comes the *Flox*," Hunt says with a delighted laugh. "She's just steaming right along." Hunt scrambles down to the dock and hollers at Webb across the water, "Come in and have some Coke and oil."

Ivy Lea

The *Flox*

Hot Rivets and High Spirits

Bruce Dingman

Bridges are heroic creations. In Norse mythology the gods rode their steeds over Bifrost, a bridge of fire. The Thousand Islands bridge never glowed with flames, but it was more than cold steel to the men who worked on it...

Bruce Dingman

The men on the Thousand Islands bridge were not exactly old Norse gods flying through the clouds. But then, working high on the girders of the unfinished arches, they did not have their feet on the ground either.

Up that high, the river and the islands were spread like a kingdom that is free for the taking. The men pitched the hot rivets as though it were a sport. A refinement was added to the game. The men waited for a tour boat full of wide-eyed visitors glorying in a meek and deferential river. Then they pitched a hot rivet through the air ten feet in front of the bow. There would be a small explosion of steam hissing in devilment and a burst of boyish glee on the bridge. Then the dizzying, dangerous work would resume.

When the Canadian span of the Thousand Islands bridge was being built through 1937 and into 1938, Bruce Dingman was there. A lad from the prairies, he worked with the fearless Mohawk rivet gangs high in the air. His life melded with the steel girders that linked Canada and the United States, changing forever the nature of the Thousand Islands.

A clear-eyed man with a cane and a neat, close-cropped white mustache, Dingman lives with his wife Dorothy in the homestead on the river built by his wife's kinfolk, the Shipmans. Just around a bend in the river to the east is Ivy Lea and then the slender arch of the bridge that was dedicated on August 18, 1938. By chance, that was the same day that the film *The Wizard of Oz* premiered and the world was introduced to another engineering feat, the fabulous yellow brick road. The praises of the more mundane bridge of iron were sung by Canadian Prime Minister William Lyon Mackenzie King and United States President Franklin D. Roosevelt. Dingman stood thirty feet away while the politicians enjoyed the applause. Roosevelt, noting the peace between the two nations, said, "The best symbol of common sense is a bridge." For his efforts, Dingman was given a small bronze medallion of the structure.

Bruce Dingman was born in 1909 in Red Deer, Alberta where the rolling foothills of the Rocky Mountains begin the disruption of the prairie flatlands. In 1929, in the heart of the Great Depression, the twenty-year-old man left Red Deer for six years of gypsylike existence riding railway boxcars from job to job. "You'd pick up a dollar here and a dollar there and keep moving," he says. "You either did that or you starved."

Dingman passed close to the St. Lawrence on boxcars but never noticed the Thousand Islands until a construction boss who hired him in Glace Bay promised, "If you get to the Thousand Islands, we're going to build a bridge there. There's a job for you there." The construction of the bridge had languished as a project since American hotel owner W. Gilbert Freeman first suggested the idea in 1926. But then the Depression spurred the project as a way to create work. So Dingman, never realizing the commitment he was making to a life by the river, clambered onto a freight car again. He landed one night in July in 1936, a year before construction of the bridge began. That night he met Thomas Truesdell loading bags of cement in the village of Lansdowne. Truesdell told him, "There's no steel work yet, but if you want a job, I've got a job for you."

Dingman started by loading bags of cement for the bridge, which were carted down to the river and across the water on a scow. Dingman calculates those days by the 110,000 bags of cement that he helped move. Next he cut timber on Hill Island for the piles that held the bridge before the permanent supports. The heat of cutting timber --- in spite of the cool water nearby --- was devastating. It was as bad as a mine. "You couldn't get a whiff of air. You just sweltered," Dingman recalls.

When the girders started to climb to the eventual two-hundred-and-twenty-foot peak of the towers, Dingman was hired as a high-rigger working with a Mohawk rivet team. The Mohawks were clannish, says Dingman, but he found them friendly and liked their "down-to-earth" spirit.

Starting in the spring of 1937 and working through the winter months with three sweaters under his overalls, Dingman's job was the rivet catcher. The rivets were heated in a small, portable furnace until the iron was red hot. Then the rivet was grabbed with tongs and thrown to Dingman, who caught it in a funnel, plucked it out with a set of tongs and thrust the slug in the hole for the hammer team.

Dingman will never forget the arm of the Mohawk who pitched the rivets fifty feet or more. The rivet would hurtle in the air towards him "like a bullet," Dingman says. "He was a good-hearted soul. It would be beautiful how he'd handle the rivet." Sometimes the rivet would be thrown while Dingman was standing above. The hot metal would arc and practically drop in his funnel.

The height did not bother Dingman. He would climb up a girder tower to take pictures for people for a five-dollar fee, and he could look down and see the tiny but powerful eddies that swirl around the bridge in the channel.

But the height was still dangerous. One day Dingman and a crew were working on a tower when a platform near them dropped a few feet accidentally. A man named Angus McDonald lost his balance. "He just went over backwards," Dingman recalls. The workers watched in a trance as McDonald fell struggling in the air. "All the way down we could see the poor fellow. He was trying to get to the water --- but he landed on the rocks eight feet in." After the death, the only casualty on the project, the work stopped for the day and the men trudged home, defeated.

The workers took pride in the bridge and Dingman admits that there was some sadness when the task was finished. "When it was all done and I walked away, I felt bad --- but I had to head out. I couldn't hang around."

Dingman would be back, though. He met Dorothy Shipman, a charming girl from a river family, and married her in 1941. Then Dingman packed for the Second War World to serve for almost four years in the engine room of a submarine chaser and escort ship on the east coast. In 1974, the two returned to the Shipman homestead on the St. Lawrence to retire, with Dingman working as a fishing guide.

Dingman thinks the Thousand Islands bridge was built to last. He knows its structure as well as others know the arcane currents and swirls of the river. He roasted in the heat on the iron girders and froze in the chill. His sweat mingled with the St. Lawrence.

Dingman remembers the engineer who designed the structure said, "It will be there long after you're gone, and your children are gone and their children." Dingman does not doubt that. He knows the rivets that he plucked out of the air fifty years ago will not fall out.

On the St. Lawrence near Ivy Lea

The Thousand Islands bridge

'He Had Never Been Bullheading Before'

Dorothy Shipman Dingman

In Norse mythology the goddess Freyja was abducted by male giants and used for ransom, as often happens to women in the hands of men. However, even without the help of myths, marriage is a risky business...

Dorothy Shipman Dingman

At sixteen Dorothy Shipman impressed a man from the West. She was rich in intelligence, maturity and poise. The newcomer, a rider of Depression-era rails, was caught off guard and thought that the young girl was a "school-marm." On their first date, however, he learned that Dorothy Shipman came from authentic river stock. She knew the mucky side of the river like a farm girl knows the barn stalls.

The young couple went fishing for bullheads one evening in Knight's Creek. The slim, sly wisp of a creek coils around the one-hundred-and-fifty-metre rise of Fitzsimmons Mountain, pouring into the St. Lawrence near Shipman's Point, where the family had homesteaded on the shoreline in the 1850s.

"He had never been bullheading before," Dorothy says of her husband, Bruce Dingman. For all his worldly experience, he would have to learn about the river. "I thought it was really peculiar because I had to bait all his hooks for him.

"You have a nice long worm on the end of a hook. And when they're really biting good all you have to do is plunk the thing in there. And they'll grab it right off. And you pull for all you're worth over your head.

"If you don't, they'll fall off because they don't have a hook in their mouth. They're hanging onto the worm."

In 1941, the twenty-one-year-old Dorothy Shipman took the married name of Dingman without breaking her ties to the river. The Shipmans were a United Empire Loyalist clan which left Vermont in the eighteenth century when their loyalty to the British Crown became perilous for them. Family lore says that Daniel Shipman, Dorothy's great-great-great grandfather, hid in a cellar to save himself from the lynch mob that came to hang him with a rope. Daniel

Shipman brought his family --- and in one swoop, all his future, still unborn descendants --- north to safer country in Canada, in the Brockville and Maitland area.

In the 1800s, Dorothy's great-grandfather David Shipman and his brother Charles moved their families to two hundred acres of riverfront farm land east of Gananoque and Landon's Bay. Part of the property would later be sold for the resort known as the Glen House. Charles Shipman gave the family name to the spur of land that juts out into the river, called Shipman's Point.

David Shipman built the farmhouse in 1852 where the Dingmans live today. Guides started to bring their American customers across the water to dinners cooked by Shipman's wife Elizabeth Cross. The dinners were good enough to launch the family in the tourism business. Elizabeth did the cooking, with help from a daughter. In later years she was partly crippled after she broke both wrists and the bones were not set properly.

The farm passed from the Shipman patriarch to Freeman Nelson Shipman, the youngest of twelve children. Dorothy remembers her grandfather Freeman Shipman seen through the "angelic light" of childhood. He was a kind, hard-working man with white hair and a mustache.

"Every night before he went to bed he made the kindling with a long knife with two handles.

"When he was sick in bed I used to sit on the end of his bed and he'd show me pictures in the Bible --- which I have now --- and sing me songs."

Freeman Shipman had a slight build. After he started his tourism home he would row fourteen kilometres across the river to Clayton for guests. He would row one St. Lawrence skiff for the passengers and tow another behind for the luggage. Then he rowed the fourteen kilometres back to Canada with his small caravan.

Around the turn of the century he bought a steam-powered boat called *Riverview*. "Then he graduated to the gasoline engine."

Shipman also ran a farm with dairy cows, sheep, horses, chickens and turkeys. His barn is still standing, though the structure had to be lifted a few feet north when the Thousand Islands Parkway was built.

The tourism business was booming, so in 1895 Shipman built the sixteen-room house known in the family as the Annex. The building sits precariously close to the water like a boat ready to be launched at any moment. In the summer Dorothy and her husband move to its uninsulated rooms. The main house is only a few feet away.

Grandpa Shipman had an unlucky star over his aging head. One day the old man slid off the roof of the barn and flew to the ground. He fractured his skull. As well, while chopping wood one day, his old hands miscalculated and he cut his foot with the axe blade. Gangrene set in and he died, at seventy-eight years of age.

Kenneth Bruce Shipman, Freeman's son and Dorothy's father, took over. He was a cheerful and ingenious man known for his loud, distinct laugh. At one time the common joke in Gananoque was, "Kenneth Shipman's in town. I hear him laughing."

Dorothy was amazed at the inventiveness of her father, who carved cogwheels out of wood and built himself a clock. He also devised a scheme to stop the chickens from laying eggs on the beams, where they rolled off and smashed on the floor. The farmer built a timer out of a clock and connected it to a light. At the right hour, the light came on, and the hens retired to their nests to lay the eggs safely.

Kenneth Shipman built a third house on the property in 1919 and added a thirty-passenger tour boat, called the *Merry Widow III*, to the family enterprise. Dorothy remembers the 1920s as a joyful time, before the gloom of the Great Depression, when guests were open and carefree. There were fewer boats on the river and the Thousand Islands bridge --- which Dorothy's husband helped build --- did not exist. The smaller tour boats like the *Merry Widow* took people down the narrower channels. "The Lost Channel was more lost in those days. You couldn't see the bridge.

"There were rocks on each side. You had to be careful that the swift current wouldn't sway you onto the rocks. It was thrilling because it was dangerous."

Dorothy spent her summers as a waitress. She remembers guests like the regal Mrs. Grier, who returned year after year for half a century and spoke with a sedate British accent. Mrs. Grier liked Dorothy's grandmother and the two would endure hours in the parlour together talking. One time Mrs. Grier objected to the bathing suit of a young woman, in the 1920s style, with a skirt and short leggings.

"Mrs. Grier was absolutely shocked to death because it looked to her like the girl had nothing on. I can remember her sitting on the porch and saying, 'I have a good mind to ask Hilda never to wear that bathing suit again.'"

Another guest was Mr. Crammer from New Jersey, a devoted angler who wore knickerbockers with long, knee-length socks. "He said the best part of fishing was the anticipation.

"He tried to be scientific about it.

"Mr. Crammer had to have the moon in the right phases, the right plug."

Just before construction began on the Thousand Islands bridge in 1937, Bruce Dingman had come to town in a boxcar with choices that would change the young woman's life. He was a rover, a quick-witted, hard-working man who suited the mood of the river. "He fit right in with the Truesdells --- and they're river rats."

After Dingman got his lesson in bullheading the two dated until they married. Then in 1941, just after the exchange of vows, Dingman enlisted in the Navy and was gone. "I felt badly when he had to go away, especially on our first anniversary, because there's never another first anniversary."

Dorothy says that now with a large, hearty laugh.

"I can remember when he went off to sea. I was trying to be brave. My heart was just breaking," she chuckles. "This lady said to me, 'Oh well, you had him a little while.' And I just broke down and cried."

Again, the bold Shipman laugh.

"It sounded as though he was gone for ever."

It was a risky venture, marriage, to a man who knew the life of a rover. Dorothy could have been caught with a husband who always wandered, like a ship. "He'd been coast to coast seven times. Somebody warned me once, 'He's done an awful lot of travelling. Are you sure he's not going to want to travel for the rest of his life?'

"But he didn't."

Dingman came back from the Navy. His wife's instincts were right.

The river and the charm of the woman held him in a single spot in a single marriage half a century. Bruce and Dorothy Dingman had six children together --- half of what patriarchs like Abraham achieved, but still respectable in less Biblical times. And the Dingmans did not need an oracle to tell them what they wanted out of life. Every spring, as soon as the river shakes free of the ice, the two pack their bags. They open the door of their home by the water and migrate a few feet across the grass to the Annex. There, in a drafty, thin-walled house under the trees, the river feels as close as a bedside lamp.

On the St. Lawrence near Ivy Lea

Genealogical Impulses

Lawrence and Marjorie Mallory

Not all the voyages on the river are forward. Some look backwards in time, and the desire for knowledge of beginnings sometimes stops dead in front of a mute tombstone ...

Lawrence and Marjorie Mallory with tombstone showing Grenadier Island homestead

Behind the wheel of a battered white tugboat called the *Dover Mule*, Lawrence Mallory reads the river with the unvanquished eyes of the old fur traders and river trappers. Mallory was raised on Grenadier Island with a six-foot-tall sturgeon fisherman for a father. Mallory knows the river and the currents, and can pilot a boat at night without hitting a shoal. "I don't known where they all are," he says with river canniness, no foolhardy boaster, "but I know where they ain't. I don't think anyone knows where they all are."

Stormy weather is the real adversary on the water, says Mallory, a veteran of more storms than he can count. He eyes some dark clouds crowding the afternoon sky, but looks down to the surface of the water to judge and pass verdict on the weather. The level of the water has dropped in preparation for a storm. "If the water is going down," Mallory tutors, "you know by tonight when the storm hits, the storm and the wind will be down river. It will be out of the east. If the water's going up, you're going to get it southwest."

Mallory has not forgotten the lesson he learned in his twenties when he was driving a tugboat during the construction of the St. Lawrence Seaway. The fog had rolled in thicker than seaweed and he refused to take a load of men out. Another tug captain mocked the weather, for which he paid later in humiliation. That captain took thirty men out and had to call Mallory on the radio in desperation when he struck a shoal. The boat had started to sink and the fog, which hid the shoal, also hid the boat from rescue. Mallory could not see on the river to find the sinking boat, so he followed the sound of the boat's horn.

"When it's foggy, it's dead quiet," he says. No one drowned that day.

His destiny sealed by the Mallory who came to the St. Lawrence years ago, Lawrence Mallory has worked as a tugboat captain, a crane worker on a barge and a marine construction supervisor. "I've never really worked on the shore," he observes. He saw the river from Grenadier as he grew up, fishing commercially at a young age, and doesn't know another life besides the river.

"It's quite a thrill to go out in a boat and pull up your nightline and get a two-hundred-pound sturgeon. And you wonder if you want to stay in the boat if it starts thrashing around." Lawrence recalls his boyhood days spent helping his father. Sturgeon fishing on the St. Lawrence has disappeared now, but in the 1940s and 1950s Lawrence and his brother helped their father. They worked on the family farm on Grenadier, fished commercially for carp themselves, and caught sturgeon in the foul weather months of the early winter and spring.

Mallory remembers the day that his father caught a three-hundred-pound sturgeon in 1956. "Just to lift three hundred pounds (into the boat) is quite a lift," he remarks. "The fish will struggle and fight until it's tired, and you're tired too. A fish that size will do a lot of struggling before it gets to the surface. When it gets to the surface it's like it's got the bends."

Mallory, the St. Lawrence River supervisor for the river construction firm Bond Marine, lives in Rockport with his wife Marjorie, within sight of the island where he was raised. His father, also called Lawrence, "came ashore" for three wretched years to work in a factory. His son was born in 1934, four years before the Thousand Islands International Bridge was finished. Lawrence junior was born near the spot where the span of the bridge touches the Canadian mainland like a steel tether binding earth and water and sky together. His wife light-heartedly calls her husband's father "the troll that lived under the bridge."

The troll reference isn't too far-fetched. The history of the Mallorys and the Williams --- Marjorie's family --- goes back so far it is lost in a fog of half-truths and folklore. The winding arabesque of their twin

Lawrence Mallory

genealogies reads like a history of the Thousand Islands. The Mallory family saga goes back through fishermen and island dwellers to the founder of Mallorytown Landing. His wife has United Empire Loyalist blood mixed with river clans like the Chisamores, Burtches, Andresses and Buells. Her family line stretches back to the sea-born Owen Williams, a Welsh child delivered on a ship sailing to New York.

Marjorie Mallory's interest in the history of the two families started one year when she was raising four children and her husband was gone for weeks working on the river. She needed a distraction. She visited local cemeteries with her children, writing down the brief, indisputable facts chiseled on tombstones, bribing the children when they wailed with promises of ice-cream cones. Her information grew into a ragged and tumbling pile of records and wayward slips of paper. She and her husband reversed the Loyalist path north to Canada and made genealogical raids for information south across the St. Lawrence.

She traced her husband's family back three generations to the notorious Archie Mallory. As far as Marjorie can tell, Archie Mallory, whose first wife died in a flu epidemic in the United States, settled in Mallorytown in the first half of the nineteenth century. He raised one family with Sally while he supported a second family nearby on a hill. "He had an extremely tolerant wife, if you ask me," Marjorie comments shrewdly. Apparently Archie Mallory was a ram brimming with love and affection. When his hormones spoke, he listened. And his hormones spoke often and louder than convention. The spare-family-on-the-hill was not his only pastoral interlude. One day an angry husband came pounding on his door, and, according to the story, Archie Mallory raised an axe, smashed the door, and killed the husband.

It was Archie's grandfather, Daniel Mallory, who Marjorie believes --- although some dispute it --- founded Mallorytown. Other sources say that Mallorytown was founded by a member of the family called Nathaniel, whose son Andrew established the Mallorytown Glassworks about 1825. Marjorie has found assessment records that show a grant of land worth a hundred pounds going to Daniel in 1795. She believes that he was an enterprising United Empire Loyalist who belonged to the rebel American army in Vermont before crossing the border into Canada. By chance, Daniel Mallory crossed the St. Lawrence to an island, wading the final three hundred feet with two other United Empire Loyalists who would become important in the Thousand Islands, the Hodges and the boat-building Andresses.

The Williams aren't as stubborn and determined as the Mallorys, Marjorie says. Her father and grandfather were both caretakers for United States Senator Joseph Hines, who had a regal summer residence, called Opawaka Lodge, on Dashwood Island. Marjorie has traced her family back to Owen Williams and Catherine Buell. Owen married one Buell sister and Reuben, his son by another marriage, married her sister. "I used to think he was a horse thief that got out of Wales, but now I know he was born in the ship," Marjorie says. The trail of Williams winding backwards in time stops in the New York Harbour. "I've gotten frustrated over Owen Williams," Marjorie exclaims. On a visit to Wales she failed to find clues that took her roots back further.

"We get a lead and follow it," Marjorie says, shuffling a stack of unruly papers. "Sometimes it's great and sometimes it just fizzles away."

Rockport

'There's No Place Better Or Worse'

Grant Haskin

The beauty of the river is the wealth of the earth. "You were in Eden, the garden of God; every precious stone was your covering, carnelian, topaz, and jasper, chrysolite, beryl, and onyx, sapphire, carbuncle, and emerald." (Ezekiel 28:13)

Grant Haskin with ice tongs

"I'm the last of a dying breed," Grant Haskin announces. He has been as versatile as the change of seasons --- farmer, ice-cutter, stone-cutter, boat-builder, transport driver, plumber, electrician, repairman, golf club superintendent and bus driver for his own one-vehicle school bus company. "I'm sort of a jack of all trades. I got my experience on the river."

Born in 1926 on a dairy farm near the village of Lansdowne, Haskin naturally assumed he would be a farmer. Ever since the staunch United Empire Loyalist Abial Haskin fled Vermont in the mid-1700s for British territory in the Thousand Islands, the Haskins have been farming the hard, stubborn land. Aside from an inclination to choose elaborate first names and odd spellings --- Lemuel, Uri, Solomon, Ithimen, Ephraim and Thaddeus --- the Haskins were God-fearing men, Methodists and Presbyterians who tended their land and "read the Bible every day at breakfast."

But the economy was changing, affecting the farmers in the Thousand Islands, whose rocky farms clung desperately to the wild countryside and gradually fell behind the larger, mechanized farms with richer soil. It was a time of flux and like many river folk the Haskins could only adapt by being as flexible as the river.

In 1937, Grant Haskin's father, Walter Horton Haskin, moved the family to land near Rockport. Then in 1948, the same year Grant Haskin married Marilyn Hunt, the father and son bought a two-hundred-acre farm belonging to Captain John Carnegie who ran tour boats. By then, farming was becoming difficult in the area and Grant Haskin took other jobs, most of them on the river, to adapt. For three dollars a day in the 1940s he helped Bill Trickey cut ice in the river for ice boxes and cheese factories. Trickey had a motorized saw connected to a modified car engine and a motorized conveyor belt that lifted the blocks out of the water. The ice was hauled by dump trucks and horse-drawn sleighs.

"It was risky," Haskin says. As the weight of men and horses and loads increased on the ice, the water would ominously spread over the surface. The danger of breaking through was always present. "There were a few got wet. I've seen horses in the river."

Coming back from Club Island one time late in winter Haskin remembers the ice was perilously thin. He and a friend were walking on a bridge of ice with black, open water rushing by on both sides like two separate rivers. Haskin walked in front of the team of horses testing the ice with an axe. As a precaution, the horses were separated from the load with a rope one hundred and sixty feet long. Behind was Bill Hunt sounding the ice with an iron spud to gauge the thickness. Hunt had one ear cocked to the differences in tone of the ice. "It's just something you learn," Haskin says. "Sound ice will ring almost like hitting a rock. As it gets thinner, that solid sound diminishes." That day --- in spite of the gossip on the telephone lines predicting a drowning --- Haskin and Hunt returned safely. Other times, while walking across the ice to the islands, Haskin sometimes sank to his chest in the wintry water.

After the Second World War Haskin helped his father-in-law Clifford Hunt build wooden tour boats in Rockport. Hunt had worked in the shop of Rockport's premier boat builder Eddy Andress, "a wise old owl," Haskin says, who loved children, the Masonic Lodge, and a card game for chatty folk called five hundred. According to Haskin, Andress "worried about saving his customers money." Andress lived to be ninety-five years old. "The night he died he played five hundred with his family until the eleven o'clock news."

Aside from building boats Haskin and his father quarried red granite from the sides of hills on their land. They used sledge hammers and crowbars to break the rock once mauled and exposed by glaciers. The rock was ideal for breakwaters and Haskin found himself drawn more and more to the river for work. In 1954, he got his first job as caretaker on an island. The summer residents needed custodians who could cut the costs by doing all kinds of work. Then in 1969 Haskin was hired at the Grenadier Island Country Club, a nine-hole course with a psychologically treacherous hole over a small inlet. When the water is low, boys in boats collect the golf balls belonging to golfers whose swings were distracted by the water. From every hole you can see the river, Haskin says. A slice on number nine puts the ball in the river for certain. The club has a croquet course and a dining room where Marilyn Haskin, who also shares bus driving duty with her husband, cooks the dinners.

Because he has worked so widely on the river, Haskin, a tanned, trim man, is well known in the Thousand Islands. He listened to the tales of the generation of rum-runners, now dead, and saw the river in its beauty and cruelty. "There's no place better or worse than the river," he says.

Haskin smiles easily, without the dour bearing of his ancestors, who refused to dance or play cards or mock the king. Still, there is an unpretentious and liberal devoutness in Haskin, Freemason and member of the United Church of Canada. Sharing space with the picture of white draft horses in his study is a row of Bibles big and little, thick and thin. Prodded into thought, he admits that faith plays a role in his life, even as a peculiar confidence on the river when the water is stormy and dangerous. And the river is his link to creation, his unbound blue-green Bible of genesis and growth and change. On the water he feels alive.

"I can go to Toronto and back by the road and never realize I've been anywhere. But on the river, if I went five miles east or west, I'd be noticing things I'd never seen before. The sun shines differently on the river. The wind is blowing differently. There's a ripple on the water."

Rockport

Scholars of Islands and Ice

The Grindstone Island School

An island can be like a small schoolhouse with room to explore what lies in a child's mind. And the discovery of risks and disappointments and joys will last a lifetime beyond the bounds of the island...

Grindstone Island Scholars and teacher Beth Marshall in front of schoolhouse

In a field quick with snakes, by a pond where imaginary icebergs are cracked by a child with a stick, sits the Upper School of Grindstone Island. For more than eighty years children from Grindstone have trooped through the front door to start their education. In the first half of the century, classes made of farm families could be as large as thirty or forty, with another group at the island's Lower School. Madgel Brown, the grandmother of one of the current Upper School scholars, went to the school in the days when there was no island school bus to cut through waist-high snowdrifts. At that time forty-five children jostled in the school. But as the year-round residents of the island dwindled so did the students. In 1988, the teacher, Beth Marshall, would say "Grade four, get out your phonetics book." Grade four was one child.

On a September morning, while the school mascot, a white rabbit, shuffles unnoticed behind the desks, the kindergarten class, one small blonde girl, wanders to a drawing board to sketch. This year six children from four families are the whole school, from kindergarten to grade six. In 1989, the grade six class, one girl, was cut and sent to the mainland, where the older children go to school.

The children on Grindstone are not aware that one-room island schools are rare. The Grindstone scholars share blond hair and common adventures, such as testing themselves on the ice until they inevitably fall through or landing a fish of monstrous proportions. Jamie Brown can boast of the eleven-pound walleye that he caught with his grandfather when he was eight. Like the others, he

Ice fishing

has a story about the game called "ice break-up" when he lost the dare to dash across thin ice and tumbled into the cold water. After that, it was a race home to a tub of warm water.

Kirk Keesling says that he would like to live across the water in Clayton because then he could buy candy with no trouble. There is no store on the island.

Johanna Cupernall, blond, brown eyed and the oldest at the school, caught a ten-pound pike when she was nine and lost the ice contest to the pond nearby. Her mother had to bring dry clothes to the school.

Erik Cupernall, Johanna's brother, warms to tales of riding his three-wheel vehicle down the narrow dirt roads of the island. He likes to slide down a hill in winter because "You get moving fast." He says, "I like to ride bikes in the winter on the ice." Once Erik caught a carp and tried to keep it as a pet, but his father explained that the fish would only survive in the river. Back the beast went.

The Cupernalls are typical island folk. They moved from a trailer to raise beef cattle on their island farm. The father, Larry, is a boat carpenter who works in Clayton. When the ice freezes around the island the Cupernalls, like the other families on Grindstone, use an airboat. The mother, Catherine Cupernall, besides raising eight children, drives the island school bus and keeps one ear tuned to the Citizen's Band radio for information. Raising a child on an island has its blessings, Catherine Cupernall says. The relatively small island is "very private" and the children "can't get lost." The restrictions are not difficult for children who are not feeling the pressure of teenage years yet. The Cupernalls skate on the ice and ride the two family horses.

Liz Keesling, the mother of Carol and Kirk, admits that she worries about her children being near the water and the ice. In spite of swimming lessons she worries about the children falling into the water while they play on the front lawn. "I make them wear their life preservers at all times in the summer. If they fell in, it would only take a minute to drown." The children have more freedom on the island, Keesling says. "They can go down to a dock and pull out a perch or a little rock bass and it puts a smile on their face --- as long as they have that life preserver on."

Liz Keelsing's grandmother and great-grandparents were born on the island. She is a caretaker at the New York State Canoe-Picnic Point Park on Grindstone.

The children at the school have difficulty describing the island that is familiar to them. It feels like home. Other places are different. Jamie says that the island is "rocky, very rocky" and "round." The island is "all different shapes." Johanna elaborates, "Sometimes it's muddy. Sometimes it's dry. I like it here because at night you don't have to lock your doors." Her brother Erik the speedster knows the change of the leaves in the fall and recalls the snow piling on the bare branches. "It makes it look like a white forest," he says.

Grindstone Island

Here in Mind and Act

Susan Smith

The Thousand Islands has two sides. The summers can be heavenly. The winters can be hellish. For anyone who wants to be a settler, that makes a tough choice...

Susan Smith

On a mild day in January Susan and Eliot Smith, bundled against the wind, skitter across the ice in their small red hovercraft. The machine has no brakes. Stopping and turning are among the mysteries of hovercraft navigation. The Smiths have hit a rocky shoreline or two, but after four years on Sagistawika Island they have mastered the technique.

On this winter day the Smiths whirl and turn in the channel, headed between two islands. The hovercraft vanishes from sight behind an island swept by misty groves of bare, sticklike trees. The sound of the engine cuts mysteriously. In a few minutes the Smiths return to Sagistawika, disappointed. The ice is starting to break in the mild spell, not normally a problem, since the hovercraft flies on a cushion of air over both ice and open water. But today the engine is not working properly. Eliot Smith does not want to risk losing power over an open patch of water.

For the rest of the day Eliot Smith and his guests fiddle with the hovercraft engine outside in the winter sunlight. In her study, lined with books and files on the islands, Susan Smith reflects on the challenges faced by a modern day island settler. The Montreal pair are as happy in the Thousand Islands as orphans who are finally given a home.

The times of ice break-up are the most treacherous, Susan Smith says. She and her husband accepted the risks when they built a large home on the island, with the intention of eventually living on the river year round. But there have been frightening times, like the day in January that Susan Smith tried to cross alone in a small aluminum boat. A wedge of broken ice had formed an almost impenetrable barrier between two islands. Smith finally pushed her way through in the boat only to find that solid ice barred her way again further down the river. "I wasn't strong enough to pull the boat across the ice. I had to make my way back through that ice bridge to get back to the island." By that time the dock was also locked in ice. Smith had to abandon the boat in frustration and walk the last few feet.

"I was really upset that I had let myself get into this predicament." Smith spent three days on the island by herself. "I must have been in a state of shock. I could not get warm for a day and a half. It put all my life in perspective.

"The third night we had a gale and all the ice blew out and then I could easily get to shore."

Once or twice a winter the Smiths find themselves marooned on Sagistawika for a few days. If the wind blows hard or the ice is treacherous, the two throw an extra log in the fireplace and phone Montreal to say they cannot come to work.

The local people shake their heads. Only the hardiest and most stubborn old-timers have refused to follow the exodus to the mainland in the winter. The Smiths are different. They decided to move against the current of the times and make their home on Sagistawika, near Gananoque. Doug Battams, a white-haired river man from Bishop's Point, where the Smiths dock their hovercraft, worries that the pair will come to harm on the river. They phone him as a safety measure when they are crossing the ice.

Susan Smith cannot explain how the romance with the Thousand Islands started, though a clue lies in the research that has absorbed her for years. The Smiths first came to the islands for a houseboat holiday in 1971. Eliot ran a family tombstone business in Montreal and Susan was in charge of raising money for a private school. The next year the two were back as boaters. They bought a thirty-foot Norwegian cruiser and sailed from Montreal through the locks on the St. Lawrence Seaway.

From the beginning Susan Smith was driven by a desire to know the history of the islands. She needed more than the social life of a boater. "I got excited about the island names. I asked who named the islands and no one seemed to know." Instead of drifting in meditation on the river, Smith jumped ashore on islands with her notebook and pursued the islanders with questions. One of the first people she talked to was the awe-inspiring science writer with an encyclopaedic mind, Helen Wright Greuter, who lived in a small cottage on Little Sagistawika Island.

Little Sagistawika was connected to Sagistawika by a bridge. Greuter owned both islands, which had been in the family since 1886. The first owner, Smith believes, was a butcher from Gananoque named Henry Campbell, who apparently kept his beef cattle on the rocky eight acres.

Helen Greuter had an impressive background. By the 1980s the stream of science books that she had written numbered thirty. Her father was a geologist who took his bride for their honeymoon to Iceland where he did a geological survey. During her childhood she spent the summers on Sagistawika in an extravagant Victorian cottage with six bedrooms and a library.

By 1977, the Smiths had taken another step closer to the islands. They were now boaters renting the sprawling Victorian cottage on Sagistawika for the summer. The cottage had gone for years without anyone living in it and the building, with its peaked roof and window sashes, seemed like a piece of the past preserved in an outdoor museum. "It was just like in the movies, all cobwebs. It was really charming." Susan Smith is not a believer in ghosts. However, she says slyly that both Greuter's grandfather and grandmother died in the cottage and that at least one guest was unnerved by the atmosphere of the building.

For eight years the Smiths spent their summers in the cottage, becoming more like settlers preoccupied with a house and an island. In 1985, they made the final commitment and built a two-storey replica of a Victorian cottage on a piece of land that Greuter sold to them.

While staying on Sagistawika, Smith was also gaining momentum with her island research. She talked to over one hundred people and her files grew as thick and lush as a well-seeded field of corn. Smith was intrigued by the days of the squatters and

The Smith hovercraft

campers and the settlement of the islands before 1910. She also wanted to know the significance of the island names, particularly in the Admiralty group, where Sagistawika lay.

The British general and statesman the Duke of Wellington is now her "patron saint," she says. By coincidence, Smith's birthday, September 23, is the date of Wellington's first great victory at the battle of Assaye in India. Many of the islands were named by a British surveyor Christopher Fitzwilliam Owen under the spell of Wellington. Owen did a survey in 1815 adopting the names of Wellington's ships and officers for the island names. Smith wanted to know the history of the people and ships whose names had been used.

Smith also added to her growing paperwork mulch heap by joining the Thousand Islands Association, which links boaters and summer residents and river folk. An energetic woman with a knack for inspiring people to action, Smith began her term as president of the association in 1986.

Another person might have been satisfied to enjoy the river and the islands, but Smith needed the research. It was as though Smith was not content to settle physically in an area. She had to settle mentally, too. Smith was taking possession of the islands the way that a student takes possession of a subject by reading books.

On a January afternoon, however, practical matters break in. Smith has to leave her computer and her study to tackle the problem of crossing the ice to return to work Monday morning. With the ice breaking up fast and the hovercraft engine beyond repair, the Smiths have few choices left.

A series of phone calls ends with Dave Williams setting out from the Gananoque River in a cumbersome aluminum iceboat built at Williams marine, near Ivy Lea. The boat is a crude, square, metal wedge with an aircraft propeller mounted aft to push it forward. It is a vehicle of the last resort. From behind the islands, over the white winter hush, the engine of the iceboat roars.

The Smiths and their guests climb into the craft. There is a single bench behind the windshield that mercifully cuts the wind and a few seat pads break the chill of the metal. The boat moves sluggishly over the ice, pushing its own dead weight grudgingly. When the ice thins, the craft breaks through in a crash. The boat lurches to one side, then rights itself, moves forward and bites at the next lip of ice. Sometimes the ice is solid enough for the craft to crawl out of the water like a mechanical slug taking a step forward in evolution. The iceboat may look out of place on the river, but like the Smiths, it is an ingenious adaptation and reaches its destination.

Sagistawika Island

Ivy Lea

A River for Creators: Getting Metafishical

"Riding The Storm Out" by Michael Ringer

'I Had to Create Something'

Rene Longtin

Not everyone can look up and point to the star that shines over a single, rare destiny. Not everyone can look inside and discover the artist waiting to be born. Rene Longtin was lucky. He wanted to be a master boatbuilder...

Rene Longtin

In the 1970s, inside Gananoque's Algan Shipyards saws rang with the sound of aluminum sheets being cut. The arc welding torches buzzed. The scent of melting aluminum filled the air as the sheets were welded together on large metal frames. Then, from 1972 to 1976, down the rusty rails and into the St. Lawrence rolled a series of four aluminum tour boats for the Gananoque Boat Line.

The foreman for the first two boats and masterbuilder for the second two was Rene Longtin. He was a small man at five feet, four inches, and the flame of pride and craftsmanship burned inside him. After starting as a mill worker and carpenter, Longtin became a builder of boats which included the world's largest trimaran.

Longtin joined an old and dying profession in the Thousand Islands, shipbuilding. In the thick French-Canadian accent that sets him apart in the Anglo-Saxon United Counties of Leeds and Grenville, he explains: "I took a bunch of plates an' a bunch a men an' put it all together an' create a boat. That's me. I had to create something. This is what was part of being ... being a shipbuilder."

Longtin was born in 1932 in a French-Canadian pocket of eastern Ontario near the village of Embrun. His father was a dairy farmer with ten children on a piece of land beside a small river called Castor, French for beaver. The family traced its lineage back to the Longuetins from a province in France on the coast of the Mediterranean. In 1734, the Longuetins came to Lower Canada, which is now Quebec.

Rene Longtin's family moved in 1940 when he was eight years old to the French-Canadian community in Cornwall, where Joseph Longtin found work as a carpenter. His son grew up on the St. Lawrence, passionate about the game lacrosse, which led him to friendships with the Mohawks on Cornwall Island. Rene Longtin fished and went swimming with the Mohawks, who, like him, later found jobs on dam and bridge construction on the river.

Moving from a French-Canadian community into English-speaking Canada was not easy. Without any bitterness or resentment Longtin says, "My accent was so bad. I got laughed at quite a bit because I couldn't pronounce my word."

Longtin's ability with English only improved when he started to work in a Cornwall cotton mill.

In 1954, he married a woman named Estelle who, by coincidence, had lived near him as a child. "I was born in the spring an' she was born in the fall, nine miles apart."

Longtin moved from carpentry to working for a shipbuilder, who brought him to Gananoque in 1971 to build the first big aluminum tour boat for the Gananoque Boat Line. The Longtins were the only French-Canadian family in town, Rene Longtin says. By the late 1980s there were still only half a dozen in Gananoque. That did not matter to Longtin, because in his heart he only wanted to build boats.

After working as foreman for the construction of the first two *Islander* boats, Longtin was hired by the boat line to build larger crafts. That was his moment of pride. "Before I said I'm building a boat; now I said I'm building a vessel."

Building with aluminum was difficult because of the characteristics of the alloy. "Aluminum is not like steel. It expands, but it doesn't retract like steel. That was one factor you had to be on guard, to give aluminum the chance to go where she would go, without buckle."

The work went well until it was time to launch the *Islander III* on the rail. While preparing the rail cradle, a steel beam fell on Longtin's foot and broke it. "I finished the boat with a cast." During the first attempt to launch the boat, a wheel snapped on the rail cradle. Then, because the river was low, the railway sank into the mud and a steel beam was jarred loose. The beam poked a hole in the hull. The boat was patched and taken to a Kingston dry dock for repair.

By then, Longtin was launched himself in Gananoque as a shipbuilder. Gananoque had a tradition of building skiffs and tour boats, but not ships, though the founder of the town, Joel Stone, built a schooner called the *Leeds Trader*. Longtin bought the Algan Shipyard company in 1978 and rented the old corrugated iron building from the boat line. There he built a series of tour boats and catamarans, boats with large twin pontoons for hulls. His work included the Kingston overnight passenger boat the *Canadian Empress*. In 1978, Scottish businessman Duncan Muirhead came from Tortola in the Caribbean with a proposal for a boatbuilding partnership with the boat line. Thus was born the *Lammer Law*, a ninety-five-foot trimaran for charter from Tortola. Longtin was the builder, helping to fill the gaps in the plans that Muirhead had devised.

Next came the trimaran *Cuan Law*. At one hundred and five feet in length the *Cuan Law* was the world's largest in 1988. After its christening in Gananoque, the trimaran sailed down the St. Lawrence under the Thousand Islands bridge with only twenty feet to spare.

Longtin was proud to complete the tour boats and the trimarans, though the end of the projects left him with a dilemma. He was a shipbuilder in a town where there was no need for ships. One giant project fell through because Longtin could not afford the million-dollar bonding required by the government. He pleaded that he was an accomplished boatbuilder with the work to prove it, but the regulations stood. "Basically I blame the government for putting me out of business."

Now Longtin is a captain aboard the *Islanders*, wearing the four-stripe epaulet, but he has a pride in the boats that few captains share. Not many captains build the vessels they sail. Sometimes on the water Longtin sees the *Canadian Empress* sail past and it stirs his heart. He has an odd word to describe the feeling.

"I call them trophies. It's part of me. I built it. I done everything to it. I go down to the river an' it's my trophy."

Gananoque

Invention as a Driftwood Philosophy

Bill Ewald

The owl seems ingenious. It has large eyes and can see in the dark. But some people are truly ingenious and in the chaos and debris and confusion of the world, they see an inventive order...

Bill Ewald and owl carving

Beachcove Island is a cunning piece of work. Only an acre in size, the isle reaches out with long, slender fingers of rock to grab, like a curious child, anything that floats past. Its four sandy coves lure ducks and Canada geese to spend an hour in meditation. A large colony of tree swallows plucks insects from the air in payment for birdhouses. And, in wry rebellion, the American owner of the Canadian island flies the Maple Leaf on his flag pole. The flag is a rebellious snub of Ewald's cruder compatriots.

Over the years Beachcove Island, facing the main Canadian channel in the Navy Island cluster, has been busy. It gathers from the current a collection of wreckage, castoffs and odd bits fleeing from their owners. Everything from driftwood to a picnic table is snared and scooped ashore. And it is all put to work by an ingenious man with a gleefully agile mind and a driftwood philosophy, Bill Ewald.

"Whenever I see a piece of something going along, I decide whether it's a keeper," says the Long Island-born *junkmeister* and duke of derelicts. "The river is a conveyor belt of used building material." The wood is stockpiled under the cottage or stashed in a packed storehouse until Ewald can think of a use for it. "I like to improvise from whatever we have."

The variety is endless. Ewald has found pieces of docks, clothes' baskets, burnt pans, a large bench, half the sign of a river restaurant, a bottle from a nineteenth-century picnic, an aluminum boat and "a lot of boat fenders." Not long ago he gazed out, saw a big blue barrow and decided to fish it out of the current. "Rather than let things like that go down the river, I say, maybe I'll have a use for that some day." He admits that he has some limits, though. "I've gotten so I just let the ice chests go by. There's so many of them."

Among the more exotic finds are an aircraft tire and mount painted in military colours, and a large flint spearhead, buried in the sand of one of the island coves. Ewald believes that the spearhead was used by Indians to hunt hundreds of years ago.

If Ewald sounds like the possessed pack rat of the St. Lawrence, he is not. He is a retired optical engineer with twenty-seven camera patents to his credit and a mind as restless as a jittery heron. He is always alert for a cast-off fragment he can convert into something useful. His mind thrives on the challenge of an unsolved problem.

While Ewald talks on his porch, within view of one of his thirty-three birdhouses for tree swallows, a humming bird hovers to take a drink of sugar water from a cylinder on a hot July day. Nothing escapes Ewald. He counts the drops of water that the tiny bird sips. "That's unusual," he comments. "He took three bubbles. Only once before have I seen him take three-bubbles worth." When he first hung the feeder, ants swarmed over the cylinder by climbing down the wire that held it in the air. Ewald saw a problem that needed a solution. He ran the wire through a plastic bottle cap and poured Tabasco sauce into the cap. The ants, with no taste for hot sauce, stayed away. "That's absolutely original," he says with quick self-irony. "That's a working system."

The rest of the island is a system tuned more finely by Ewald's ideas. Ewald moves small trees to improve the view when he is in the mood. In spite of the natural impulses of the trees, the island has Ewald touches, such as the low walls of rock that run here and there like small dikes built for a long-forgotten ceremony. Ewald started toying with the stones when he built a jogging path over the nettle surface of the island. Rather than just toss the stones aside, he was compelled to make a pattern. In the low swampy parts, he built wooden ramps and walkways from driftwood, using the aircraft wheel as a support in one spot.

Ewald doesn't know why his mind has a restless, ingenious turn, but he suspects the fault lies, not in the stars, but in himself, his genes. "I had a grandfather who was a prolific inventor," he explains. His grandfather, John Henry Scholding, invented the heat-activated fire extinguisher used to spray water from ceilings. Scholding also invented mines that explode in the water.

As a boy, Ewald would build and experiment in his grandfather's workshop, once even catching his arm in the gears of a grinding machine. When he was young he became fascinated with optics, which led to a university degree in science and a stint during the Second World War in the United States Navy as a specialist. His navy rank was artificer optics, third class. At the American submarine base in Pearl Harbour he repaired periscopes and designed a submersible gun sight.

After peace was declared, Ewald returned to the product development department of Eastman Kodak, where he worked for thirty-seven years and invented camera systems like the automatic focus on slide projectors. The patents, by agreement, were turned over to the company for one dollar. Although he has no regrets about the arrangement, Ewald says that the patents and the royalties would probably be worth over one million dollars today.

Yet time started to catch up with Ewald when computers were used to design lenses. The inventor deplores the use of computers as an attack on the personal touch. But Ewald had prepared his escape from technology. In the 1950s, "bitten by the island bug," he was determined to buy a rock on the Canadian side of the border. The Canadian side was quieter, less developed and had been left in rugged shape by the glaciers scraping across the Canadian Shield centuries ago. Edwin Nuttall, the elderly tax assessor of the Township of the Front of Leeds and Lansdowne, took the Ewalds in his boat from Gananoque to the Thousand Islands bridge hunting for available land. In 1958, Ewald and his wife Betty bought Beachcove for $1,200 and built a modest cottage among the white pine, oak and dogwood.

Then Ewald turned the island into another workshop. He collected small boats and concocted a foot pedal to steer his canoe. A tree stump was carved in the image of an owl. Ewald altered the ecology of the island by adding birdhouse after birdhouse for the tree swallows, who responded by growing in numbers. He tamed the coves with a rake and built his rock-lined jogging path, quacking like a duck when he ran to give the birds fair warning that he was coming.

Now, watching the river from his porch, Ewald is on guard for driftwood and unsolved problems. While he talks the humming bird comes back for a second drink and a great blue heron, a fellow collector and connoisseur of castoffs, hovers over a clump of seaweed. The heron dives and catches his prize. The sails of four sailboats in the channel hang limply, without inspiration, wind and current forgotten for the moment. The stalled sailboats prod Ewald to a thought about his windy, wave-tossed self. "I find it difficult to sit still," he admits.

Beachcove Island

A River Mixed from Oil

Michael Ringer

The old myths are full of stories about people who violate the sanctity of nature. For their crime they are changed into rocks and trees and birds. Still, no one can resist trying to rip aside the veil to have a look...

Michael Ringer

Fog and storms and treacherous ice floes bring Michael Ringer out on the river. He spends hours afloat or tramping through island brush. Through a scuba mask he peers at perch and bass and pike under the water. He has been close to the skittish great blue heron. His hair has been swept by a draft from the wings of a low-flying hawk.

Getting close to the river is important for Ringer. He says that he cannot paint what he has not seen and felt and smelled. One particularly good expedition was a trip to the rookery of the great blue heron on Ironsides Island. Ringer --- who teaches art at Alexandria Centre in Alexandria Bay --- had heard so much about the birds that he decided to visit their island on an evening in mid-October.

"There was an absolute deluge of rain. There was no wind, but the rain was coming down so hard in sheets that everything was blocked out. You couldn't see anything ahead of you. It would stop and be absolutely still. Then fifteen minutes later it would start to deluge again."

Ringer climbed ashore on the fortresslike island and let the primitive, forbidding mood of the place fill him. "It's an absolute jungle. You have to crawl over everything. There are tremendous red roots that are coming out of things. As I went around the pines, all of the sudden I came upon the rookery. Of course, there were no birds there. There were huge dead trees with stick nests on top of them and everything was shrouded in a kind of a fog. It sent a chill right down my spine. It seemed so prehistoric and remote. It felt as if I was witnessing what I could have seen one hundred years ago."

Only when he reached the island did he realize that the herons had left for the year. Yet Ringer had what he wanted, a sense of the strange island with a lingering mood like the tomb of a Celtic king.

Later, after a dozen trips to Ironsides to observe the reclusive great blue heron, Ringer produced a series of paintings. In a work called *Standoff at Ironsides* four herons face each other in an outdoor stalemate. The heavy, almost rank green of the plants and the water --- that elusive "olive-yellow-brown kind of green" of the river --- is overwhelming.

On his first trip to Ironsides Ringer absorbed the solitary atmosphere of the island. On the way back, that solitude mixed with a new image of the river for Ringer. The result was a muted, impressionistic watercolour of a foggy island called *The River*. "Again the rain started. I saw a freighter coming up-river and I went to the head of Resort Island and sat there and waited because I wanted to get a photograph of the freighter in exactly the right position. The rain let up just in the nick of time. I couldn't do any sketches because it was too wet."

Mid-October became in the painting "an August morning, a misty, humid day."

In the centre of the picture the island is braced against swells unusually calm for the St. Lawrence. The lines of the waves are straight, almost like abstract figures in an hallucination. To the right, visible in spite of the fog, someone is sitting in a St. Lawrence skiff. On the other side, veiled in the mist with its power and mass subdued by distance, is a mighty freighter.

The St. Lawrence skiff was painted later to add what Ringer and Harold Herrick felt was missing. The scene summed up the river so well that Herrick, an expert skiff sailor, put the painting on the cover of the book he published, *The River and the Skiff*. The skiff, Ringer says, gives the picture the dimensions of time and tradition. In contrast, the freighter in the fog is "subdued and sublimated and brings us back to modern days."

"It's the time that I probably like the river the best. That's that peaceful time when the river is most natural, the river is doing what the river wants to do, as opposed to being ripped up by five-hundred-horsepower engines that tear back and forth."

For the river folk the picture may look odd and unnatural. It shows the St. Lawrence as tranquil as if it were a lake. But the calm is one side of an ever-changing river, Ringer says.

"This is definitely one of the faces of the river. There is always hidden danger in it. I think the people that see this painting understand that even though you have that placid, calm feeling, there are still shoals that lie underneath the water. If you aren't careful, they can kill you. The river can easily destroy you."

"The freighter is now a natural part of the river. The freighters --- I always enjoy hearing that whump, whump sound --- they're not tearing up anything. You can feel it. You can sense it. You can hear it. It's another sensation."

Ringer put his feelings about freighters into a work called *The Vandoc at Heart Island*. The massive black stern of a Canadian freighter leaves a modest, white-capped line in its wake as it passes Boldt Castle. The tiny light bulbs shine from the ceiling of a dark deck mimicking stars in the sky.

The slow-moving freighters treat the St. Lawrence with respect, Ringer says, much as he does. He takes his sketching boat out to observe the river and the wildlife undisturbed. In his boat --- with a heron decoy that tells the ducks that no danger is present --- Ringer gets close enough to the herons to touch them. "They will pick up on the absolute slightest movement ... If I move my finger or drop a pencil, their heads will go straight up. And they'll watch you. They may not know something is there, but they'll stay alert until they do know something is there. They can out-wait anybody."

"They've got a personality. They talk to you." If the heron is approached with the right combination of courtesy and protocol, it will not fly. "If I sneak up on them, they don't like it. However, if I make myself noticeably visible and then get up-wind from them and drift down very slowly, they will accept my presence. When you get too close --- thirty five or forty feet --- they'll squawk and fly away. You just sit there very quietly and sketch. They'll let you sketch them. They don't like the sound of a camera."

The moment that a heron takes to the air it looks awkward. Then the flight becomes smooth and graceful, Ringer says. "Their wing tips turn back a little bit. It's almost like they're rowing or paddling down the river."

Redwood

Courtesy of Save The River!

"St. Lawrence River Muskellunge" by Michael Ringer

Out of the Mould of St. Brendan, the Seafarer

John Boxtel

The river casts its blessing over many people. It invigorates. It stimulates. And yet some folk have to look beyond for an answer to what stirs them...

John Boxtel

On the high rock bluff at Rockport a nine-foot-high statue of St. Brendan, the patron saint of seafarers, may some day stand facing the wind and water of the St. Lawrence River. St. Brendan clutches a cross to his chest with one hand and spreads his other hand out over the river. Behind him is a white, wooden Roman Catholic church.

That was the concept of the sculptor, a tribute to the energy and inspiration of the river. The sculpture remains only a concept. It was not immediately approved by the church council because of cost. It waits in the limbo of the artist's mind to be given form and substance.

For John Boxtel, the stillborn St. Brendan is disheartening. He would like his St. Brendan to keep watch over the water like his other sculptures. His Neptune stands at a private harbour on Lake Ontario ready to raise a conch shell to his lips and blow.

"All these things are self-portraits. I am in Neptune looking out on Lake Ontario. Now when I sit here I can think of me being there. I really feel that I am there because my sculpture is there."

Boxtel also sees a part of himself in St. Brendan, the sixth-century Irish saint who was fabled to navigate a small boat across the Atlantic Ocean and, as some claim, discover North America. Boxtel is another seafaring adventurer. A Dutchman born in the same nordic climate as the saint, he also crossed the Atlantic, to make his home in the Thousand Islands.

In 1979, John Boxtel --- a carpenter, architect and high school art teacher who immigrated to Canada in 1954 with fifty-six dollars and a box of tools --- decided the moment was ripe to dedicate himself, at forty-eight, to art full time. Practically sight unseen, he was determined to buy a cottage on an island in

232 A River for Creators: Getting Metafishical

Boxtel sculpture *River Watchers* in front of artist's home

the St. Lawrence and live year round with a painter named Rose Stewart.

The ad for the cottage sounded perfect. It was an island paradise fit for a dreamer. It was also "an absolute lie," declares Boxtel, his voice a husky exuberance punctuated by a high-pitched laugh. "I bought it anyway."

Life in the remote seclusion of the ice-bound winter on Wallace Island seemed eccentric in the 1970s. The days when people lived and farmed on the smaller islands were gone. The numbers had fallen over the past half-century on Grenadier after most of the families of the pioneers retreated to the comforts of the mainland. Only large islands like Howe and Wolf, with their ferry service, or Hill and Wellesley with their giant bridges, still held residents. Even local people in Rockport doubted that the Dutchman with the wildly curly hair would survive his own enthusiasm. "They thought I was absolutely stark raving mad," Boxtel shrieks with delight. In spite of the restrictions of two people living alone on an island and the occasional twinge of fear at their vulnerability, Boxtel and Stewart fed on the freedom. The two artists could follow inspiration without interruption or distraction. Their studios sprouted a crop of paintings and sculptures.

Boxtel's first task was to rebuild the decrepit cottage with its rotting porch. The building was originally constructed out of pine on Wallace Island by a lighthouse keeper named Wallace. The lighthouse keeper tended a kerosene lamp lighthouse which has now been replaced by an electric lamp. Boxtel fashioned his own version of a lighthouse to guide the wanderer, a seven-foot-high statue of Diogenes made out of weather-resistant fibreglass in a bronze patina coating. Boxtel modified mythology to suit himself. Diogenes was an ancient Greek philosopher whose cynicism led him to wander with a lamp in search of an honest man. Boxtel's more sociable Diogenes stood at the end of a dock with a lighted lamp as a friendly beacon on the dark river.

The winter ice could slice through an ordinary aluminum boat with ease, so Boxtel designed and built an iceboat out of plywood. The boat had iron runners on the bottom to slide across the ice. Retractable handles allowed the boat to be pushed

Boxtel in his studio

over the ice and gave support if the boat broke through. Boxtel discovered that winter on the island was not as deadly or as reckless as it looked, even if you had to cross the ice in a primitive iceboat to go shopping. "In five years I never got my feet wet," he claims.

From their island home Boxtel and Stewart watched the leaves change colour across the swift-flowing current by Ash Island. Then they noticed the change. As soon as boats became scarce on the river in the fall, summer in the islands seemed a mere circus show, an illusion meant for a gullible throng. The two felt the depth of the solitude on the river. But with their creative impulses to lead them and give them strength, the artists were not lonely. "When we had the need to go and look at people, we would go to Toronto for a day and be saturated with people," Boxtel says.

Still, the desire for solitude was odd for a man like Boxtel, a gregarious artist who finds his material in the human form and personality. He explains that it is not the commotion of the city or the beauty of the natural landscape which motivates him. "I think your immediate experiences never show up in your art work. You gather experience in life. It has to go through a period of gestation inside before you translate it into art."

Boxtel found some of the inspiration for his passionate nature in physical work. He felled pine trees on his property. He lugged the logs by hand, often still frozen, into his studio. With one exception, he says that he has never cut down a living tree. "It's such a shame because you can't replace a tree," he says.

The exception was a huge, hollow white oak. The tree was dead except for a single aspiring branch as long as an arm with green leaves still thrust out of it. One day a psychic who came to the island to fish pointed from his chair in the kitchen and announced, "There is a tree over there that you're going to carve." A mark was put on the kitchen wall to record the direction. Boxtel and Stewart searched for the tree that fall, without luck. Then in the spring Boxtel found the one-armed oak in the direction that the psychic had predicted.

"I carved a bird out of it," he says. The seven-foot-high bird now perches on a rock on Pine Island, near Rockport. Like many of Boxtel's creations it is only happy facing water. "There is a sense of movement, of time passing on the river that some art work has to participate in," the sculptor says. "If you turned them away from the river, they would be as lonely as hell."

"I'm always turned towards the river. I have to be able to see the river when I'm working. I like to see the water moving. It's so alive. If it was a lake, it would be dead because the water wouldn't be going anywhere."

After five years Boxtel and Stewart moved from Wallace Island to a home that the sculptor designed on the shore west of Gananoque. The daily complications of life had worn them down. But Boxtel's statues of pine and bronzed fibreglass --- totems that proclaim his spiritual stand to the world --- continue to face the river whenever possible.

For Boxtel, the river is a demonstration of the might of creation. One spring day he was standing on his dock on Wallace Island and spotted an immense floe of ice quickened by wind and current. The floe was larger than the channel where it was aimed. Mesmerized, Boxtel watched. It was pure uncensored drama. The floe slugged a rock, swung round and drove the dock six inches into the island with the force of a pile driver. "It was just unbelievable --- the power. I love that power."

That same power Boxtel tries to put in his statues, which leaves him grappling with the riddle of creation. Is a statue dead or live? Is there a spirit in nature? Are men and women created or do they create themselves?

These days St. Brendan, the spiritual ancestor and altar ego of the adventure-loving sculptor, stands as a model only in the artist's studio. The tiny arm is spread to cast his blessing abroad and calm the waters. He is full of power and might and spirituality. And yet he is a statue, not a man.

"My statues have no soul. They have no living spirit. Only by the mood I create in the sculpture do they express soul. But they don't have any and they aren't animated. They don't think and they don't talk."

St. Brendan, poor lump of clay, has fallen outside the created world that he represents.

"He is imposing his will on the water. He didn't create the water and he didn't create the stillness that would fall on the water. He just tried to impose his will on the elements. And that has nothing to do with creation..."

On the shore west of Gananoque

Paint Your Iceboat Fire-engine Red

John Boxtel's Journal

Someday, centuries hence, when the St. Lawrence is only a dry river bed dreaming of tall granite cliffs, there will be a mythology of the river rat. It will come from what is happening now in stories whose endings are unwritten . . .

Scene from Machar's Woods bluff, Gananoque

The first winter on Wallace Island John Boxtel kept a journal as a way to explore the experience. He starts his journal by talking about his fears. He was worried whether he could make a living for Rose Stewart and himself as a sculptor on an island. He did not know if the task would be too difficult at his age or whether winter on an island would defeat the pair. Yet Boxtel reasoned that fear was something he had learned, that raw emotions could be conquered. So Boxtel writes with the delight of a belated pioneer self-consciously preparing for winter and a new life. There are blackberries and apples and wild grapes to pick and fish to be caught. Stewart experiments by baking pies made from wild berries picked on the island. The two cut and haul firewood for the winter. From the handwritten, one-hundred-and-sixty-one-page document here are a few excerpts of a winter of discovery.

SEPTEMBER: The sunlight is pale and delicate, without the shimmering heat of summer, yet penetrating and warm, carefully etching shadows in the grass. It is a light one can look at without being blinded by the glare ... The wind is getting stronger. It bends the trees and almost reverses the current of the river. I feel comfortable and protected in this house. After all, it has been here for one hundred and fifty years.

It is fall. The colours are starting to change and the wind is trying its level best to blow the leaves off the trees. I don't see what is the hurry and why the wind uses such devastating force. In the end the leaves will fall anyway.

We took the raft I had built and loaded it with firewood in order to transport it around the island.

There I was for all to see sitting on my knees on the raft, which was below the surface because of the weight of the wood, and it looked as if I was pushing the firewood through the water.

OCTOBER: The trees are shedding their leaves gradually so that we can see further into the forest all the time. Only where there are a lot of evergreens the mysterious quality remains ... We lit the wood stove in the kitchen for the first time today to help create the right atmosphere for Thanksgiving.

NOVEMBER: The winds have stripped the trees bare and the cats cry because there are no more mice around ... The water is a very deep green, clear right to the bottom. The water is down at least two feet, making all the docks stick out of the water as if they were on stilts. The weather was mild with a grey sky... The weather is gradually getting colder. There is a very small rim of ice on the river in calm areas that does not go away.

DECEMBER: So you expect company at nine at night and it is pitch dark and pissing rain and they have just phoned to tell you they are there waiting for you at the government dock. What can you do but go there and collect them?

We still go to the shore at least once a week for mail and for a cup of coffee at the Boston Cafe [in Gananoque]. We try to sit facing the window together so that we can see the people walking by all duffelled up in their mackinaws and ski-doo suits.

It seems now that we are further away from people, we are closer to them in our minds. Ken is worried about us. He does not come out anymore because his boat is out of the water and his boathouse is frozen. But he will come out on the road and tell us that it is getting colder and to be careful not to overload the boat.

It turned out, one, the pipes were frozen, and two, the toilet backed up into the sink and water cascaded all over the kitchen floor creating one hell of a mess. I rushed up when I heard the commotion and quickly grabbed a bucket after running upstairs to shut off the toilet. Rose swore she would take the house and throw it into the river.

Winter shoreline

DECEMBER 31: The river is freezing fast and the ice along the shore supports the iceboat with four adults The stove has been lit since early November ... The only boat on the river is our little iceboat.

JANUARY: It seems that the man across the river had gone home today and got into trouble. His boat had accumulated about four inches of ice on the bottom and with a lot of ice on the river his motor gave out. Bud Hunt saw him coming and went to his rescue, but he broke a shear-pin on his motor, so Ken and Wilson had to rescue the two of them. It would not take long before one would freeze to death in this weather, drifting around in the St. Lawrence, and with the mist coming off the water it is hard to see a boat on the water. I painted the iceboat fire-engine red so that it is easily visible on the ice.

Our friends on the shore tell us that if we make it through this winter all the rest will be easy. It is so far the coldest winter since time began in this country ... At the head of our island there is a little open water, but above Ash [Island] all is a frozen waste ... The channel is only open about thirty feet across, some places less. The ice extends from the shoreline far into the river.

My mother is dying. I received a letter yesterday [from Holland]. It was her last. She only wrote four sentences and my brother had to finish it ... It is one of the hardest things for one that goes to make a new life in another country.

FEBRUARY: The snow was falling when we got up this morning, great fat snowflakes with lots of spaces [in between], falling slowly straight to the ground. They were falling so slowly that you could count them and, if you wanted to, examine each individual snowflake ... We had a great storm last week that blew a lot of ice into the channel and created a barrier there, huge ice blocks lying helter-skelter on large floes of ice interspersed with holes. Ducks land on the open spots to fish. They dive under the ice and come up on the other side of an ice floe.

We go to Toronto for a few days and get so tired from the crowds that it takes two days to find our equilibrium ... We also have become vulnerable to colds and things because we are so isolated that we lose our immunity to disease and catch a bug very easily ... Rose and I end up passing it back and forth until it is worn out.

MARCH: We are now more than halfway through March and winter is still hanging in there ... The wind was whipping the snow over the water so that I could hardly see where I was going. This made things tricky as there was a lot of ice drifting around ... We got home and within ten minutes it snowed so badly that we could not see the boathouse.

We are storing a boat for our farmer neighbour ... I keep hitting my head against the beam that I have installed to haul it. The beam is just at head level. I am going to charge him fifty dollars for storage --- not for storage actually, but for the ten times that I hit my head against that damn beam.

Last night it rained. It was not the cold, driving rain of late winter, but a quiet, balmy rain of spring. I could smell it already in the late afternoon.

Both Ken [a friend] and I felt somewhat sorry for the fish as it was lying in the boat flapping around. It looked like a pet dog lying there in the bottom between the two seats. Rose left quickly when Ken raised the axe to chop off its head. She had been summoned to take pictures for posterity and she, too, said it was too bad we had to kill such a beautiful fish. I was happy we only caught one.

Wallace Island

A River for Creators: Getting Metafishical 239

Gananoque boathouses

Odin's Eye Laid to Rest

Rock bluff on St. Lawrence, Gananoque.

It is nightfall in the islands.

The sun sets over the frail line of Lake Ontario, past Wolfe Island, where Bruce Woodman chews the last smoldering cigar of the day, where the ferry cuts sideways across the current.

The water has gradually lost its colour, drained from blue and green to cool, lustrous grey, then an obliterating blackness like a fire extinguished. The islands are great, dark, significant shapes against the open sky.

In the distance, the Thousand Islands bridge is hard iron no longer. It is a string of lights hung out at points, reflected like airy shapes on the water.

Allen Cook's nets lie hidden in the dark oblivion of water. They have the veil-like coherence of a dream. The nets wait all night for the fish to fill them like great pods.

The sea gulls have retired. Some gather in flocks to ride the slow roll of the waves in the lee of an island.

The guides and the lucky anglers are cleaning the catch of the day. Their tools are set in order for the morning. The hunters are sleepily anticipating the first heave out of bed before the sun rises, when the river seems its freshest.

Muskie Jake, with the stroke of a knife blade, opens the flesh of a fish. It is gritty, spiked with tiny filaments, as ripe as a fruit packed with seeds.

In a dark tavern Clayton Ferguson relives the day. Abruptly, for no reason, he utters dark words. He is strumming the blues on his guitar again, this time more sharply. After a long fight a muskie has beads of blood on its red back fin, he says.

For Ferguson, that sums it up, catches the matter on the right barb. It sounds like an epitaph. Blood on the fin. Beads of life.

The fishing guide knows too much. He has gazed into the reflection of his own uninhibited self. The words pour out of him as though he were a flask knocked over on a table.

Yet not all the river rats have spoken.

Brendan Reid, the great Gananoque fisherman, is dead. His name is still invoked in admiration. His river is still here.

The bold, husky-voiced Harold Herrick, self-proclaimed radical publisher and master sailor of the skiff, is dead. He died of cancer after his skiff book was published.

Others passed away long ago, such as the drowned Thomas Horne, whose terror and loss and hopelessness in the last moment of a full life went unheard. Only his skiff remained to tell his tale. Poor wooden lyric with a hole in the bottom.

Some made their farewell cries from the water. So the voices lifted of the three from Pennsylvania, fishermen sinking in the cold, choppy water of October off Horseblock Point. A woman in a cottage yelled to them in the dark to hang on. Just a little while longer. Hang on. Hang on.

Too late.

Drowning, the life rushed out the bunghole of their bodies into the one boundless current.

The river is not for amateurs, not for romantic fools.

A few cross the water at night when the moon is as bright as a harrow blade. Only those who know the shoals can take the risk. Others have died or been spiked by a sudden dock, a jutting stone.

But tonight the boaters lie at anchor.

The islanders are safe. They feel good when the night wraps around the coastline again. The islands are given back their solitude, their meditative lines. Margaret Reid has turned on her lamp and picked up a travel book. The pages are turned slowly.

Bill Browning is laughing loudly with a group of friends at Camp Browning. His voice is his genius -- a flint striking sparks of friendship, the flame of conversation drawing people together in a circle.

In the end, the best talkers are the ripe old folk, the melons of the fall, the balm of the crushed berry. They are the Fred Hodges, the Leonard Turners, the Allen Cooks...

Others bred in cities have poorer material. They are small fry.

Think again and remember the last, late prologue before the river freezes. Never forget the men and women who stayed with the river when it sundered itself into ice and cold currents.

In winter, time of death and memories and farewells, the river freezes. A bridge of ice grows from the land and links island to island. The folk come out and walk on the river as though tempted by forbidden pleasures. For a brief season they can cross without a boat. They can stand below the cliffs and look up unhurried by the current. The ice fishermen come out and cut holes with their augers. They look down. The holes -- as round as a bright full moon -- are full of river life.

The Thousand Islands

OVERVIEW MAP OF THE THOUSAN[D]

ONTARIO

Gananoque

Ivy

HOWE ISLAND

THE ADMIRALTY ISLANDS

THE NAVY ISLANDS

THE LAKE FLEET ISLANDS

Eel Bay

Lake

WELLESLEY IS[LAND]

GRINDSTONE ISLAND

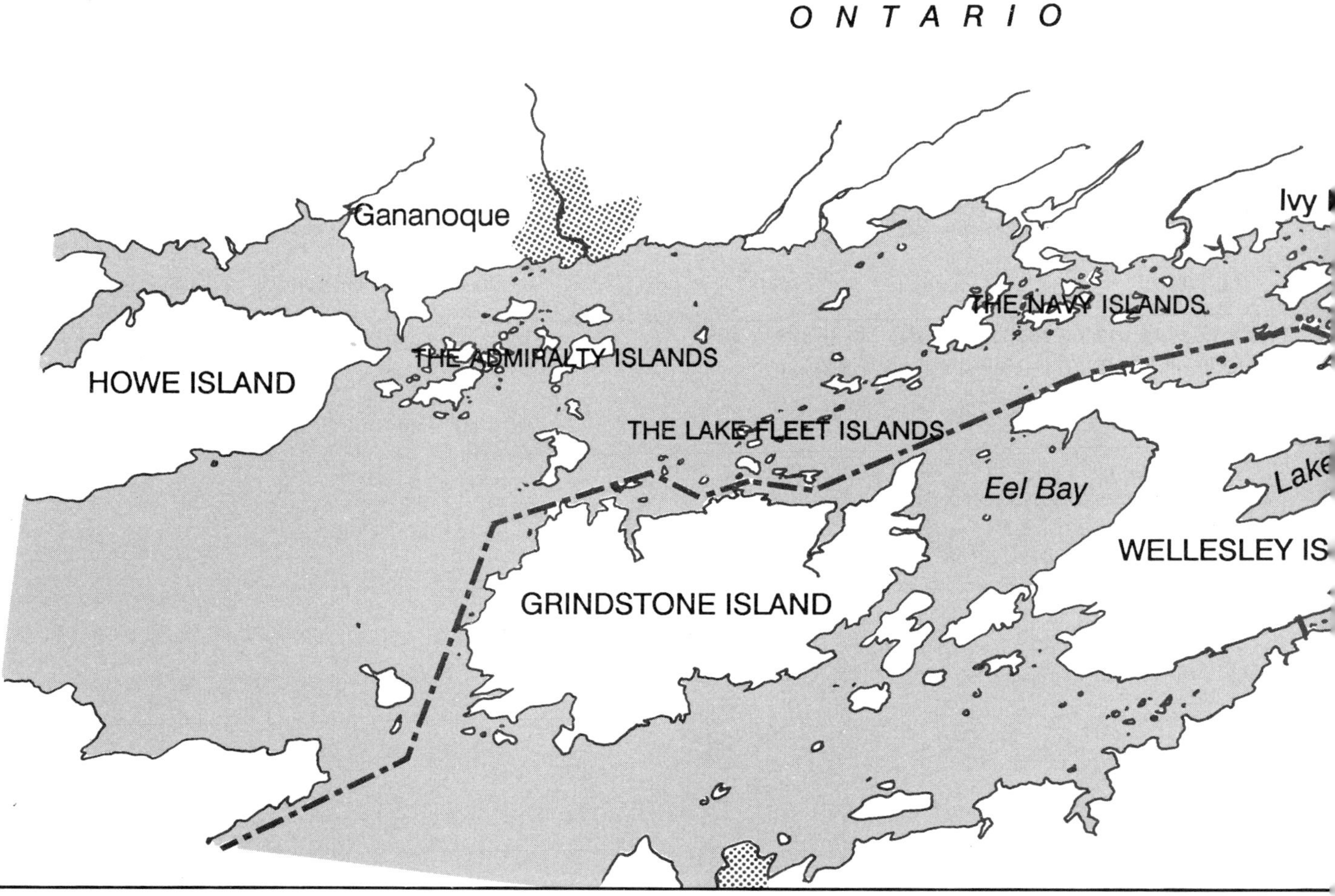

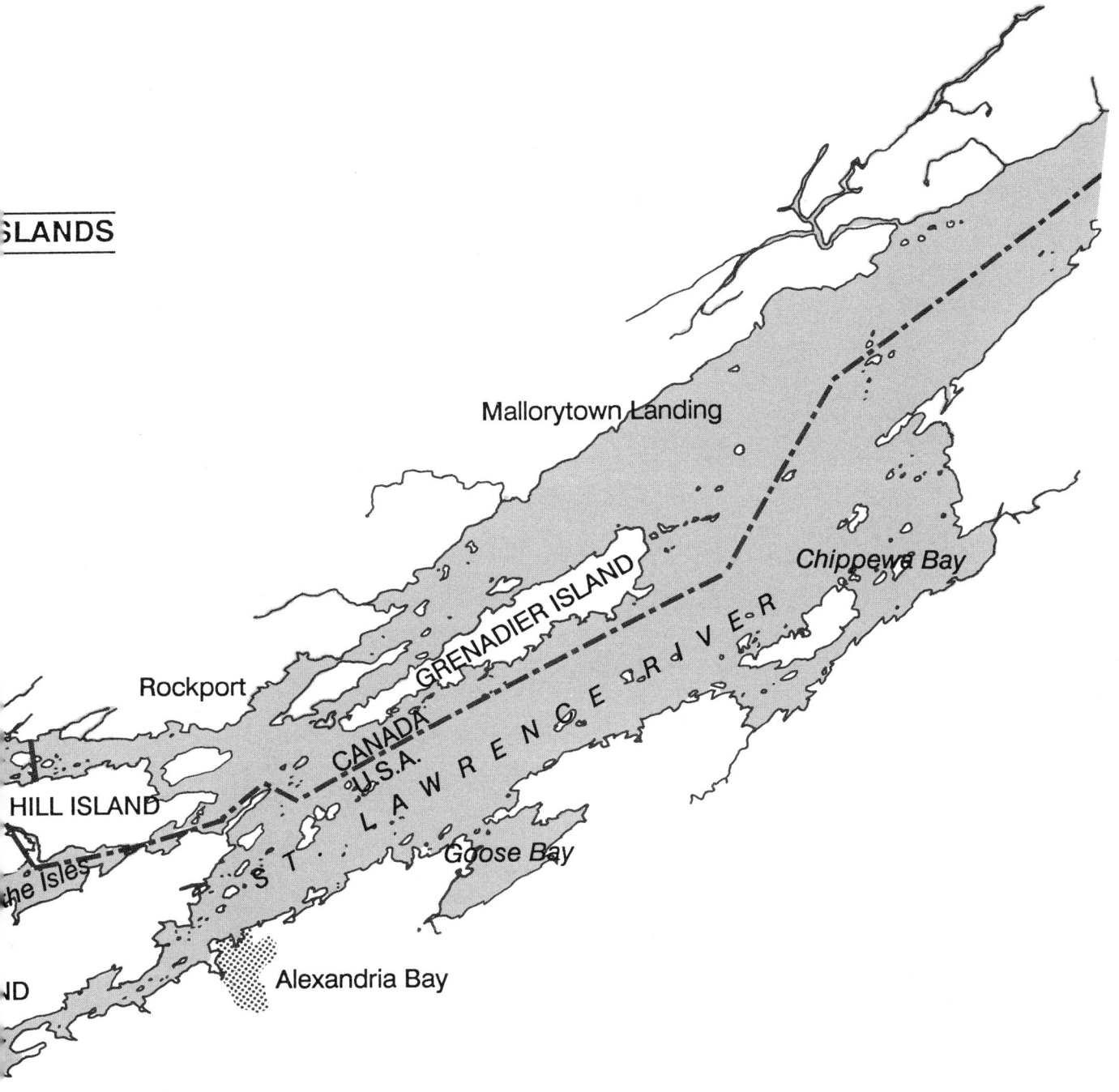

Legend

1	Lindsay I
2	Bostwick I
3	Blackduck I
4	Sagistawika I
5	McDonald I
6	Tremont Park I
7	Hay I
8	Little Huckleberry I
9	Huckleberry I
10	Juniper I
11	Leek I
12	Flat Huckleberry I
13	Camelot I
14	Endymion I
15	Sugar I
16	Prince Regent I
17	Gray's Beach
18	Gordon I
19	Halsteads Bay
20	Landons Bay
21	Horseblock Pt
22	Stave I
23	Downie I
24	Mulcaster I
25	Spilsbury I
26	Shipmans Pt
27	Hickory I
28	Flynn Bay
29	Calumet I
30	Picton I
31	Murray I
32	Fishers Landing

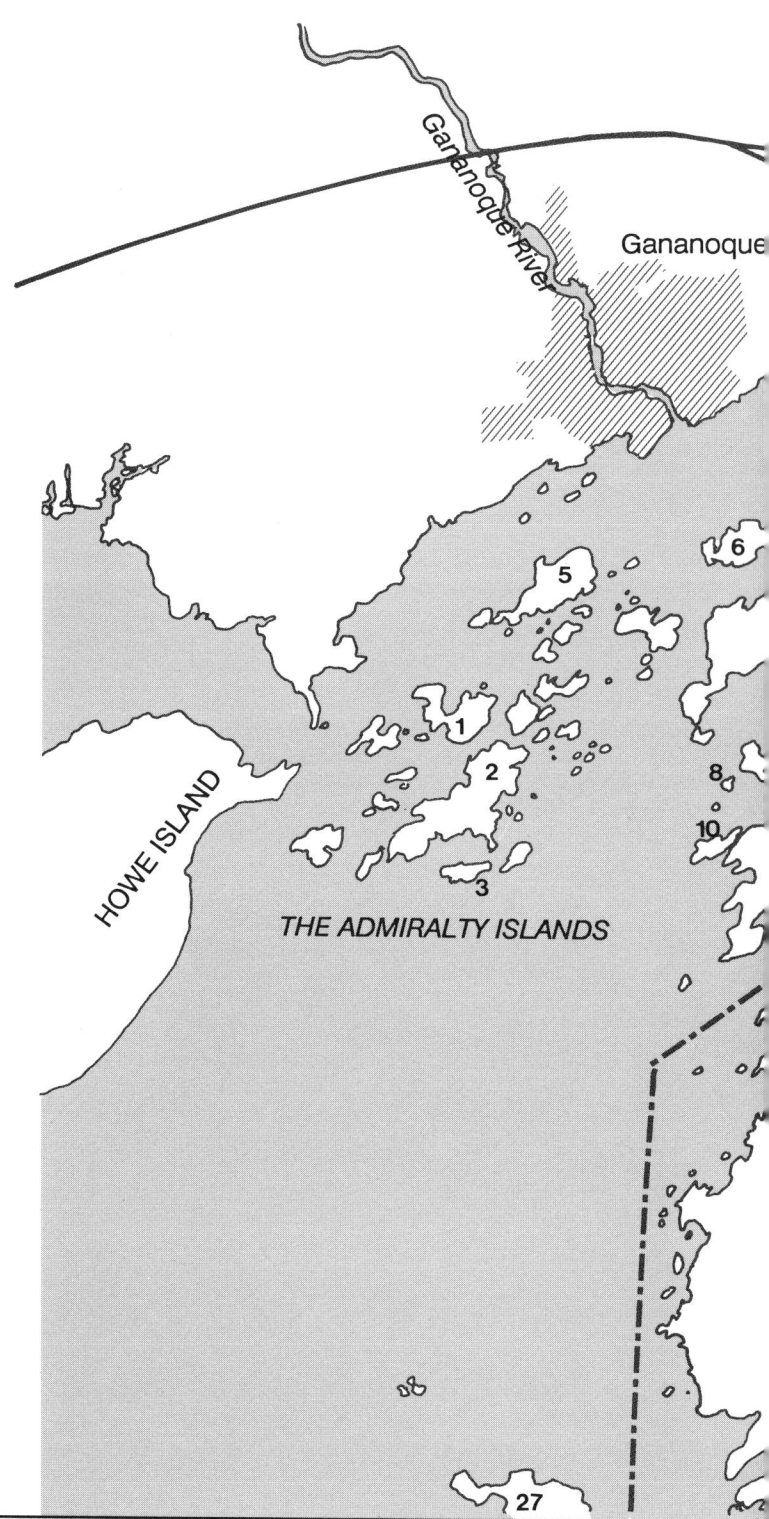

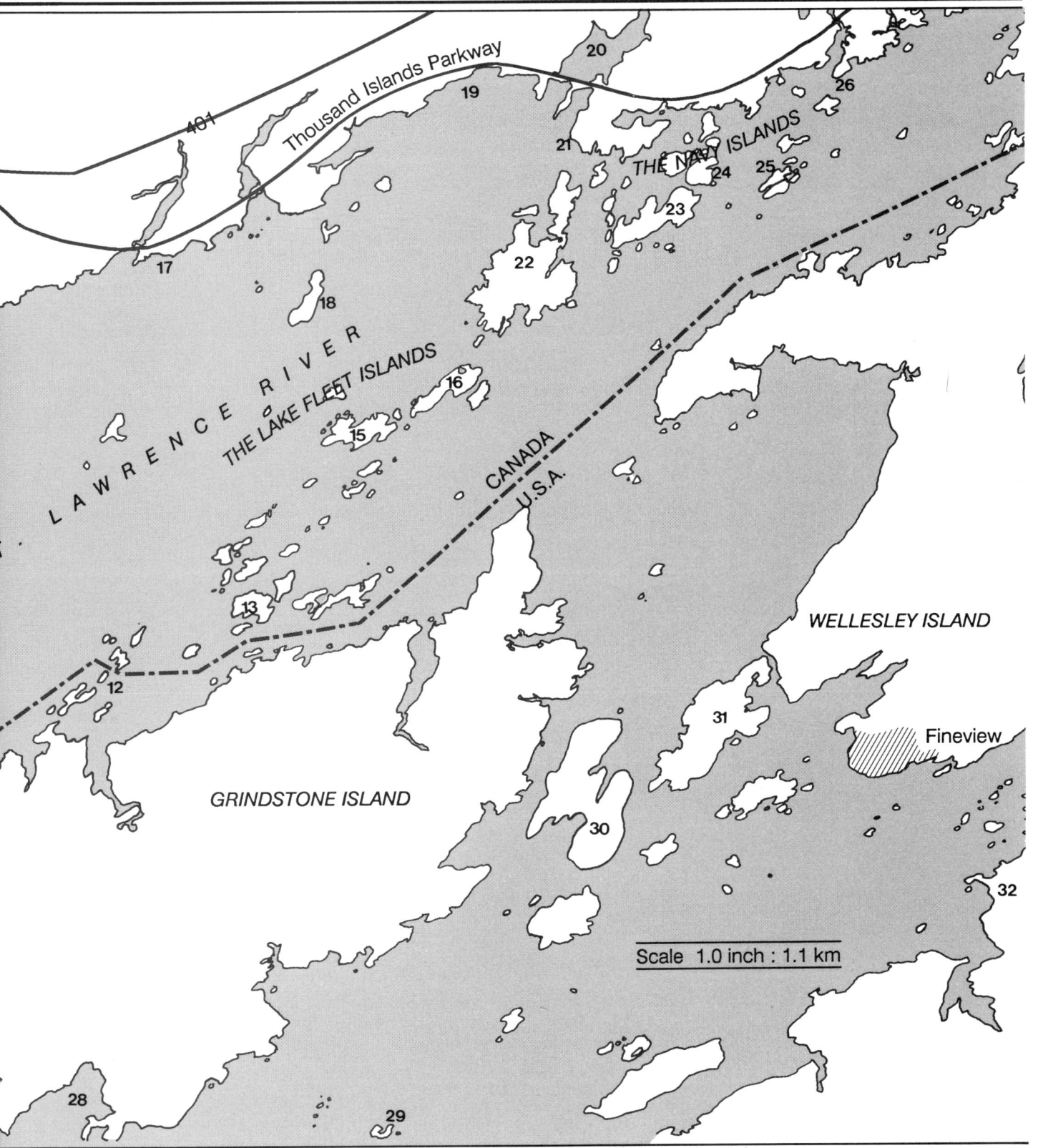

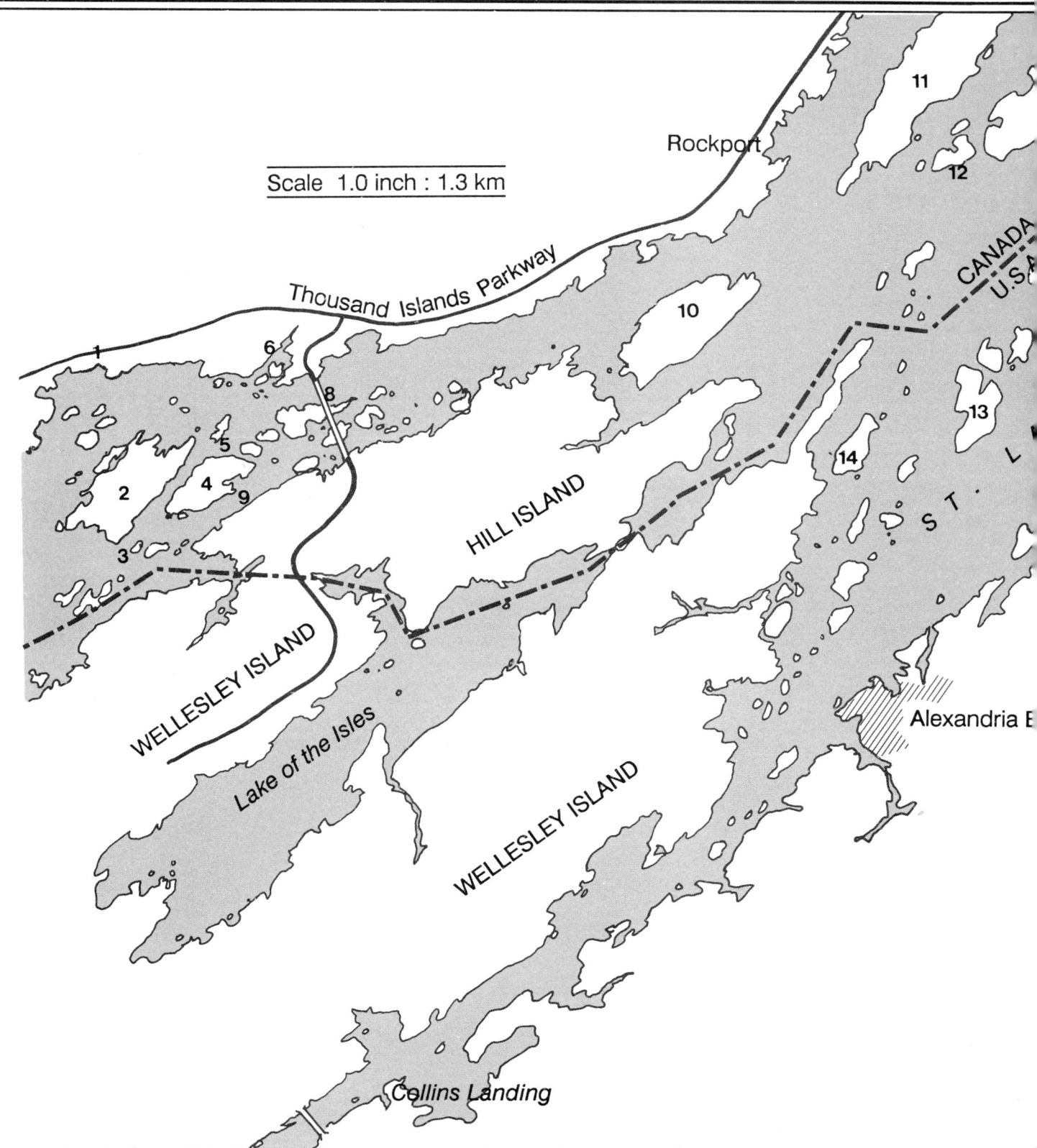

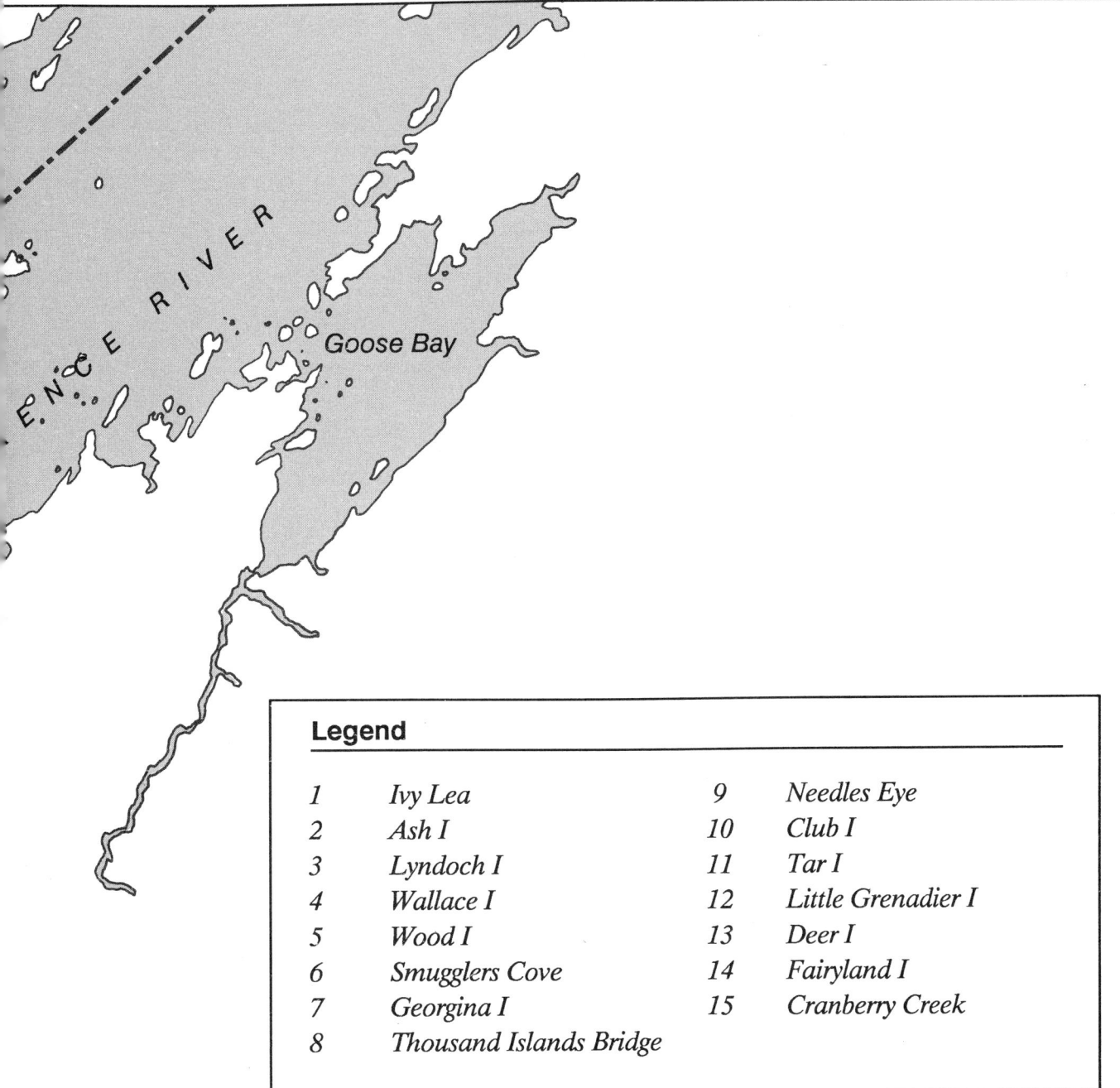

Legend

1	Ivy Lea	9	Needles Eye
2	Ash I	10	Club I
3	Lyndoch I	11	Tar I
4	Wallace I	12	Little Grenadier I
5	Wood I	13	Deer I
6	Smugglers Cove	14	Fairyland I
7	Georgina I	15	Cranberry Creek
8	Thousand Islands Bridge		

Legend

1. *Tar Island Narrows*
2. *Squaw I*
3. *Pooles Resort*
4. *Buell's Pt*
5. *Little Grenadier I*
6. *Ironsides I*
7. *Little Ironsides I*
8. *Chokecherry I*
9. *Jorstadt (Dark) I*

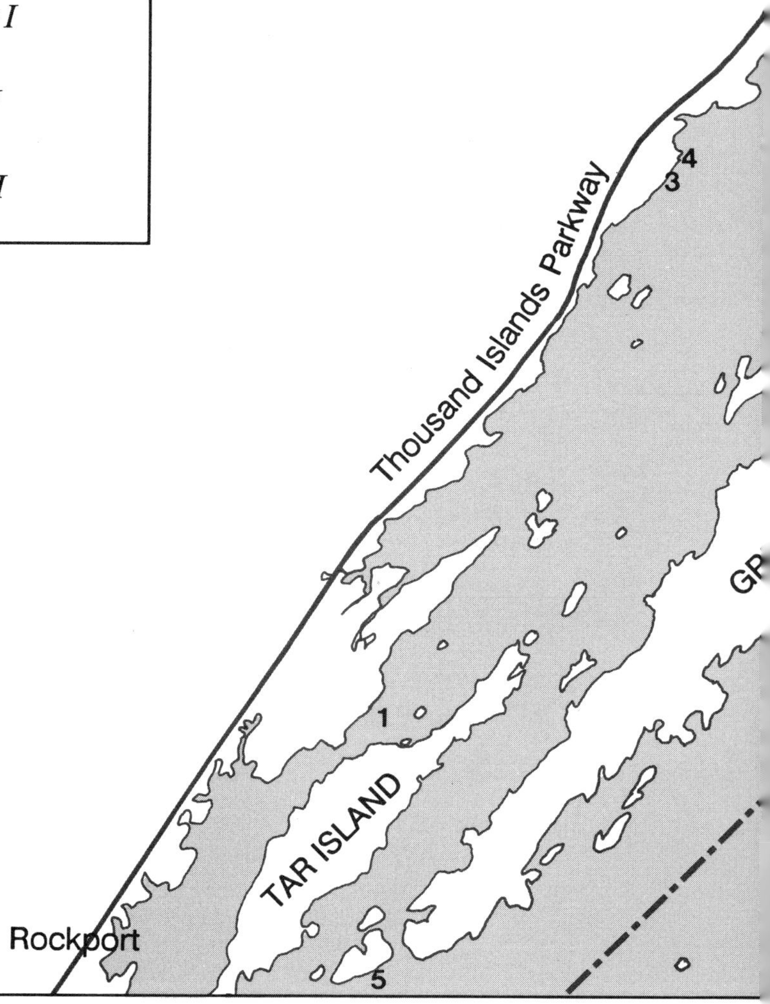

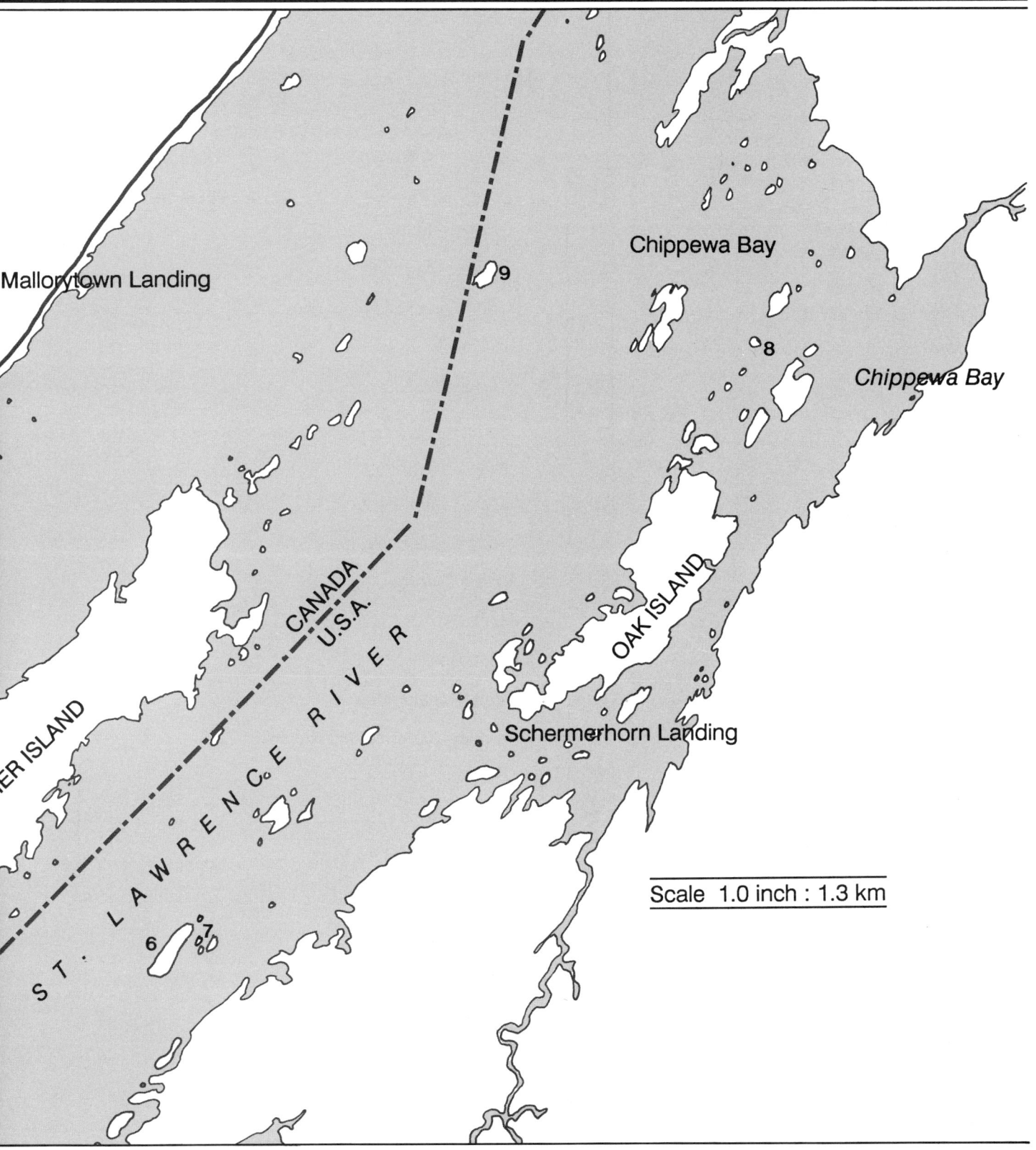

Name Index

Baird, Clover Boldt 118
Balcom, Lawrence 77
Bangma, Albert 134
Bovey, Jack 127
Boxtel, John 231
Browning, Bill 130
Burley, Ben 43
Burt, John 25
Burtch, Kathleen 40

Casselman, Dr. John 31
Cook, Allen 165
Copp, Martin 153
Cox, Bob 115

Dingman, Bruce 202
Dingman, Dorothy Shipman 205
Dowd, Walter 59

Ewald, Bill 225

Fenzel, Tom 49
Ferguson, Clayton 156

Gavin, Basil 46
Grimes, Hunter 68
Grimes, Martha Service 66
Grindstone school scholars 213

Haskin, Grant 211
Herrick, Harold 71
Hickey, Lawrence R. 80
Hodge, June Senecal 187
Hodge, Ralph and Mary Ann 182
Horne, George 101
Huck, Ron 106
Hunt, Bud 199
Hunt, Donald "Moe" 74
Huntley, Clarence "Muskie Jake" 161

Jasper, Bruce 142
Johnston, Ethel Andress 191
Jones, Roland 145

LaPan, Steve 37
Liles, Coit 148
Longtin, Rene 223

Index

Mackintosh, Anne "Blu" 51
Mackintosh, Douglas 109
Mallory, Lawrence and Marjorie 208
Manse, Ernie 174
Martin, Dr. Harold 121
McCarney, Hal 112
McCready, Clark 83
McCune, Shannon 16
McIntosh, Rolly 62
McNally III, Andrew 103

Omohundro, Dr. John T. 28

Reid, Margaret 97
Ringer, Michael 228
Rusho, Leon and Marjorie 179
Russell, Bob 13

Senecal, Richard 168
Service, Robert Gareth 195
Shaw, Ed 171
Small, Peter 137
Smith, Susan 216
Snider, Everett 92
Sykes, Mike 22

Truesdell, Helen 86
Turner, Leonard 89

Wilder, Patrick 19
Wiley, Rick 139
Woodman, Bruce 159

Younge, David 94

Acknowledgements

Courtesy of Pieter Bergen and the Museum of the Great Lakes, Kingston

Lake o' Isles

Thanks to:

Sergeant Jack Hatch of the Ontario Provincial Police, Gananoque detachment;

Jack McEligot, Federal Bureau of Investigation:

Dave Warner, superintendent, and Keith Dewar, chief of visitor activities, St. Lawrence Islands National Park, Canadian Parks Service;

Ida Van Brocklin, executive secretary, and the Alexandria Bay Chamber of Commerce;

Cindy Chaltain and the Thousand Islands International Council;

Shane Sanford, Boldt Castle operations manager, and the Thousand Islands Bridge Authority;

Maurice Smith, executive director, and Michele Dale, registrar, the Museum of the Great Lakes in Kingston;

Jan W. Maas and the St. Lawrence-Eastern Ontario Commission:

Gaetane Hemsley and the St. Lawrence Seaway Authority:

Claude William Hunt of Belleville, author of *Booze, Boats and Billions: Smuggling Liquid Gold!*;

Douglas Mock, Department of Zoology, the University of Oklahoma;

George Maxwell, State University of New York, College at Oswego;

John Nalon, president of the Gananoque Historical Society;

Linda Gibson, Springfield House;

Hugh Reynolds of Rockport for historical information;

Kenneth Hill of Lansdowne for information on the Rockport Cheese Factor;

Brian and Jean Mabee of BJM Photographics for discounted film.

Special thanks to:

Ted Hewitt, for his care in the darkroom printing the photos;

Barbara Sibbald, for her work as book editor;

Dave Yacaginsky, Soft Landings Balloons, for a balloon flight across the St. Lawrence River;

Martha and Hunter Grimes, for help, guidance and a meal of island deer;

and Brenda Thompson, for her sacrifices and help as a loving wife.

Permission was kindly given from the following to quote copyright material: The Canadian Parks Service and Christina Bates for information in the unpublished report on Grenadier Island filed at the St. Lawrence Islands National Park, Mallorytown; John Burt Productions, to quote from *The Slick of '76 - A Musical Catastrophe*, commissioned and produced by River Barge Productions in 1986 and 1987 in the Thousand Islands, with music by Barry Keating, book by David Schechter, lyrics by Barry Keating and David Schechter; The Conservationist magazine for quotations from Harold Herrick (top of page 156) and James Brabant (top of page 161); Pantheon Books, a division of Random House, for a quotation (top of page 94) from *Memories, Dreams, Reflections*, by C.G. Jung, recorded and edited by Aniela Jaffe, translated by Richard and Clara Winston; Vanguard Press, a division of Random House, for a quotation from *The Island*, by Robert Russell (page 15).

A Note About The Author

Photo by Brenda Thompson

Shawn Thompson

Born in dear landlocked London, Ontario in 1951, the author migrated one spring day to Gananoque in the Thousand Islands. He lives there now in a shipshape house --- only a sea gull's cry from the water, no less --- with his Celtic wife Brenda and their Celtic daughter, Caitlin.

Thompson has an Honours B.A. in English literature from the University of Western Ontario --- he was the Rhinegold medal winner of his graduating year --- and an M.A. in English from dear doubtless Queen's University. As a graduate student he held two government scholarships and worked as a teaching assistant for five years. He left a shipwrecked Ph.D. thesis to become a scribbling reporter.

He was editor of the weekly newspaper, the Gananoque *Reporter*, for four years. As editor of the newspaper he won an award from the Ontario Community Newspaper Association for a series of articles on river rats. The series was judged the best multiculturalism writing of all community newspapers in Ontario in 1987. There is no nautical class in the awards.

Thompson wrote *River Rats* while working for the Kingston *Whig-Standard* as a rim rat or copy editor. In 1989 he became the Gananoque bureau reporter for the *Whig-Standard*.

The author drew on a variety of experiences as a nautical hitchhiker to write *River Rats*. He crossed the water by iceboat and hovercraft. He saw the St. Lawrence from a hot-air balloon, a helicopter and the deck of the oldest tall ship still sailing the seas, the *Cuidad de Inca*, renamed the *Maria Asumpta*.

By way of ending, the author remains yours sincerely, boatless in Gananoque, but rich in river folk.

For more copies of
River Rats
The People of the Thousand Islands

send **$19.95 plus $2.00** for shipping and handling to :
General Store Publishing House Inc.
1 Main Street, Burnstown,
Ontario, Canada   K0J 1G0
Telephone (613)432-7697   Fax (613)432-7184